D0368096

1001 Government Freebies and Cheapies

by
Matthew Lesko

with
Mary Ann Martello

Contributing Editors
Mercedes Sundeen; Andrew Naprawa

Researchers
Emily Subler; Lynda Burns; Caroline Pharmer

Publicity
Debbie Samson

Senior Production Editor
Toni Murray

Production
Meserve Associates

Production Designer
Stevan Meserve

Production Staff
Beth Meserve; Peggy Yates; Patricia Riggs

Cover Design
Lester Zaiontz

Original Art
Karen Schirmer and Bruce Wallis

1001 GOVERNMENT FREEBIES AND CHEAPIES, Copyright 1994 by Matthew Lesko with Mary Ann Martello. All rights reserved. Printed in the United States of America. Published by Information USA, Inc., P.O. Box E, Kensington, MD 20895.

Clip art used in this publication © New Vision Technologies, Inc.; Dynamic Graphics, Inc.; Totem Graphics; One Mile Up; Techpool; Image Club Graphics, Inc. and Corel Corp.

FIRST EDITION

Library of Congress Cataloging-in-Publication Date
    Lesko, Matthew
    Martello, Mary Ann

1001 Government Freebies and Cheapies

ISBN #1-878346-22-9 (paperback)

The information in this book is continually updated on-line through the CompuServe Information Service. For subscription information call (800) 524-3388 and ask for Representative 168.

Other books written by Matthew Lesko:

Getting Yours: The Complete Guide to Government Money

How to Get Free Tax Help

Information USA

The Computer Data and Database Source Book

The Maternity Sourcebook

Lesko's New Tech Sourcebook

The Investor's Information Sourcebook

The Federal Data Base Finder

The State Database Finder

Government Giveaways for Entrepreneurs

The Great American Gripe Book

What To Do When You Can't Afford Health Care

Lesko's Info-Power

IRS Secrets, Shortcuts and Savings

Table of Contents

Who Doesn't Love a Freebie?

We All Have Our Limits 2

Dealing with Bureaucrats:
Ten Basic Telephone Tips 3

For Your Baby

Are You Having a C-Section? 7

A Healthy Start — The Early Years 7

Pregnancy Care 8

Bill Welcomes Your Baby! 9

Start Early 9

Can I Have a Drink? 10

Eat for Two 11

Is Smoking Really Dangerous
for My Unborn Baby? 12

Breastfeed or Bottlefeed? 12

What If I Become Diabetic
While I'm Pregnant? 13

Uncle Sam's Answer to Dr. Spock 14

For Your Business

Flex Your Time, Not Your Muscles 17

Complaint Hotline 18

Build a Better Mousetrap — In Tahiti 19

Hot Tips for Trade Trendies 19

A Credit to the Gender... 20

From Beets to Rutabagas 20

Oh Tax-Me-Not 21

One Glass Ceiling
Is Another Woman's Floor 21

The "Better Boss" Book 22

Facts on Working Women 23

Break the Glass Ceiling 24

The Fruitcake's in the Mail 24

Free Help Finding
Guardian Angels 25

What a Great Idea! 25

Some Nighttime Reading 26

Is Your Business in a "Sick Building"? 27

Simply By Design 27

Free Consultants Make Your Company
a Safe and Healthy Place to Work 28

Go to the Bank 29

What's Hot, What's Not 30

Open a Bed and Breakfast
in the Pines 30

Video Display Terminals — User Friendly? 31

Cholesterol, High Blood Pressure,
Smoking, and the Workplace 32

Plants Eliminate 90% of Office Pollution 33

Help Your Employees
Clean Up Their Own Act 34

No Money — No Problem 35

Dial-A-Porn Business Boom 36

Take a Class 36

Workers' Comp for Federal Employees 37

Plant Closing 37

Lend a Helping Hand 38

Teach Your Workers English 39

Check Out the Mail 40

Got A Great Idea? 40

Mom's Home Office 41

Should My Company Go Public? 42

Your Technology Phonebook 42

Be Your Own Financial Manager 43

Energy Business 44

MBA without the Degree 44

First, the Idea 45

More than Running the Cash Register 46

Carpal Tunnel Syndrome 46

Maternity and Family Leave 47

Overseas Carry Out 48

Wheelchairs: A Hot Business Opportunity? 49

For Your Career

Check Out the Head Hunters 53

Landing an Excellent Job 53

Check It Out 54

Get The Scoop on Dirt 54

Weigh Yourself on the Salary Scale 55

Is Jacques Cousteau Your Idol? 55

Turn Off the Weather Channel 56

Solar Power 57

Your Job Magazine 57

Put Your Mouth to Work 58

Check Out the Options 58

Free Instructions 59

Co-op with the Experts 60

Don't Be Tied to a Desk 60

Fly Right 61

Reach for the Stars 61

Work for the CIA 62

Statistics Headquarters 63

Gone Fishin' 64

For Some Direction 64

Bank On It 65

Volunteer 66

Defense Work 66

Astronaut Training 67

A Matter of National Security 68

Dig In 68

$3,000 to Design a Stamp 69

Astronaut Application 69

Summer Jobs 70

Practice MBA 70

Energy Education 71

Summer Aid 71

Join The Team 72

Stay-In-School 72

Energize 73

20 Occupations Most Desired by Feds 74

Women Doing the Jobs of Men 74

Free Job Training for Teens 75

Does a College Degree Guarantee a Job? 75

For Your Community

Neighborhood Watch 79

Consumer Resource 79

Adopt A Roadway 80

Chemicals in Your Community —
Learn What You Need to Know 80

Clean Up the Air
in Your Part of the World 81

Is It Safe to Drink the Water? 82

Recycling Efforts 82

Changed Your Oil Lately? 83

Bringing Art To Life 84

Tourism in Your Town 85

Are Drugs Invading Your Town? 86

Spruce Up the View 86

Look within to Help Your Town 87

Wetlands Protection 88

Base Closure Catastrophe 89

Community Theater 89

The Endangered Species Hit List 90

Environment Dictionary 91

Stop Crime 91

In Your Neighborhood 92

Don Quixote Would Be Proud 92

Clean the Air 93

Clean It Up 94

Cable Catastrophe 95

Environmental Awareness 96

Roadside Improvements 97

For Your Diet

Getting Fit, Losing Fat 101

Anorexia Nervosa and Bulimia 101

Some Dinner Reading 102

The Fountain of Food 103

Eating Right To Lower Your Cholesterol
and High Blood Pressure 104

Are the Kids and I Eating Right? 105

Information for Community
Nutrition Services 106

Know What
the Most Informed People Know 106

Just Can It 107

What's on a Label? 108

The Road to Good Health 108

Talk Turkey 109

Your Food Magazine 110

Change the Channel 110

For Your Education

Crash Course in College Economics 113

Birth Control or Self-Control 113

The GI Bill 114

What's a Pound Worth? 114

Speed Trap 101 115

Back to School Zits? 115

Majoring In Stress? 116

What's Fair's Fair, Scientifically Speaking 116

College-Bound and Gagged 117

Native American Programs 118

Last-Minute Tans Have a Dark Side 118

Your Neighborhood College 119

Flight Schools 119

CD-ROM vs. Floppy Disks? 120

I'm Studying Abroad 120

Free Engineering Degree 121

SATs Get Tested 121

Pilot Tests 122

Scholarships and Internships 122

For Your Garden

Plant Facts 125

Lawn Care Do's 126

Don't Move Gypsy Moth 126

Garden Chemical Free 127

Don't Plant It Here 128

The Dirt People 128

Dig In 129

Work the Soil 130

For Your Grandparents

Jog the Dog 133

One Depression Was Enough 133

Over the Rainbow Coalition 134

No More Forget-Me-Knots 134

Retirement Travel Made Easy 135

Make Their 80th Special 135

The Downside of Longevity 136

Smoke Signals 136

Senior Citizen C-Sections? 137

Hearing is Believing 137

Should My Diet Change as I Get Older? 138

Stronger Medicine 139

A Special 50th Wedding Anniversary 140

Now's the Time 140

Your Ship Has Come In 141

Grandma Getting a Little Shorter? 141

Your Grandparents' Boat 142

When It Is Time To Move 142

Medicare Made Easy 143

Service Hotline for the Elderly 144

For Your Health

Don't Let One Setback Ruin Your Health 147

What Your Children Should Know 147

You Can Cure a Cold with Chicken Soup 148

Think You Can't Get Pregnant
Because You Have Endometriosis? 148

Lead Poisoning is the Number One
Preventable Childhood Disease 149

Down Syndrome, Mental Retardation,
and Learning Disabilities 150

Help For Handicapped and Gifted Children 151

Understanding Childhood Immunizations 152

Sudden Infant Death Hotline 153

Programs for Children of Alcoholics 154

Caring for Children with AIDS 154

There Is Help for Those
Helping Low-Income Mothers 155

Call For The Answer...The Smoking Hotline 156

Children and Mental Health 157

Parents of Disabled Children
Are Not Alone 158

Does Your Child Have Asthma? 159

Illegal Drug Use in Youth 160

A Wealth of Family Planning Information 160

Special Health Care Needs 161

What the Experts Say
about How to Quit Smoking 162

Parent Guides for Alcohol
and Drug Information 162

Mental Health and You 163

The Pain People 164

Cerebral Palsy in Children 164

Clearinghouse
on Disability Information 165

Did Your Lifetime Membership Expire when Your
Health Spa Closed a Year Later? 166

For Your Hobbies

Socks Included 169

Get Out of the House 169

Do You Know Someone
Who is a Gold Digger? 170

Borrow the Battle 170

A Thousand Words 171

For the Would-Be Wine Connoisseur 171

The Wild, Wild West 172

Paint the Chinese Way 172

GOLD Rush 173

This Land Is Your Land 173

Bring The Birds to You 174

What's the Name of that Bird? 174

An Armchair Walk in the Woods... and Time 175

Stamp It! 175

What's This? 176

Going Fishing without Mosquitoes 176

For Your Home

Kung Fu Movers 179

Home Shopping Tips For Veterans 179

Concerned about Pesticides? 180

The Masking Tape Deduction 181

Safe Houses for the 90s 181

Mortgage Money Guides 182

Bought Some Swamp Land In Florida? 182

Before You Even Start Looking for a House 183

This Old House 183

Energy Efficiency for You 184

Unseen, but Deadly 184

Exactly What's It Going To Cost? 185

Let Me Light Your Fire 186

Pesticide Safety 187

For a Different Look 187

Make It as Nature Intended 188

Counseling for Homebuyers, Homeowners,
and Tenants 188

Pest Free Home 189

Efficient Houses 190

For Your Investments

Your Own Investment Counselor 193

Credit Handbook 193

Save With Savings Bonds 194

Save For The Future With Futures 194

Commemorative Coins Bring Big Bucks 195

Minerals into Money 195

Get Rich Quick Schemes 196

Van Gogh for $1,000? 196

Did Your Broker Make You Broke? 197

For Your Kids

Why Do Leaves Change Colors? 201

For a Clean Environment 201

Shake It Up Baby! 202

Step Out of the Way 202

What Does the Coast Guard Do? 203

How Do Things Grow? 203

Do You Dream of Flying High in the Sky? 204

Let the Sun Shine In 204

Learn Fire Safety with Big Bird 205

Money, Money, Money 205

Water 206

Do You Like to Second Guess
the Weather Channel? 206

Want to Learn about the Capitol? 207

Do You Know Who
the World's First Black Pilot Was? 208

Having Trouble Breathing? 208

Give a Hoot! Don't Pollute! 209

Help Your Kids to Read and Write a Fun Way .. 209

Help Your Kids Hit the Books 210

Listen To Your Elders 211

How Old Is the Tree Out Front? 211

Safety First 212

Swim with the Sharks 212

Get in Shape a Fun Way 213

Read Me a Story 213

Creatures Great and Small 214

For Your Little Scout 214

The School Bus Is Not A Zoo 215

De-Video the Kids 215

Pueblos in Pittsburgh 216

Send Your Kids to the Moon 216

Images for Space 217

A View from Above 217

Shopping Made Safe 218

Help Them To Read 218

Get Out the Crayons 219

Ready for Kindergarten? 220

Helmets are the Rule 221

Solar System Puzzle 221

Right To The Moon 222

Color Me 222

For Your Love Life

The Marriage-Go-Round 225

Keep Up with the Joneses 225

Impotence... When Love's a Letdown 226

The Top Nine 226

The Condom People 227

Bigger Breasts: Sure, but How Safe? 228

AIDS: Changing Sex in the Nineties 228

Are Your Hot Flashes Getting Hotter? 229

Free Condoms! 230

Norplant — The Latest Thing 230

Contraceptive Risk and Effectiveness —
Get the Facts 231

Fearless Sex Hotline 232

The Way to a Man's Heart
Is through His Stomach 233

For Your Mantel

Superheros, For Real 237

And the Emmy for Exports Goes to.... 237

When The Little Guy Sees Big 238

Physics Fun 238

Bringing Technology to the Common Man 239

Be True to Your School 239

Beam Me Up, Scotty 240

It's Just Gas 241

Honors for a Class Act 241

Uncle Sam's Star Awards 242

Grade the Principal 243

Start by Jogging Your Dog 243

Intellectual Athletics 244

Top Ten Quality Control Freaks 244

For Your Mind

News of the Day 247

All Aboard 247

How Much Is too Much? 248

Labor Pains 248

A Raise is a Raise 248

Time For A Sale? 249

Pick a Job, Any Job 249

Just the Facts, Ma'am 250

Be Your Own Economist 250

How Much Can You Really Take with You? 250

What Comes in Goes Out 251

Bills, Bills, Bills 251

Who Do You Believe? 252

An ARM and A Leg 252

The Latest Dirt 253

Invitation Lost in the Mail? 253

Better than a Rolex 253

Project Blue Book 254

Flowerpower Plus 254

Ready to Hit the Open Road? 255

Recall Their Bluff 255

How Much? 255

Does Money Grow on Trees? 256

A Job Bank for Globetrotters 256

Share the Wealth 256

Televidiots, Fight Back 257

Let Your Fingers Do The Walking 257

Better than Sitting Home 258

Legal or Not? 258

Plan Ahead 258

Uncle Sam's Poor Box 259

Your Travel Agent 259

Stars in Your Eyes 260

Aye and Nay 260

UFOs 261

Disappearing Towns 261

Tally Up 262

Cost of Illegal Drugs 262

Television Interference Problems 263

How Schools Spend Your Tax Money 263

April 15th Seems to Come Earlier
Each Year 264

Social Security: Another Wrong Number? 264

The Economic Outlook 265

Don't Be A Broke Bookworm 265

A Big Number For Small Business 266

The Safe Sex Buzz 266

Understanding Lemons,
Roadkills, Grouchy Drivers 266

Cancer Answers 267

Medicare Madness...
Keep Tabs on Benefit Erosion 267

When Meat's a Mystery, Call Uncle Sam 268

Loose Lips Save Ships 268

The Dump Snitchline 269

Spreading the Clean (and Sober) Word 269

Confessed Under Hypnosis? 270

For Your Nonprofit

Tons of Free Books 273

Learn the Ropes 274

Giveaway Wish List 274

Step Inside the Loop 275

Strike Up the Band 275

A Home for the Holidays 276

Soup's On 277

Pledge Drive Propaganda 278

For Your Pets

And You Thought They Were Just Cute 281

It Was Love at First Sight 281

Mommy, Mommy,
May I *PLEASE* Have a Dog? 282

Take Good Care of Fido 283

Vet Speak 283

For Your Pocketbook

America's Most Wanted 287

Mileage Meter Mess 287

Mother Nature's Watchdogs 288

Don't Get Mad, Get Even 288

And That $60,000 Toilet 289

Ton 'O Trash Ahoy 289

Lassie, Call Flipper 290

Bowling For Drug Kingpins 290

Me and My Bogus Kalvins 291

Double-Dipping Doctors 291

Free Muggers Money 292

For Your Pleasure

Turn On The Ocean Blue 295

Science and You 296

Up, Up, and Away 296

Outer Space in Omaha 297

Yodeling Cowboys 298

The Latest Technologies 298

Some Enchanted Evening 299

Silver and Gold 300

Star Wars Speaker 300

Foreign Affairs Films 301

Banking On Screen 302

For Your Retirement

Pension Central 305

Pensions — An Investment for Your Future 306

Social Insecurity 307

Don't Let Yourself Become a Victim 307

Social Security Speakers 308

For Your Soul

For that Special Day 311

Against Your Conscience 311

Need a Pick-Me-Up 312

Testimony to Service 312

Stars and Stripes 313

Volunteer Service 313

And They Said It Would Never Happen 314

Don't Panic, Take Leave 314

Disabled Act On Your Rights! 315

Are They Regular Voters? 315

A New Set of Wheels 316

Home Shopping 316

Where Did You Begin 317

International Peace 318

For Your Summer

Show Them the One that Got Away 321

Secret Fishing Holes Revealed at Last 321

Boating and You 322

Importing Pleasure Boats 322

Man Overboard 323

Go to the Source 323

Stern and Bow 324

Get Your Notice 324

Updates for Mariners 325

For Your Teacher

Save the Rainforests 329

Smokey the Bear and You 329

Your Guide to Outer Space 330

Where the Heck Is Timbuktu? 330

Bring Your Paints to School 331

Armchair Archeologists 331

You and Your Wildlife 332

Free Flights of Fancy 332

Send Your Students to the Moon 333

Them Bones, Them Bones 334

Environmental Hazards in Your School 334

Connect the Dots to Pirate Booty
and Ghost Mines 335

Geology on Screen 336

Shaking in Their Seats 337

Cloudy With a Chance of Eagles 337

Art of the U.S. 338

Everything Old Is New Again 339

In the Footsteps of T-Rex...Utah Canyon
Boasts Fossils Galore 339

Bring a Cast-Iron Umbrella 340

English as a Second Language 340

Speak Out 341

Make African Art Come Alive 342

Scientific Americans 343

LEAP Back in Time 343

Carbons to Computers 344

Build a Better Light Bulb 344

Take Your Class to the Park 345

The Original Jurassic Playground 345

Indian Ancestry 346

Teaching Science Close to Home 346

Powwow with the Experts 347

Party Animals on Parade 347

Following in Godzilla's Footsteps 348

Free Land Films and Videos 348

Calling Mother India 349

Wild and Woolly Neighborhoods 350

Help Students Clean-Up 350

Drug Abuse Teaching Aids 351

River and Water Films 352

The Mummy Walks at Midnight 353

The Idea Factory 354

Your Travel Journal 354

Separation of Church and State? 355

Science Horizons 355

For those Budding Actors and Actresses 356

Art Assistance 357

The Noble Path 357

Celebrate the Asian Way 358

Draw Me a Map 358

Turn the Tide 359

One with Nature 359

Social Studies Simplified 360

Explore Mars 361

What's Happening in the World? 361

Every Day Should Be Earth Day 362

Free Science Lab Equipment 362

For Your Travels

Know Before You Go 365

Right-On Write-Offs 365

Far Shores, Far Out 366

Where to Go 366

Fly Right 367

Call Mother Nature 367

Why Are You Taking My...? 368

Travel Scams 368

Camp USA 369

Take the Train 369

Travel on Uncle Sam's Expense Account 370

Not Just a Trip, but an Adventure 370

George Washington Never Slept Here 371

Do Some Research 371

You Can Only Bring So Many 372

3-2-1-Lift Off! 372

The White House 373

Row, Row, Row Your Boat 373

Be Your Own Tour Guide 374

For Your Worries

The Bomb's in the Mail 377

Before Your Boss
Sends You on a Foreign Affair 377

Security Tips for the Briefcase Bunch 378

Experts TRAC Terrorists Here 378

Bombs and Guns 379

Global Terrorism Tallied, Get the Free Report .. 379

Water Questions 380

It's Your Fault 380

The Worst Winter in a Hundred Years 381

The Check's in the Mail...or Is It? 381

When a Disaster Strikes 382

Insured, I'm Sure 382

First Aid 383

Panic City 383

Safe At Any Speed 384

Call in the National Guard 385

Army Downsizing 385

A Boss with Itchy Fingers 386

This is Not a Drill 387

Good News: Aviation Accidents Are Down!
Bad News: Fatalities Are Up! 388

You've Survived the Flood, Now What? 388

Who's Got the Energy? 389

Pipeline Safety 389

Did I Remember to Turn Off the 390

On the Wrong Track 391

Your Guide to More Freebies: Directory of State Information

Alabama 394

Alaska 395

Arizona 396

Arkansas 397

California 398

Colorado 398

Connecticut 399

Delaware 400

District of Columbia 401

Florida 402

Georgia 403

Hawaii 404

Idaho 404

Illinois 405

Indiana 406

Iowa 407

Kansas 408

Kentucky 408

Louisiana 409

Maine 410

Maryland 411

Massachusetts 412

Michigan 413

Minnesota 414

Mississippi 415

Missouri 416

Montana 417

Nebraska 417

Nevada 418

New Hampshire 419

New Jersey 420

New Mexico 421

New York 421

North Carolina 422

North Dakota 423

Ohio 424

Oklahoma 425

Oregon 426

Pennsylvania 426

Rhode Island 427

South Carolina 428

South Dakota 429

Tennessee 430

Texas 431

Utah 432

Vermont 433

Virginia 433

Washington 434

West Virginia 435

Wisconsin 436

Wyoming 437

Index

Index.. 439

Who Doesn't Love a Freebie?

Times are tough, and we're all looking for more ways to save a few bucks, right? So here are more than 1,000 freebies and cheapies to get you started. They are not all free; only 923 of them are. The rest cost less than $10! But they're well worth it.

Actually, we could have made the book one million and one freebies because the government is so huge that it has at least that many great freebies to offer taxpayers. Remember, these freebies are not really free — you already paid for them with your tax dollars.

What we've done here is put together the government's greatest hits. It's all the neat stuff you can get your hands on and put to use for gifts, self-help, teaching aids, toys, investment decisions and more. Every member of the family can use these freebies.

For Grandma:
- Turn her home into that little bed and breakfast she always wanted.
- Publications that can make her the next "Queen of the Dancing Grannies."

For Mom:
- A "Top Gun" pilot as the featured speaker for her next women's club meeting.
- Break into the world of business with help from the Women's Business Ownership Program.
- Check lead levels in house paint and water to see if it's safe to go home again.

For Dad:
- Extra money reporting the neighborhood tax cheat to the IRS.
- Beat a speeding ticket with a report from the National Institute of Standards and Technology.
- Get a raise, using information from the Bureau of Labor Statistics.

For the kids:
- Dig up real dinosaur bones with some help from the National Park Service.

- Convince mom pizza is good for you with studies from the Food and Nutrition Information Center.

For your mother-in-law:
- Send her to the moon as a NASA civilian astronaut.

- Send her on a free trip to Jamaica as a Peace Corps volunteer.

For Grandpa:
- Let Bill and Hillary send him his next birthday card.

- Make him the life of the party with a free videotape of his prostate surgery.

For your church:
- A free drug-confiscated limousine from the General Services Administration.

- A thousand free books to sell at your next yard sale from the Library of Congress.

For your boss:
- Close down your office until they replace that smelly copier with help from the Environmental Protection Agency.

- Warn him that if he makes a pass at you at the office Christmas party, you and your friends at the Equal Employment Opportunity Commission will see him in court.

For yourself:
- Let the Bureau of the Census point you in the direction of single men and women.

- Let the National Park Service find the best place for you to escape the rat race next summer.

- Have the IRS show you how to write off your vacation expenses.

We All Have Our Limits

Despite our best efforts to make the information in this book as timely and accurate as possible, it is sure to be outdated by the time it reaches your hands. Government policies change every day; and supplies of some items are limited. But you can use this to your advantage.

If the item or publication you call about is no longer available, ask if they have anything new. You may be amazed at what you find. Our researchers, for example, called one department to ask about a publication on commodities trading, only to be told that it was no longer in print. The department, however, offered three more up-to-date booklets and a new information hotline.

If you call one of the numbers listed in this book and find that you have reached the chinese laundry now using a phone number once assigned to the Department of Commerce, try calling the federal information directory at (202) 555-1212. Another good source for phone numbers is the Federal Information Center in your state. These numbers are listed by state in the last chapter of this book.

Dealing with Bureaucrats: Ten Basic Telephone Tips

An important part of your success in using this book is the careful handling of bureaucrats. Whether you are dealing with your local power company or with the government, you will be speaking to another human being. If you deal with them pleasantly and patiently, you will get quicker service and more publications and information.

Here are a few important tips to follow when you attempt to get information of any kind from a government agency over the telephone. Above all, remember that patience is often rewarded — even by weary government bureaucrats!

- **Introduce Yourself Cheerfully**
  Starting the conversation with a cordial and upbeat attitude will set the tone for the entire interview. Let the official know that this is not going to be just another mundane telephone call, but a pleasant interlude in an otherwise hectic day.

- **Be Open And Candid**
  Be as candid as possible with your source. If you are evasive or deceitful in explaining your needs or motives, your source will be reluctant to provide you with anything but the most basic information.

- **Be Optimistic**
  Relay a sense of confidence throughout the conversation. If you call and say "You probably aren't the right person" or "You don't have any information, do you?" it's easy for the person to respond, "You're right, I

can't help you." A positive attitude encourages your source to dig deeper for an answer to your question.

- **Be Courteous**
  You can be optimistic and still be courteous. Remember the old adage that you can catch more flies with honey than you can with vinegar? Government officials love to tell others what they know, as long as their position of authority is not questioned or threatened.

- **Be Concise**
  State your problem simply. Be direct. A long-winded explanation may bore your contact and reduce your chances for getting a thorough response.

- **Don't Be A "Gimme"**
  A "gimme" is someone who expects instant answers and displays a "give me that" attitude. Be considerate and sensitive to your contact's time, feelings, and eccentricities. Although, as a taxpayer, you may feel you have the right to put this government worker through the mill, that kind of attitude will only cause the contact to give you minimal assistance.

- **Be Complimentary**
  This goes hand in hand with being courteous. A well-placed compliment ("Everyone I spoke to said you are the person I need to ask.") about your source's expertise or insight will serve you well. We all like to feel like an "expert" when it comes doing our job.

- **Be Conversational**
  Briefly mention a few irrelevant topics such as the weather or the latest political campaign. The more conversational you are without being too chatty, the more likely your source will be to open up and want to help you.

- **Return the Favor**
  You might share with your source information or even gossip you have picked up elsewhere. However, be certain not to betray the trust of either your client or another source. If you do not have any relevant information to share at the moment, call back when you are farther along in your research.

- **Send Thank You Notes**
  A short note, typed or handwritten, will help ensure that a government official source will be just as cooperative in answering future questions.

For Your Baby

Are You Having a C-Section?

The National Institute of Child Health and Human Development can provide data and medical information about this health issue. A 13-page booklet, *Facts About Cesarean Childbirth*, discusses cesarean delivery, types of incisions, current thinking about repeat cesarean, and the pros and cons of this method of birth.

Contact: National Institute of Child Health and Human Development, Building 31, Room 2A32, 9000 Rockville Pike, National Institutes of Health, Bethesda, MD 20892; 301-496-5133.

A Healthy Start – The Early Years

Your hormones and body are going through drastic changes now that you are pregnant. *Prenatal Care - A Resource Guide* lists publications, videos, and other resources to contact to receive information on pregnancy, labor and delivery, breastfeeding and infant care.

For your copy, contact: National Maternal and Child Health Clearinghouse, 8201 Greensboro Drive, Suite 600, McLean, VA 22102; 703-821-8955, ext. 254.

Pregnancy Care

You are pregnant. Now what do you do? How much weight should you gain? Can you keep exercising? The Maternal and Child Health Clearinghouse has several free publications dealing with prenatal care to get you and your unborn child off to a good start.

Some of the publications include:

- *Caring for Our Future: The Content of Prenatal Care.*

- *Health Diary: Myself-My Baby*, a new publication which takes you step by step through your pregnancy.

Contact: National Maternal and Child Health Clearinghouse, 8201 Greensboro Dr., Suite 600, McLean, VA 22102; 703-821-8955, ext. 254.

Bill Welcomes Your Baby!

The Ultimate Announcement! Let the President welcome your newest newcomer to the world with a special congratulatory notice sent directly from the White House. Just send a copy of the announcement or write a note with the date of birth.

Contact: White House, Greetings Office, 1600 Pennsylvania Ave., NW, Washington, DC 20500; 202-456-2724.

Start Early

Starting Early: A Guide to Federal Resources in Maternal and Child Health is a free resource directory which includes a description of more than 500 publications and audiovisual materials, an annotated listing of over 80 federal agencies and information centers, and a directory of federal, regional, and state maternal and child health programs.

Contact: National Maternal and Child Health Clearinghouse, 8201 Greensboro Dr., Suite 600, McLean, VA 22102; 703-821-8955, ext. 254.

Can I Have a Drink?

There are many concerns regarding alcohol use while pregnant.

The National Clearinghouse for Alcohol and Drug Information has several free publications dealing with drinking and drug use during pregnancy.

Some of the titles include:

- *Alcohol, Tobacco, and Other Drugs May Harm the Unborn,* which presents the most recent findings of basic research and clinical studies (PH291).

- *How To Take Care of Your Baby Before Birth*, a low-literacy brochure aimed at pregnant women that describes what they should and should not do during their pregnancy, emphasizing a no use of alcohol and other drugs message (PH239, also in Spanish).

- "An Inner Voice Tells You Not to Drink or Use Other Drugs", a poster which depicts an artistic rendition of a pregnant American Indian Woman (AV161).

- *Prevention Resource Guide: Pregnant/ Postpartum Women and Their Infants,* a resource guide which targets pregnant and postpartum women, women between the ages of 15-44, counselors, health care providers, and prevention program planners. It provides a high-demand, comprehensive resource for information concerning alcohol and other drug prevention among pregnant and postpartum women and their infants (MS420).
- *Pregnancy and Exposure to Alcohol and Other Drug Use* provides information about preventing drug and alcohol use amont women of childbearing age (BKD94).

Contact: National Clearinghouse for Alcohol and Drug Information, P.O. Box 2345, Rockville, MD 20847; 800-729-6686.

€at for Two

Now that you're pregnant, your doctor is going to tell you to gain weight. *All About Eating for Two* is an article describing the types of food and vitamins you will need to maintain a healthy pregnancy.

Once you've had Junior, you have to feed and clothe him. *Feeding Baby: Nature and Nurture* and *Good Nutrition and the High Chair Set* are articles which discuss breast feeding, formula and vitamin supplements.

For your free copies contact: Food and Drug Administration, Division of Consumer Affairs, HFE-88, 5600 Fishers Lane, Rockville, MD 20857; 301-443-3170.

Is Smoking Really Dangerous for My Unborn Baby?

The Office on Smoking and Health can provide you with information on smoking as it affects pregnancy and newborns. Some of the free pamphlets available include: *Is Your Baby Smoking?*, which explains the dangers of passive smoke on the baby; and a "Pregnant? Two Reasons to Quit" poster, which reminds pregnant women that when they smoke, they smoke for two.

Contact: Office on Smoking and Health, Centers for Disease Control, 4770 Buford Hwy., Mail Stop K-50, Atlanta, GA 30341-3724; 404-488-5705.

Breastfeed or Bottlefeed?

Are you debating whether you should breastfeed or bottlefeed? The National Maternal and Child Health Clearinghouse can refer you to several organizations, as well as provide you with free publications dealing with breast feeding, including:

- *Breastfeeding Catalog of Products*, which includes a listing of videotapes, posters, brochures, journal articles, data bases, curricula and training aids.

- *Nutrition During Lactation*, which discusses your diet while you are breastfeeding.

- *Surgeon General's Workshop on Breastfeeding and Human Lactation*, which covers the physiology of breastfeeding, the unique values of human milk, current trends, and cultural factors relating to breastfeeding.

Contact: National Maternal and Child Health Clearinghouse, 8201 Greensboro Dr., Suite 600, McLean, VA 22102; 703-821-8955, ext. 254.

What If I Become Diabetic While I'm Pregnant?

Understanding Gestational Diabetes: A Practical Guide to a Healthy Pregnancy addresses questions about diet, exercise, measurement of blood sugar levels, and general medical and obstetric care of women with gestational diabetes.

It answers such questions as: Will my baby have diabetes?, What can I do to control gestational diabetes?, and Will I have diabetes in the future? This is a free booklet.

Contact: National Institute of Child Health and Human Development, National Institutes of Health, Building 31, Room 2A32, 9000 Rockville Pike, Bethesda, MD 20892; 301-496-5133.

Uncle Sam's Answer to Dr. Spock

The hospital hands you a new baby and you don't even have to take a test, but you have a thousand questions.

Infant Care, a free publication from the National Maternal and Child Health Clearinghouse, answers all your questions, such as:

- When do babies need shots?

- What should they eat and when?

- When should they sit up?

A video, "Before It's Too Late Vaccinate", explains the importance of immunizations. The pamphlet, *Parent's Guide to Common Childhood Illnesses,* gives a brief overview of things you need to look for when your child is sick.

Contact: National Maternal and Child Health Clearinghouse, 8201 Greensboro Dr., Suite 600, McLean, VA 22102; 703-821-8955, ext. 254.

For Your Business

flex Your Time, Not Your Muscles

The U.S. workplace is changing quicker than President Bill's cabinet appointments. Companies have discovered that helping workers with day care  and eldercare pays off, and that flexible work schedules mean fewer cases of burnout.

The Work and Family Clearinghouse has written materials and a database where they can match your company with a company of similar needs and geographic area. You can then see how they succeed with these innovative programs.

The Work and Family Resource Kit is a free publication which provides information on all of the above, plus provides references and resources for further information.

Contact: Work and Family Clearinghouse, Women's Bureau, U.S. Department of Labor, 200 Constitution Ave., NW, Washington, DC 20210; 800-827-5335.

Complaint Hotline

Need some help resolving a complaint? What about setting up a complaint handling procedure for your business?

The Office of Consumer Affairs works with the business community on behalf of consumers and assists consumers with marketplace problems.

To help businesses improve customer relations and the quality of goods and services, the Office develops cooperative projects with companies, trade and professional associations, consumer organizations, and more.

They have many free publications.

- *Consumer Services Directory* describes consumer-related activities and services of Commerce Department agencies, and lists publications and audiovisuals.

- *Consumer's Guide to Complaint Handling* is a brochure to help consumers resolve their complaints with specific steps to follow for complaints about auto repair, mail order, banking and credit, and travel.

- There is also *Helping Small Business Respond to Consumers' Needs*, which is a manual for state and local consumer protection agencies.

Contact: Office of Consumer Affairs, U.S. Department of Commerce, 14th and Constitution Ave., NW, Room H5718, Washington, DC 20230; 202-482-5001.

Build a Better Mousetrap – In Tahiti

Starting up a factory overseas does not make you Benedict Arnold. You can play Albert Schweitzer, and a New Age business guru in many small countries, and still be a good U.S. citizen at home. Learn the best countries to do business in with Foreign Labor Trend reports prepared by American Embassy staff in 70 foreign countries.

Contact: Office of Foreign Relations, U.S. Department of Labor, 200 Constitution Ave., NW., Room S5006, Washington, DC 20210; 202-219-6257.

Hot Tips for Trade Trendies

If you picture the global marketplace as a horse race, the racing form is the U.S. Small Business Administration's Export Information System (XIS), a database of hot products and trends on 25 world trade markets, including growth trends over the last five years.

Contact: Office of International Trade, U.S. Small Business Administration, 409 Third St., SW, Suite 6100, Washington, DC 20416; 202-205-6720.

Oh Tax-Me-Not

When the Internal Revenue Service (IRS) knocks, you need a friend not an accountant.

To make sure you have all your records in order, order Publication 334, *Tax Guide For Small Business*, which explains what can be deducted and how, as well as what records you need to keep.

Contact: Internal Revenue Service, U.S. Department of the Treasury, 1111 Constitution Ave., NW, Washington, DC 20224; 800-829-3676.

One Glass Ceiling Is Another Woman's Floor

Do you feel like you are the only woman in town trying to run a business? Ever wonder how you stack up against other businesswomen in the U.S., or whether you should be in another line of work? What about your chances of rising to the top of the heap?

If you're interested in finding out more about women in the workforce, including trends and future projections, you might find the free series of fact sheets on women business owners very interesting.

Some of the topics include:

- *Working Mothers And Their Children*, which provides statistics on working mothers, and

- *The Family and Medical Leave Act of 1993*, which explains the Act, requirements, and exclusions.

Contact: Women's Bureau, U.S. Department of Labor, 200 Constitution Ave., NW, Room S3309, Washington, DC 20210; 202-219-6652.

The "Better Boss" Book

One reason so many women-owned businesses succeed is that they simply care about their lowly workers. Is it nature, nurture, or just good business sense?

The Small Business Handbook: Laws, Regulations and Technical Assistance Services is a free handbook which explains employees' rights and can help you become the boss you always wanted to have.

Contact: The Assistant Secretary of Policy, U.S. Department of Labor, 200 Constitution Ave., NW, Room S2006, Washington, DC 20210; 202-219-6181.

Facts on Working Women

Women will account for 62% of the net growth in the labor force over the next ten years.

As part of their free *Facts on Working Women* series, the Women's Bureau has put together interesting fact sheets including the following:

- *Women Workers: Outlook To 2005* examines where women will fit into the labor force and the occupational outlook.

- *Women With Work Disabilities* explains the Americans With Disabilities Act, employment profiles, and employment assistance programs for women.

- *Earnings Differences Between Women and Men* show the earnings gap and the factors that affect it.

Contact: Women's Bureau, U.S. Department of Labor, 200 Constitution Ave., NW, Washington, DC 20210; 800-827-5335.

Break the Glass Ceiling

The Glass Ceiling Commission was created to identify artificial barriers that prevent women and minorities from advancing to mid- and upper-level management positions in the corporate world and to determine how such barriers could be removed.

They have a free brochure, *Breaking The Glass Ceiling*, which gives a brief overview of the Commission's work. They also have articles and other reports dealing with this issue.

Contact: Glass Ceiling Commission, Office of the Secretary, U.S. Department of Labor, 200 Constitution Ave., NW, Room S2233, Washington, DC 20210; 202-619-6652.

The Fruitcake's in the Mail

Many products are best marketed by mail, but this takes more than stamps and a zip code directory. It takes some knowledge of Federal Trade Commission's Mail Order Rule, which requires companies to ship purchases made by mail when promised or to give consumers the option to cancel their order for a refund.

For a free copy of *A Business Guide to the Mail Order Rule* contact: Enforcement Division, Federal Trade Commission, 6th and Pennsylvania Ave., NW, Washington, DC 20580; 202-326-3768.

Free Help Finding Guardian Angels

Look no more. The Investment Division of the U.S. Small Business Administration licenses, regulates, and funds some 320 Small Business Investment Companies (SBIC) nationwide, which supply equity investments to qualifying small businesses.

A free *Directory of Small Business Investment Companies* is available which lists names, addresses, telephone numbers and investment policies of SBICs.

Contact: Investment Division, U.S. Small Business Administration, 409 Third St., SW, Washington, DC 20416; 202-205-6510.

What a Great Idea!

To help you get started with patenting your invention, the Patent and Trademark Offices will send you a free booklet upon request called *Summary of How the Patent Process Works*, which explains the steps you need to take to be awarded a patent.

For your copy contact: Commissioner of Patent and Trademark, U.S. Department of Commerce, U.S. Patent and Trademark Office, P.O. Box 9, Washington, DC 20231; 703-308-HELP.

Some Nighttime Reading

Read every line before you sign. The Federal Trade Commission has three free publications to help you learn your way around the franchise business.

When you go in for the big meeting, you'll know the right questions to ask.

- *Franchise and Business Opportunities* is a four page guide about what to consider

- *The Franchise Rule: Questions and Answers* is a one page summary of the disclosure rule and penalties

- *Franchise Rule Summary* is a seven page explanation of the federal disclosure rule.

For your free copies contact: Franchise Rule Information Hotline, Federal Trade Commission, Pennsylvania Ave. at 6th St., NW, Washington, DC 20580; 202-326-3220.

Is Your Business in a "Sick Building"?

Do you suffer from headaches and have difficulty concentrating only while you are at work? You could be working in a Sick Building, a term used to describe situations where workers experience acute health or comfort effects when they are at work, but no specific illness can be identified. The Indoor Air Quality Information Clearinghouse can answer all of your indoor air quality questions and has many free publications on this topic including, *Indoor Air Facts: Sick Building Syndrome.*

Contact: Indoor Air Quality Information Clearinghouse, IAQ INFO, P.O. Box 37133, Washington, DC 20013-7133; 800-438-4318, 301-585-9020.

Simply By Design

Thinking of doing your own publishing? *Simply By Design: Desktop Publishing Guide* ($1) provides detailed instruction with sample illustrations for publishing your own documents. It covers such basic design concepts as planning a publication and developing a format; use of logotypes, and more.

Contact: Superintendent of Documents, Government Printing Office, Washington, DC 20402; 202-783-3238.

Free Consultants Make Your Company a Safe and Healthy Place to Work

The Occupational Safety and Health Administration (OSHA) was created to encourage employers and employees to reduce workplace hazards and to implement new or improve existing safety and health programs.

They provide research on innovative ways of dealing the these problems, maintain a recordkeeping system to monitor job-related injuries and illnesses, develop standards and enforce them, as well as establish training programs.

OSHA has an extensive list of publications on a variety of job hazards. Some of the titles include:

- *Asbestos Standard for Construction Industry*

- *Hearing Conservation*

- *Respiratory Protection Program Highlights*, a one-sheet description of hazards, standards, of OSHA programs or policies.

- *FatalFacts*, a one page periodic news sheet that summarizes fatal accidents occurring in the construction industry, the citations issued against the company involved, and the precautions that could be taken to avoid such accidents.

- *SafeWorks*, a one-page news sheet that provides a brief summary of the results of a small business employer's request for workplace safety and health assistance from OSHA-funded consultation services.

Contact: Occupational Safety and Health Administration, U.S. Department of Labor, 200 Constitution Ave., NW, Room N3101, Washington, DC 20210; 202-219-4667.

Go to the Bank

Think you don't have the money to start a business?

A Guide To Business Credit For Women, Minorities, and Small Business is a free publication which describes the various credit opportunities for industrious entrepreneurs. Don't let the lack of funds hold you back.

Contact: Publications Services, MS-138, Board of Governors, Federal Reserve System, Washington, DC 20551; 202-452-3244.

What's Hot, What's Not

The Federal Procurement Data Center (FPDC) can tell you how much the federal government spent last quarter on products ranging from pasta to real estate.

It also can tell you which agencies made those purchases, and who the contractors were. FPDC summarizes this information through a free, annual standard report, and provides customized reports on a cost recovery basis.

Contact: Federal Procurement Data Center, General Services Administration, 7th and D St., SW, Room 5652, Washington, DC 20407; 202-401-1529.

Open a
Bed and Breakfast in the Pines

If Cheerios and sleeping bags don't cut it anymore, the Office of Rural Affairs and Economic Development will help you pick up a cheap country inn and have you turn a profit turning down sheets. *Working Together: A Guide to Federal and State Resources for Rural Economic Development* lists loans, counseling, publications, assistance, and special programs available to encourage development in rural areas.

Contact: Office of Rural Affairs and Economic Development, U.S. Small Business Administration, 409 Third St., SW, Washington, DC 20416; 202-205-6485.

Video Display Terminals – User Friendly?

Over a million people each day sit down to work in front of a terminal, inputting and outputting information.

There have been concerns about the risks these terminals present.

Are we destroying people's eyesight? Are they at risk for carpal tunnel syndrome?

The National Institute For Occupational Safety and Health (NIOSH) has put together an information booklet titled *Video Display Terminals* describing video display terminals, the current research on their use, a listing of articles for further information.

Contact: National Institute For Occupational Safety and Health, 4676 Columbia Parkway, Cincinnati, OH 45226; 800-356-4674.

Cholesterol, High Blood Pressure, Smoking, and the Workplace

Get your employees on the road to good health. The National Heart, Lung, And Blood Institute (NHLBI) Workplace Initiative promotes research and educational projects and materials that promote the reduction of cardiopulmonary morbidity and mortality among workers and their families.

The "Workplace Initiative Kit" contains materials for professionals and workers related to risk factors for cardiovascular and pulmonary disease, especially the three major modifiable risk factors: high blood pressure, high blood cholesterol, and cigarette smoking.

Materials include: technical documents for health professionals, guides for workplace program planners, brochures and materials for workers, order forms for additional publications, and audiovisual materials.

Some of the free publications and posters include:
- *It's Your Business...*

- *Smoking Policies for the Workplace*

- *Make Workplace Wellness Programs Work for Your Company*

- *A Reading List for Heart and Lung Health at the Workplace*

- *A Resource Guide for Heart and Lung Health at the Workplace*

- *Small Business Basics: Guidelines for Heart and Lung Health at the Workplace*

- *Workplace Facts on Heart Disease and Stroke: A Data Fact Sheet*

- *NHLBI Kit '90*

Contact: National Heart, Lung, And Blood Institute (NHLBI), Information Center, 7200 Wisconsin Ave., P.O. Box 30105, Bethesda, MD 20824; 301-251-1222.

Plants Eliminate 90% of Office Pollution

Office plants are great places to hide microphones, but they also clear up 90% of office pollution, according to a National Aeronautics and Space Administration (NASA) study called, *Interior Landscape Plants for Indoor Air Pollution Abatement.*

The study shows that house plants remove chemicals from the air and clean up indoor air pollution.

The report is free from NASA Library, Bldg. 1100, S170A, Stennis Space Center, MS 39529; 601-688-3244.

Help Your Employees Clean Up Their Own Act

Making your workplace clean and safe should also include looking at your employees. Are some coming in late often or not at all? Are there problems with some employees' work habits? It could be that drugs or alcohol are involved.

The National Institute on Drug Abuse is developing programs to eliminate illegal drug use in the workplace. Its programs include research, treatment, training, and prevention activities, as well as projects related to the development of a comprehensive Drug-Free Workplace programs.

The Clearinghouse distributes the following four-part videotape series on drugs at work:

- "Drugs At Work" (employee/employer versions), presents information about the nature and scope of the alcohol and drug problem in the workplace and about the Federal Government's initiative to prevent and reduce the problem.

- "Getting Help" (employee/employer versions), highlights the benefits of an effective employee assistance program to employees and employers through comments by business, labor, and government leaders and Employee Assistance Program professionals.

- "Drug Testing: Handle With Care" (employee/employer versions), describes the options available for designing a drug testing component as part of a comprehensive drug-free workplace program.

- "Finding Solutions", Drug abuse in the workplace is portrayed as a community-wide problem. The solutions offered through education and prevention are presented as personal, workplace, and community responsibilities.

Contact: National Clearinghouse for Alcohol and Drug Information, P.O. Box 2345, Rockville, MD 20847; 800-729-6686.

No Money – No Problem

Raising capital is a little bit like raising kids; it's a pain, but worth the effort.

How To Raise Money for a Small Business is a fact sheet outlining the basics of raising money, where to find it, borrow it, types of business loans, how to write a loan proposal, and U.S. Small Business Administration (SBA) financial programs (you'll have to do the kids yourself) .

For your free copy contact: Publications and Graphics, U.S. Small Business Administration, 409 3rd St., SW, Suite 6400, Washington DC 20416; 202-205-6665.

Dial-A-Porn Business Boom

Thinking about getting rich quick by starting a dial-a-porn phone service? Before you do, better make sure you know the federal laws concerning these services and how to comply with them.

For the free fact sheet, *Commission Adopts Final Rules to Regulate Indecent Communication by Telephone*, contact: Federal Communications Commission, Consumer Assistance and Small Business Division, Office of Public Affairs, 1919 M St., NW, Room 254, Washington, DC 20554; 202-632-7000.

Take a Class

Nothing like going back to school. Many U.S. Small Business Administration (SBA) offices run seminars for people interested in buying a franchise. You can learn the ins and outs, as well as financing information available from the SBA. The SBA also has a free 4 page brochure titled, *Evaluating Franchise Opportunities*, for people considering franchises as a way to start a business.

Contact: Your local SBA office for more information or Answer Desk, U.S. Small Business Administration, 409 3rd St., SW, Washington, DC 20416; 800-827-5722.

Workers' Comp for Federal Employees

Do you work for Uncle Sam and were injured on the job? *Federal Injury Compensation* is a free publication which lists questions and answers regarding the Federal Employees' Compensation Act. They can also provide you with claim forms and checklists for evidence required in support of claims for occupational diseases.

Contact: Federal Employees' Compensation Division, Office of Workers' Compensation Programs, Employment Standards Administration, U.S. Department of Labor, 200 Constitution Ave., NW, Room S3229, Washington, DC 20210; 202-219-7552.

Plant Closing

Is your plant closing?

Cooperative Labor-Management Worker Adjustment Programs is a free study of companies and unions using techniques and procedures which provide invaluable lessons for management, unions, state and local officials, and others involved in plant closing and dislocated worker issues.

For your copy contact: Information Office, Bureau of Labor-Management Relations, U.S. Department of Labor, 200 Constitution Ave., NW, Room N5402, Washington, DC 20210; 202-219-6098.

Lend a Helping Hand

Want to help your employees recover from drug or alcohol addiction? Want to institute a "drug-free workplace" program, but aren't sure how?

The National Clearinghouse for Alcohol and Drug Information has several free publications and videos (for $8.50) dealing with drugs and the workplace to get you started.

Some of the titles include:

- *An Employer's Guide to Dealing with Substance Abuse*

- *Listing of Drug Testing Laboratories Certified by the Department of Health and Human Services*

- *NIDA Capsule: Resources to Address Drugs in the Workplace*

- *NIDA's Drug-Free Workplace Helpline*

- *Research on Drugs and the Workplace*

- *What Works: Workplaces Without Drugs*

- *Workers at Risk: Drugs and Alcohol on the Job*

Contact: National Clearinghouse for Alcohol and Drug Information, P.O. Box 2345, Rockville, MD 20847; 800-729-6686.

Teach Your Workers English

Want to set up a workplace literacy program? The National Clearinghouse on Literacy Education covers all aspects of literacy education for adults and out-of-school youth with limited English profi-  ciency. They publish digests, bibliographies, resource guides and more on the topic.

Two free digests include:

- *Workplace Literacy Programs for Nonnative English Speakers*, which compares workplace-based programs and traditional classroom-based programs; and

- *Learner-Centered Worker Education Programs* which describes how city workers in Vancouver convinced management and union to support a program where language is developed around workers' experiences and interests.

For more information contact: National Clearinghouse on Literacy Education, Center for Applied Linguistics, 1118 22nd St., NW, Washington, DC 20037; 202-429-9292.

Check Out the Mail

Even the mail isn't safe anymore. Mail fraud and mail theft seem to be big business. How do you protect yourself, your employees, and your company?

A free booklet, *Postal Crime Prevention: A Business Guide*, shows business owners how to protect themselves from con artists and thieves whose business is mail fraud and mail theft. It includes information on different types of mail fraud to watch for, check cashing precautions, guidelines for mailroom security, bombs in the mail, as well as additional information.

Contact: Public Affairs Branch, U.S. Postal Service, 475 L'Enfant Plaza, SW, Room 5541, Washington, DC 20260; 202-268-4293.

Got A Great Idea?

Got a great idea that just can't wait? The Patent and Trademark Office administers the patent and trademark laws, examines patent applications, and grants patent protection for qualified inventions. For more information on what is required for patents and trademarks, several free publications are available including:

- *Basic Facts About Patents*

- *Basic Facts about Trademarks*

- *Disclosure Document Program*

Contact: Public Affairs, Patent and Trademark Office, U.S. Department of Commerce, Washington, DC 20231; 703-308-4357.

Mom's Home Office

Starting a home-based business is often an economic necessity, because of the cost of childcare, the desire to be home with the kids, and more.

- *The Business Plan For Home-Based Business* ($1) is a publication of the U.S. Small Business Administration (SBA) and provides a comprehensive approach to developing a business plan for just such a venture. Once you've got your plan, all the rest you need is courage.

- *Selling By Mail Order* ($1) provides basic information on how to run a successful mail order business and includes information on product selection, pricing, testing and writing effective advertisements.

To order write: SBA Publications, P.O. Box 30, Denver, CO 80201; 202-205-6665.

Should My Company Go Public?

If my company becomes public, what do I have to tell? Are there legal ways to sell securities without registering with the Securities and Exchange Commission (SEC)?

The free booklet, *Q&A: Small Business and the SEC* discusses capital formation and the federal securities laws and is designed to help you understand some of the basic necessary requirements that apply when you wish to raise capital by selling securities.

Contact: U.S. Securities and Exchange Commission (SEC), Publications Section, M/SC-11, 450 5th St., NW, Washington, DC 20549; 202-272-7461.

Your Technology Phonebook

Need help finding the right expert? The *Technical Assistance Directory* is a free publication which lists programs, areas of expertise, and primary contacts in each of the major research and development areas within the U.S. Environmental Protection Agency (EPA). This information is provided to improve communication and technology transfer, and would be useful for the environmental community, other federal agencies, and individuals who need to locate specific programs.

For your copy contact: Center for Environmental Research Information, ORD Publications Unit, U.S. Environmental Protection Agency, Cincinnati, OH 45268; 513-569-7369.

Be Your Own Financial Manager

Just make sure you know what you are doing.

The Small Business Administration (SBA) has a series of publications dealing with financial management, designed to educate you on budgeting, money management issues, and record keeping. Some of the titles include:

- *ABC's Of Borrowing* ($1)

- *Basic Budgets for Profit Planning* ($1)

- *Accounting Services For Small Service Firms* ($.50)

- *Budgeting In A Small Service Firm* ($.50)

- *A Pricing Checklist For Small Retailers* ($1)

To order write: SBA Publications, P.O. Box 30, Denver, CO 80201; 202-205-6665.

Energy Business

The National Energy Information Center is the central distribution point for most U.S. Department of Energy (DOE) publications, including the free *Energy Information Administration Publications Directory: A Users Guide*.

The Directory includes current program information sources; an index of DOE, State, and Federal Agency contacts; a directory of DOE technical information with descriptions of computerized databases and other resources and more.

For your copy contact: National Energy Information Center, Energy Information Administration, U.S. Department of Energy, 1000 Independence Ave., SW, Room E1-231, Washington, DC 20585; 202-586-8800.

MBA without the Degree

Your business is up and running, so keep it headed in a good direction with a little help from the Small Business Administration (SBA).

They have publications on management and planning, which can help you look at the decisions you need to make. Some of the publications include:

- *Locating Or Relocating Your Business* ($1)

- *Problems In Managing A Family-Owned Business* ($.50)

- *Planning And Goal Setting For Small Business* ($.50)

- *Should You Lease Or Buy Equipment?* ($.50)

- *Small Business Decision Making* ($1)

To order write: SBA Publications, P.O. Box 30, Denver, CO 80201; 202-205-6665.

First, the Idea

Inventors are idea people. To help them become business people, the U.S. Small Business Administration (SBA) has several publications on what step two needs to be.

- *Ideas Into Dollars* identifies the main challenges in product development and provides a list of resources to help inventors ($2).

- *Avoiding Patent, Trademark and Copyright Problems* shows how to avoid infringing the rights of others and the importance of protecting yours ($1).

- *Trademarks and Business Goodwill* teaches what trademarks are and are not and how to get the most protection ($1).

To order write: SBA Publications, P.O. Box 30, Denver, CO 80201; 202-205-6665.

More than Running the Cash Register

Good employees are worth more than gold. Learn how to find and hire the right employees.

- *Employees: How To Find and Pay Them* ($1) gives you some guidelines for your personnel search.

- *Checklist For Developing A Training Program* ($.50) describes a step-by-step process for setting up an effective employee training program.

- *Managing Employee Benefits* ($1) describes these as one part of a total compensation package and discusses the proper management of benefits.

To order write: U.S. Small Business Administration Publications, P.O. Box 30, Denver, CO 80201; 202-205-6665.

Carpal Tunnel Syndrome

Carpal tunnel syndrome is a tingling sensation in the hands and fingers and can be caused or aggravated by repeated twisting or awkward postures, particularly when combined with high force. The population at risk includes persons employed in such industries or occupations as construction, food preparation, clerical work, product fabrication, and mining.

The National Institute For Occupational Safety and Health (NIOSH) has a *Carpal Tunnel Syndrome* booklet, which contains information on the syndrome, including current research, preventive recommendations, a bibliography, and articles.

Contact: National Institute For Occupational Safety and Health, 4676 Columbia Parkway, Cincinnati, OH 45226; 800-356-4674.

Maternity and Family Leave

Thirty-four States, Puerto Rico, and the District of Columbia have enacted some form of State maternity/family leave law to meet the changing needs of the American work force.

To find out what States have these laws and the scope of the law, request the free publication, *State Maternity/Family Leave Law*, available through the U.S. Department of Labor's Women's Bureau.

The publication outlines the law for each State, the employees covered by the law, temporary disability insurance, and enforcement or administration of the law for each State.

Contact: Women's Bureau, U.S. Department of Labor, 200 Constitution Ave., NW, Washington, DC 20210; 202-219-6652.

Overseas Carry Out

Do you have some food you would like to start exporting overseas? The Foreign Agricultural Service (FAS) are the experts in exports.

They have agricultural attaches and counselors stationed around the world who can help you market and sell your products.

Some of the free publications they have to offer include:

- *Agricultural Trade Offices*

- *Partners in Trade Promotion*

- *Agriculture's Emissaries Overseas*

- *Food and Agricultural Export Directory*

- *FAS Circulars*

For more information on the services that are available contact: Foreign Agricultural Service, Information Division, U.S. Department of Agriculture, Washington, DC 20250; 202-720-7937.

Wheelchairs: A Hot Business Opportunity?

Whoever thought that wheelchairs might have a bright future as a business venture?

What will wheelchairs look like in the 21st century?

Find out from the free executive summary of the report, *The Market for Wheelchairs: Innovation and Federal Policy.*

Contact: Office of Technology Assessment, Publication Order, U.S. Congress, Washington, DC 20510-8025; 202-224-8996.

For Your Career

Check Out the Head Hunters

When you are out looking for that perfect job, you will run into many companies that offer job hunting assistance. The Federal Trade Commission (FTC) often receives complaint letters about job counseling and placement services which charge large fees and misrepresent their services.

They publish two free publications: *Job Ads, Job Scams*, which explains things you need to look out for, and *Job Hunting: Should You Pay*, which explains about head hunter services and things you need to consider before you sign on.

Contact: Federal Trade Commission, Bureau of Consumer Protection, 6th and Pennsylvania Ave., NW, Washington, DC 20580; 202-326-2222.

Landing an Excellent Job

Tap the government for tips on finding the best work opportunities. *Tips For Finding The Right Job* helps you to evaluate your interests and skills, and provides information on resumes, application letters, job interviews, and more.

For your free copy contact: Employment and Training Administration, U.S. Department of Labor, 200 Constitution Ave., NW, Room N4700, Washington, DC 20210, 202-219-6871.

Check It Out

Want to check out the possibilities before you commit yourself to a four year degree? The Office of Museum Programs has put together *Internship Opportunities at the Smithsonian Institution* ($5), which is a comprehensive guide to 40 museums and offices at the Smithsonian that offer internships. Although the programs described are directed at the college level and above, this book gives valuable information about museum careers and provides details on the rich variety of research and museum functions at the Smithsonian, which may be of interest to high school students.

Contact: Office of Museum Programs, P.O. Box 37481-OMP, MRC 427, Smithsonian Institution, Washington, DC 20560; 202-357-3103.

Get The Scoop on Dirt

Does a career in archeology or anthropology interest you? Are you a teacher and want to learn more? *Summer Fieldwork Opportunities* is a free survey of opportunities for teachers and students aged 16 and above to participate in summer fieldwork.

Contact: Anthropology Outreach and Public Information Office, National Museum of Natural History, MRC 112, Smithsonian Institution, Washington, DC 20560; 202-357-1592.

Weigh Yourself on the Salary Scale

If you've got the itch to pull up stakes, know your worth wherever you're going by contacting the Bureau of Labor Statistics. They publish the *Occupational Compensation Surveys* which contain information on jobs and salary wages and occupation hourly wage for different cities across the country.

For a copy of a survey contact: Division of Occupational Pay and Employee Benefit Level, Office of Compensation and Working Conditions, Bureau of Labor Statistics, U.S. Department of Labor, Postal Square Bldg., Room 4160, 2 Massachusetts Ave., NE, Washington, DC 20212, 202-606-6220.

Is Jacques Cousteau Your Idol?

Thinking about a career in oceanography? The Department of Vertebrate Zoology has a free bibliography and listing of sources entitled *Careers in Biology, Conservation, and Oceanography* which can help you learn about the various fields you are considering.

Contact: National Museum of Natural History, Department of Vertebrate Zoology, Room 369, MRC 109, Smithsonian Institution, Washington, DC 20560; 202-357-2740.

Turn Off the Weather Channel

Think you can do better than the weather man? Study hard and a career could be in the making. You can learn a great deal about the weather from the National Weather Service. They have free publications covering every weather condition imaginable from floods to tornadoes.

Some of the freebies include:

- *Hurricane Tracking Chart*

- *Spotter's Guide for Identifying and Reporting Severe Local Storms*

- *Hurricane! A Familiarization Booklet*

- *Advanced Spotter's Field Guide*

- *Mariner's Guide to Marine Weather Services*

- *Key to Manual Weather Observations and Forecasts*

- *Flash Floods and Floods...The Awesome Power!*

For information about the publications and more contact Office of Public Affairs, National Weather Service, 1325 East-West Highway, Silver Spring, MD 20910; 301-713-0622.

Solar Power

A career in an efficient energy field might be just what you need. The Conservation and Renewable Energy Inquiry and Referral Service has a free publication titled, *Careers in the Renewable Energy and Conservation Professions and Trades* which gives an overview of the jobs available.

Another free publication, *Energy Education Resources*, provides a listing of reading material to get you started in your studies.

For these publications and more contact: Conservation and Renewable Energy Inquiry and Referral Service, P.O. Box 3048, Merrifield, VA 22116; 800-523-2929.

Your Job Magazine

Want to figure out what's happening on the career front? Get a subscription for only $8 for the *Occupational Outlook Quarterly* which covers such topics as job training, internships, profiles of workers, and matching personal and job characteristics.

There is also information on how to get a Federal job and the occupational projections to the year 2005.

For your subscription contact: Bureau of Labor Statistics, Publication Sales Center, P.O. 2145, Chicago, IL 60690; 312-353-1880.

Put Your Mouth to Work

Has your mouth gotten you into some trouble or does it make you the hit of parties? You could be a natural for a job as a D.J. Most disc jockeys need to be licensed, so get a licensing application packet from the Federal Communications Commission.

Contact: Federal Communications Commission, 1919 M St., NW, Washington, DC 20554; 202-632-7000.

Check Out the Options

Don't waste four years of college to get a degree that won't get you a job. Check out the job market through a series of Bureau of Labor Statistics publications titled *Occupational Outlook Handbook* reprints.

The series is broken down into various occupational groupings, and outlines degrees needed, job availability forecast, and even what area of the country the demand for you will be higher. There are 20 different reprints which include:

- *Tomorrow's Jobs: Overview* ($1.25)

- *Business and Managerial Occupations* ($2.75)

- *Computer and Mathematics-Related Occupations* ($2.00)

- *Health Technologists and Techniques* ($1.50)

- *Clerical and Other Administrative Support Occupations* ($1.50)

- *Sales Occupations* ($1.50)

- *Engineering, Scientific, and Related Occupations* ($1.75)

You can order your reprint (or a complete set for $24) from Bureau of Labor Statistics, Publication Sales Center, P.O. 2145, Chicago, IL 60690; 312-353-1880.

Free Instructions

The Mine Safety and Health Administration is responsible for the safety and health of our mines, and has a *Catalog of Training Programs For the Mining Industry*, which contains free instructional programs. Although these programs focus on mining, they are not exclusive to this field. Some of the programs include:

- *Cement: On-The-Job Training Modules*

- *First Aid Book*

- *Mining Accident Prevention*

- *Underground Coal: On-The-Job Training Modules*

For a copy of your free catalog contact: Office of Information and Public Affairs, Mine Safety and Health Administration, U.S. Department of Labor, 4015 Wilson Blvd., Room 601, Arlington, VA 22203; 703-235-1452.

Co-op with the Experts

The Peace Corps offers a Cooperative Education Program which is designed to give students paid work experience in their academic field of study.

Students must be enrolled on a full-time basis in their schools Cooperative Education Program. In addition, they must be working towards a degree, whether it be high school, undergraduate, graduate or professional.

For more specific information, contact: Office of Human Resource Management, Peace Corps, 1990 K St., NW, Washington, DC 20526; 202-606-3630.

Don't Be Tied to a Desk

If the outdoors is where you want to be, then look into a profession where hiking boots are part of the uniform. "A Challenge And An Adventure" is a free loan video that describes the various kinds of work the Fish and Wildlife Service is involved in. This could be the key to your future.

To borrow a copy contact your regional office, or you may contact the Office of Public Affairs for information regarding the Office nearest you: Office of Public Affairs, Fish and Wildlife Service, U.S. Department of Interior, Washington DC 20240; 202-208-5611.

Fly Right

Thinking of a career in aviation?

For every one pilot, there are 1500 other aviation professionals supporting aviation operations on the ground.

To help you learn more about the aviation field, the Federal Aviation Administration has several films and videos which outline the various careers, technical requirements, and educational backgrounds. Some of the titles include:

- *Looking Up to Your Aviation Career*

- *Put Wings On Your Career*

- *These Special People*

For a free catalog that includes free loan information, contact Public Inquiry, Federal Aviation Administration, U.S. Department of Transportation, Washington, DC 20591; 202-267-3476.

Reach for the Stars

No need to stay on the ground when the sky is the limit. *Careers in Aerospace* can give you an idea of the choices and options you have if you always dream of the stars.

For your free copy contact: National Aeronautics and Space Administration, Publication Center, 300 E St., SW, Washington, DC 20546; 202-453-1287.

Work for the CIA

The Central Intelligence Agency (CIA) offers four different Student Programs.

Each program has specific qualifications and benefits, and gives practical hands-on experience and work in a field that pertains to the students area of study such as: graphic design, languages, economics, printing/photography and more. The programs are as follows:

- Undergraduate Scholar Program - offers graduating high school students, especially minorities and individuals with disabilities who have a financial need for tuition assistance, the opportunity to work in a challenging position every summer through college.

- Minority Undergraduate Studies Program - provides students the opportunity to gain good work experience during the summer while making a competitive salary. Employment starts the summer of the students sophomore year.

- Undergraduate Student Trainee Program - gives practical experience in combination with academic studies. Individuals will also receive a competitive salary, as part of the program work is alternated with school on a semester or quarter basis.

- Graduate Studies Program - available to students entering their first or second year of graduate school, students are given the opportunity to work at the professional level and receive a competitive salary. Usually internships are in the summer, but some are available other times.

For more information on the various programs contact: Central Intelligence Agency Employment Center, P.O. Box 1255, Pittsburgh, PA 15230; 703-281-8365.

Statistics Headquarters

Get your foot in the door. The Bureau of the Census offers the Cooperative Education Program with opportunities in several different fields including, geography, statistics, cartography, computer and information systems. Each area offers different experiences. For example, in the area of geography, a co-op student would prepare reports and geographic materials, as well as respond to geographic inquiries within and outside the Census Bureau. In the area of statistics, a co-op would be designing questionnaires, preparing analytical studies, and many other related duties. Scheduling is flexible and you will be eligible for employment after graduation.

If you are interested contact: U.S. Bureau of Census, College Relations Office, Room 3124 FB-3, Washington, DC 20233; 301-763-5398.

Gone Fishin'

The Fish and Wildlife Service has a Cooperative Education Program that is available in Washington as well as in the different regions.

The program is very competitive but gives students the opportunity to get paid while working and learning.

Students can be undergraduate or graduate and are assigned based on their academic studies or career goals. Positions can be administrative or technical depending on your expertise and availability within the Fish and Wildlife Service.

For more information contact: U.S. Fish and Wildlife Service, Chief Office of Human Resources, 1849 C St., NW, Room 3058, Washington, DC 20240; 703-358-1724.

For Some Direction

Career decision making and career change are affecting more and more people as the job market seems to be changing.

The ERIC Clearinghouse for Adult, Career, and Vocational Education covers all areas of career and vocational/technical education from basic literacy training through professional skill upgrading.

Although they cannot tell you what career is best for you, they can provide you with a series of free ERIC Digests to help you look at the job market in a variety of ways. Some of the titles they have include:

- *Job Search Methods*

- *Adults in Career Transition*

- *Jobs In the Future*

- *Locating Job Information*

- *Labor Market Information and Career Decision Making*

For your copies or for more information available from the Clearinghouse contact: ERIC Clearinghouse for Adult, Career, and Vocational Education, The Ohio State University, 1900 Kenny Rd., Columbus, OH 43210; 800-848-4815.

Bank On It

The world of high finance may be for you. The Export Import Bank (EXIM Bank) has opportunities for college students to get valuable experience working in an international banking atmosphere. The Bank has Student Volunteer Internship Programs which are offered throughout the year. The student is assigned a mentor and either analyzes data or works on special projects.

For more information contact: Director of Human Resources, Export Import Bank of the United States, Suite 1005, 811 Vermont Ave., NW, Washington, DC 20571; 202-566-8834.

Volunteer

The Volunteer Service Program offers unpaid work experience to students who are in high school or college. You will get academic credit for the work that you perform. Most students will be involved in professional projects and activities.

The projects could involve research on environmental concerns or congressional issues. Most students work three to four months eight during the school year or the summer. You must contact the Federal Agency you would like to work with directly.

For additional information on the program contact: U.S. Office of Personnel Management, Washington Area Service Center, 1900 E St., NW, Washington, DC 20415; 202-606-3283.

Defense Work

The U.S. Department of Defense offers two different programs through the Office of the Secretary of Defense (OSD). Security clearance is needed in order to work for the Defense Department and can take four to six months, so apply early.

These programs are:

- Salaried Internships - available through the Washington Headquarters Services which fills the personnel needs of OSD. The positions are usually announced in December by the

Office of Personnel Management
(202-632-7484).

- Unsalaried Internships - available throughout the year based on the needs of OSD.

For more information write: Assistance Director for Employee Career Development and Training Division, U.S. Department of Defense, Washington Headquarters Services, Room 3B347, The Pentagon, Washington, DC 20301; 703-607-3422.

Astronaut Training

If you always wanted to be an astronaut, then this book is for you. *Astronaut Selection and Training* gives a basic overview of the requirements, steps and stages one must complete before becoming an astronaut. Historical information is supplied as well.

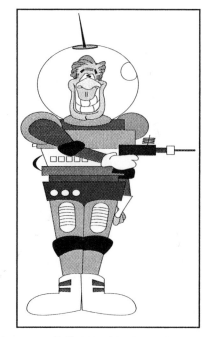

Free from: National Aeronautics and Space Administration Educational Publications, Code FEP, Washington, DC 20546; 202-453-1287.

A Matter of National Security

The National Security Agency (NSA) has a Cooperative Education Program that gives students responsibility right from the start. The Co-op Program is based on a series of semester-long "work tours". They are planned, supervised experiences with increased responsibilities each time. The projects will also be different each tour which gives you the opportunity to try new things. The four main disciplines are: electrical or computer engineering, computer science, languages, and mathematics.

For more information contact: National Security Agency, Attention M322 Co-op (FAE), Fort Meade, MD 20755-6000; 800-962-9398.

Dig In

The U.S. Department of Agriculture has a Summer Internship Program that gives students the opportunity to get good experience as well as pay during the summer months. Positions are usually scientific, technical, administrative or professional. The experience that one would get would depend on which Agency they were working for, but most positions are administrative.

For more information write: U.S. Department of Agriculture, Office of Personnel, Recruitment and Employment Division, Attention Summer Intern Program, Room 301 W. Administrative Building, Washington, DC 20250; 202-720-6905.

$3,000 to Design a Stamp

If you are an artist and think you might have a great idea for a post-age stamp, the U.S. Postal Service might pay you to design one- $3,000 for a single stamp. First you will need to have your work reviewed by their staff, and if they like your stuff, they might hire you as a freelancer to do a stamp.

Contact: Stamp Marketing Division, Office of Phila-telic and Retail Services, U.S. Postal Service, 475 L'Enfant Plaza, Room 4461-E, Washington, DC 20260-6810; 202-268-7700.

Astronaut Application

John Denver has submitted one, why don't you? The Space Shuttle program accepts applications from private citizens interested in contributing to the National Aeronautics and Space Administration (NASA) space flight program.

For an application contact: NASA, Lyndon B. Johnson Space Center, Mail Slot AHX, Houston, TX 77058; 713-483-5907.

Summer Jobs

If you are looking for a summer job that will offer you challenges, diversity, and a salary the Federal Government might be just the place for you. The type of work you will be assigned depends on your experience and what is available. Positions range from office support to trade and labor jobs to professional positions. Work is usually full-time and begins after May 12 and ends September 30. Positions are listed in the *Summer Jobs Announcement #414*.

For more information contact: U.S. Office of Personnel Management, Washington Area Service Center, 1900 E St., NW, Washington, DC 20415; 202-606-3283.

Practice MBA

Get a step ahead of other business students. The Financial Management Service of the U.S. Department of the Treasury offers the Cooperative Education Program. The type of positions available are in the areas of computer systems, finance, business administration, and accounting with students being assigned based on their major. In addition to getting good experience you will receive a competitive salary.

For more information write: U.S. Department of the Treasury, Financial Management Service, Cooperative Education Coordinator, 401 Fourteenth St., SW, Washington, DC 20227; 202-874-7090.

€nergy €ducation

Education has always been an important part of the U.S. Department of Energy's mission. The Office of University and Science Education Programs coordinates education programs within the U.S. Department of Energy. The free *Education Programs Catalog* details U.S. Department of Energy programs at the pre-college, undergraduate, graduate and general public level. It also contains a list of the National Laboratories run by or affiliated with the U.S. Department of Energy and the education programs they sponsor.

For your free copy contact: Office of Energy Research, Office of University and Science Education Programs, U.S. Department of Energy, 1000 Independence Ave., SW, Room 3F-061, Washington, DC 20585; 202-586-8949.

Summer Aid

No need to just hang out at the corner. The Summer Aid Program is designed to provide economically disadvantaged youths employment. Through special training and work experiences individuals will develop new skills. Positions are usually full-time in the summer. To be eligible for the program you must be at least 16 years of age, and qualify under the financial need criteria based on family income.

For more information contact: U.S. Office of Personnel Management, Washington Area Service Center, 1900 E St., NW, Washington, DC 20415; 202-606-3283.

Join the Team

Be a mover and a shaker. The Presidential Management Internship Program (PMI) is an entry level career development and training program designed to attract outstanding men and women to careers in public service. If chosen to be a PMI, one would be a part of a very challenging two year program.

You would participate in training conferences, seminars, and Congressional briefings, and will have the opportunity to learn at an accelerated pace and sharpen your management and leadership skills. PMIs are rotated to different Federal Agencies to get addition experience. Opportunities are also available in regions outside of Washington.

Contact: Office of Personnel Management, Washington Area Service Center, 1900 E St., NW, Room 2458, Washington, DC 20415; 202-606-2525.

Stay-In-School

The Stay-In-School Program is designed to provide Federal employment for financially needy students that attend high school or a post-secondary institution.

Every effort is made to assign students to positions that are career related or of interest to the full-time student. Stay-In-School students work part-time during school and full-time during the summer. Salary is based on work experience and education.

To get additional information and qualifications contact: U.S. Office of Personnel Management, Washington Area Service Center, 1900 E St., NW, Washington, DC 20415; 202-606-3283.

Energize

The U.S. Department of Energy offers the Cooperative Education Program in many of its different agencies and administrations.

The student will be given the opportunity to work in their area of expertise, which are usually in engineering, sciences, and business.

In the area of business, a co-op would be doing accounting, finance, or general business. Another possibility would be in the area of science, where a co-op would be doing computer work or physics.

For more information contact: U.S. Department of Energy, Personnel Operations Branch, 100 Independence Ave., SW, Washington, DC 20585; 202-586-4494.

20 Occupations Most Desired by Feds

Looking for a job, but can't seem to find anything? The Bureau of Labor Statistics has a free report from the summer of 1993 on the twenty occupations most often hired by the federal government. If yours happens to be one of those, maybe it's time for you to think of working for Uncle Sam.

Contact: Bureau of Labor Statistics, U.S. Department of Labor, Washington, DC 20212; 202-606-7828.

Women Doing the Jobs of Men

It's no longer necessary for women to settle for low paying, dead end jobs at fast food restaurants and offices. More and more, women are landing good paying jobs in what used to be traditionally only male jobs; carpenters, electricians, masons, plumbers, auto mechanics, welders, and so on. The free *Directory of Non-Traditional Training and Employment Programs Serving Women* outlines many of the free training programs all across the country for women interested in landing these "male" jobs.

Contact: Women's Bureau, U.S. Department of Labor, Washington, DC 20210-9990; 202-219-6653.

Free Job Training for Teens

You don't have to pay to go to an expensive trade school to learn how to become a welder, mechanic, nurses aide, or even a draftsman. If you're a low-income teen, you may qualify for free training through the Job Corps. There's even help getting your GED. You can find out what Job Corps programs are available in your area and elsewhere. Free publications include: *Job Corps in Brief, Train for Your Future*, and *Job Corps: A Chance To Make It*.

Contact: National Job Corps Alumni Association, 607 14th Street, NW, Suite 610, Washington, DC 20005; 800-733-JOBS.

Does a College Degree Guarantee a Job?

A recent report from the Bureau of Labor Statistics shows that a college degree will not guarantee you a job after graduation, nor will it even guarantee you a job, when you get one, that requires a college degree.

The free report *The College Labor Market: Outlook, Current Situation, and Earnings*, is reprinted from the summer 1992 issue of the *Occupational Outlook Quarterly*.

Contact: Bureau of Labor Statistics, U.S. Department of Labor, Washington, DC 20212; 202-606-7828.

For Your Community

Neighborhood Watch

Worried about safety in your neighborhood and considering trying to get a neighborhood watch program started?

The National Institute of Justice has a free publication, *Improving the Use and Effectiveness of Neighborhood Watch Programs*, which provides a wealth of information on the program. The Institute also has information on community policing programs which involve the police force making their presence known by increased foot patrols, and other services.

Contact: National Institute of Justice, NCJRS, Box 6000, Dept. AID, Rockville, MD 20850; 800-851-3420, 301-251-5500.

Consumer Resource

A free *Consumer's Resource Handbook* shows you how to communicate more effectively with manufacturers, retailers and service providers.

The first section features tips on avoiding purchasing problems and getting the most for your money by giving steps for handling your own complaint and writing an effective complaint letter. The second section, the *Consumer Assistance Directory*, lists consumer offices in both public and private sectors that provide assistance for consumer complaints. Handbooks are available by written request.

Contact: Handbook Publication Request, U.S. Consumer Product Safety Commission, Washington, DC 20207.

Adopt A Roadway

Embarrassed driving home, because the highway or roadway looks like a dump?

Become active in roadway beautification. Junkyards and outdoor advertising along federally aided and interstate highways are regulated under a program conducted through this office. The publication, *Junkyards, the Highway, and Visual Quality*, offers information on this program.

Contact: Special Programs and Evaluation Branch (HRW-12), Program Requirements Division, Office of Right-of-Way and Environment, Federal Highway Administration, U.S. Department of Transportation, 400 7th St., SW, Room 3221, Washington, DC 20590; 202-366-2017.

Chemicals in Your Community – Learn What You Need to Know

Congress passed a law designed to help America's communities deal safely and effectively with the many hazardous substances that are used throughout our society.

The law is called the *Emergency Planning and Community Right-to-Know Act*, and this booklet has been written to help you understand and take advantage of your rights and opportunities under this far-reaching law.

The first part of the guide describes how the law works, what its provisions were intended to accomplish, and how all members of the community can play an active part in making sure the law is carried out. The second part discusses specific groups and organizations affected by the law, describes what they can do or are required to do to make it work, and tells how they can benefit from it.

Contact: Public Information Center 3404, U.S. Environmental Protection Agency, 401 M St., SW, Washington, DC 20460; 202-260-7751.

Clean Up the Air in Your Part of the World

Fuel efficiency is something important to consider when buying a new car. The gas tax will effect you less, and your car will run more efficiently. The U.S. Environmental Protection Agency publishes a free annual *Mileage Guide* which contains fuel

economy estimates for all new makes and models. Peruse the list before you hit the showrooms.

Contact: Public Information Center 3404, U.S. Environmental Protection Agency, 401 M St., SW, Washington, DC 20460; 202-260-7751.

Is It Safe to Drink the Water?

The Safe Drinking Water Hotline can answer any question or concern you may have regarding drinking water, and provide you with publications and referrals to water testing companies. Some of the free publications they have include:

- *Safe Drinking Water Act*

- *Lead In Your Drinking Water*

- *Buying A Home Water Treatment Unit*

Contact: Safe Drinking Water Hotline, U.S. Environmental Protection Agency, 401 M St., SW, Washington, DC 20460; 800-426-4791.

Recycling Efforts

Land fills are overflowing and now is the time to take action. *Recycling Works!* is a free booklet that provides information about successful recycling programs initiated by state and local agencies. It also describes private recycling efforts and joint recycling ventures of government and businesses.

Contact: Resource Conservation and Recovery Act Docket, U.S. Environmental Protection Agency, 401 M St., SW, Washington, DC 20460; 202-260-9327.

Changed Your Oil Lately?

We all know that we are supposed to change our oil regularly in our car, and many of us do it ourselves to save money. But what do we do with the old oil? Can you throw it in the sewer?

Oil is a valuable resource when properly recycled. Recycling can conserve our nation's natural resources, protect the environment, and save consumers' money. However, when improperly disposed of, used oil can contaminate the soil and surface and ground waters.

The Resource Conservation and Recovery Act (RCRA) Hotline has several free publications dealing with recycling used oil including:

- *How to Set Up Local Program to Recycle Used Oil*

- *Recycling Used Oil: 10 Steps to Change Your Oil*

- *Recycling Used Oil: For Service Stations and Other Vehicle-Service Facilities*

- *Recycling Used Oil: What Can You Do?*

Contact: RCRA Hotline, U.S. Environmental Protection Agency, 401 M St., SW, Washington, DC 20460; 800-424-9346, 703-920-9810.

Bringing Art To Life

The National Gallery of Art's Extension Program is an attempt to develop awareness in the visual arts and make its collections accessible to everyone, no matter how far away from the Gallery they may live.

The programs are loaned free of charge to educational institutions, community groups, and to individuals throughout the United States.

Nearly 150 programs are offered in a variety of mediums, including slides, videos, films, and videodiscs, and covered specific topics or time periods.

The slides sets usually come with an audiocassette and text. A complete catalog of programs is available at no charge from the Extension Programs Office.

Some of the programs include:

Slide Sets:

- "Survey of American Painting"

- "Famous Men and Women in Portraits"

- "Introduction to Understanding Art"

- "African Art"

- "Impressionism"

Videos:

- "The Christmas Story in Art"

- "Leonardo: To Know How To See"

- "The Eye of Thomas Jefferson"

- "John James Audubon: The Birds of America"

- "Matisse in Nice"

- "Art of Indonesia"

Contact: Department of Education Resources, Education Division, National Gallery of Art, 4th St. and Constitution Ave., NW, Washington, DC 20565; 202-842-6875.

Tourism in Your Town

Tourism can be big business for your town. For those communities interested in initiating or developing tourism as part of their economic development plan, the United States Travel and Tourism Administration (USTTA) has several free publications dealing with travel industry market research.

Outlook for International Travel to the United States provides a one-year forecast of international travel to/from the U.S. *Marketing Tourism Abroad: USTTA's International Cooperative Marketing Manual* provides information concerning the cooperative marketing programs offered by USTTA.

Contact: Office of Research, United States Travel and Tourism Administration (USTTA), U.S. Department of Commerce, 14th St. and Constitution Ave., NW, Room 1868, Washington, DC 20230.

Are Drugs Invading Your Town?

If you don't feel safe on your own front porch, because of an increase in drug related crimes, then maybe it is time to do something. ACTION Drug Alliance helps people develop community based volunteer organizations to address the issue of drug abuse in America.

A free booklet entitled *Take Action Against Drug Abuse: How to Start a Volunteer Anti-Drug Program in Your Community* provides information on how to get started, discusses fundraising, volunteer recruitment, publicity and more.

Contact: ACTION, 1100 Vermont Ave., NW, Washington, DC 20525; 202-606-4849.

Spruce Up the View

Tired of looking at the billboard on the highway, when you could be enjoying a scenic overlook? Find out who controls outdoor advertising, the rules regarding their placement, and who to contact for more information by requesting two free publications from the Federal Highway Administration. *A Summary: Control of Outdoor Advertising* explains the laws regarding outdoor advertising and provides a state by state listing of contacts for more information. *Outdoor Advertising Control and Acquisition* explains how signs are approved, how to get offending signs removed, defines the different types of zoning, and more.

Contact: Special Programs and Evaluation Branch (HRW-12), Program Requirements Division, Office of Right-of-Way and Environment, Federal Highway Administration, U.S. Department of Transportation, 400 7th St., SW, Room 3221, Washington, DC 20590; 202-366-2026.

Look within to Help Your Town

Tired of seeing troubled youths hanging out? What about lonely or bored senior citizens? ACTION is Uncle Sam's domestic volunteer agency and supports many programs designed to provide lasting solutions to the challenges of crime, hunger, poverty, illiteracy, drug abuse, and homelessness.

If you or your organization are looking for ways to improve your community, look to ACTION for help. Some of their programs include Volunteers in Service to America (VISTA), the Foster Grandparent Program, the Retired Senior Volunteer Program, the Senior Companion Program, the Student Community Service Program, and the Program Demonstration and Development Division. For an information packet on how you can volunteer or for more information on any of the programs, contact ACTION today.

Contact: ACTION, 1100 Vermont Ave., NW, Washington, DC 20525; 202-606-4849.

Wetlands Protection

What are wetlands and why are they important? The U.S. Environmental Protection Agency's (EPA) Wetlands Protection Hotline is responsive to public in-

terest, questions and requests for information about wetlands, and options for their protection.

The hotline can provide you with may free publications on the topic.

- *Wetlands Protection: A Local Government Handbook* is available which reviews federal and state laws and programs that promote wetlands preservation.

- The *White House Policy on Wetlands* outlines President Clinton's focus on wetlands protection. The Hotline also has a packet of 32 fact sheets which cover a variety of topics relating to wetlands including information on the Clean Water Act, EPA's regional offices, as well as general information on the importance of wetlands.

Contact: Wetlands Protection Hotline, Gao/Resource Consultants, Inc., 1555 Wilson Blvd., Suite 500, Arlington, VA 22209; 800-832-7828.

Base Closure Catastrophe

With cutbacks in defense, bases are being closed all across the country. The Office of Economic Adjustment assists local communities, areas or states affected by U.S Department of Defense actions, such as base closures, establishment of new installations, and cutbacks or expansion of activities. It publishes a number of free publications on these issues, including: *Communities in Transition*, and *Planning for Civilian Reuse of Former Military Bases*.

For these publications or additional information for communities concerned about base closings contact: Office of Economic Adjustment, U.S. Department of Defense, 400 Army Navy Dr., Suite 200, Arlington, VA 22202; 703-695-1800.

Community Theater

Community Arts: Partnerships in Education is a booklet ($7) which provides a broad overview of more than 45 school-community partnerships that bring the arts into the lives of young people, their families, and the community at large. Each profile reflects community arts and education collaboration strategies that are integral to current education reform efforts.

Contact: Education Department, John F. Kennedy Center for the Performing Arts, Washington, DC 20566; 202-416-8800.

The Endangered Species Hit List

Most people know that the California condor and the bald eagle are on the endangered species list, and the spotted owl saga has been on the front page a great deal lately.

The U.S. Fish and Wildlife Service has a free series of one page biologies on a variety of endangered species, including the three listed above.

They also can provide you with the Endangered Species Act, a copy of the Federal Register titled *Endangered and Threatened Wildlife and Plants* which lists endangered or threatened species, and an informational brochure entitled *Endangered Species*.

For your copies, contact: Fish and Wildlife Service, Publications Unit, Mail Stop 130 Arlsq., U.S. Department of Interior, Washington, DC 20240; 703-358-3484.

Environment Dictionary

Tired of not understanding a newspaper article dealing with the environment because of the technical terms or abbreviations they use? *Terms of Environment: Glossary, Abbreviations, And Acronyms* defines in non-technical language the more commonly used environmental terms appearing in U.S. Environmental Protection Agency documents. This free publication is your dictionary for everything from acid rain to zooplankton.

Get your copy by contacting U.S. Environmental Protection Agency, Information Access Branch, Public Information Center, 401 M St., SW, 3404, Washington, DC 20460; 202-260-7751.

Stop Crime

One of the fastest growing, most visible crime control programs in the United States is Crime Stoppers, also known as Crime Solvers, Secret Witness, Crime Line, or other names. These self-sustaining programs join the news media, the community, and law enforcement as an alliance to involve private citizens in the fight against serious crime.

Crime Stoppers-A National Evaluation is a free publication which describes these programs, their effectiveness, and more. For your copy contact: National Institute of Justice Clearinghouse, NCJRS, Box 6000. Dept. AID, Rockville, MD 20850; 800-851-3420.

In Your Neighborhood

The Cooperative Extension Service, part of the U.S. Department of Agriculture, uses research, knowledge, and educational programs to assist people in making practical decisions. Its mission is to help people improve their lives through an educational process that uses scientific knowledge focused on issues and needs.

Located in almost every county across America, the Cooperative Extension Service provides information on topics ranging from diet to finances, from families to farming. Most of the information provided at the local level is free or low cost. *The Cooperative Extension System* is a series of fact sheets describing the Service. *Patterns Of Change* outlines the plan for the future of the Service.

For your free copies or for information about an office near you contact: Extension Service, U.S. Department of Agriculture, Room 3328, Washington, DC 20250; 202-720-4111.

Don Quixote Would Be Proud

Windmills are not a thing of the past, but a thing of the future. The U.S. Department of Energy's Wind Energy Program assists utilities and industry in developing advanced wind turbine technology to be economically competitive. The Conservation and Renewable Energy Inquiry and Referral Service has several free publications which describe wind energy programs, such as:

- *Wind Energy: Program Overview FY1992*

- *Energy From Wind*

- *Office of Utility Technologies Success Stories*

- *Is the Wind A Practical Source of Energy for You?*

For these publications and more information on wind energy contact: Conservation and Renewable Energy Inquiry and Referral Service, P.O. Box 3048, Merrifield, VA 22116; 800-523-2929.

Clean the Air

There is help close to home for your indoor air concerns. The *Directory of State Indoor Air Contacts* is a guide to locating individuals who can provide information and assistance on indoor air quality problems. It brings together information on more than 17 issues, from asbestos to wood preservatives, for the range of agencies involved in addressing those issues, from health agencies to energy departments. In most states, as well as at the federal level, indoor air quality issues are dealt with by a variety of agencies with the authority or expertise to focus on a particular problem or set of problems.

This free directory is available from: Indoor Air Quality Information Clearinghouse, P.O. Box 37133, Washington, DC 20013; 800-438-4318.

Clean It Up

Tired of all the pollution? It's time for you to act and learn how to reduce, reuse, and recycle.

- *The Consumer's Handbook for Reducing Solid Waste* describes how individual consumers can help alleviate the mounting trash problem by making environmentally aware decisions about everyday things like shopping and caring for the lawn.

- *What You Can Do To Reduce Air Pollution* explains the major air pollutants, the goals of the Clean Air Act, and the actions you can take to reduce pollution.

Both are free from U.S. Environmental Protection Agency, Information Access Branch, Public Information Center, 401 M St., SW, 3404, Washington, DC 20460; 202-260-7751.

Cable Catastrophe

Is your cable bill going up yet again? Who regulates the cable companies?

The Federal Communications Commission (FCC) can provide you with the facts.

- *Cable Television Rate Regulation*, which explains basic cable service rates and where you need to complain regarding the rates.

- *Cable Carriage of Broadcast Stations: Questions and Answers* explains a new cable law which requires cable systems to receive a stations' permission to carry them.

- *FCC Cable Information Line* provides consumers, cable companies, and other interested parties with information on cable regulation.

You can use this service to find out how to file complaints, learn about cable programs that have been dropped, and to obtain copies of cable forms, cable rules, and regulations.

For more information contact: Federal Communications Commission, 1919 M St., NW, Washington, DC 20554; 202-632-0004.

Environmental Awareness

Communities are be-
coming more aware of
the need to take a
close look at the de-
mands they place upon
their environment.
Recycling is becoming
more prevalent.
Conservation is taking
place, and communi-
ties are examining
other types of energy

such as solar. The Conservation and Renewable
Energy Inquiry and Referral Service has a series of
publications and fact sheets on a variety of energy
related topics, such as:

- *Recycling Waste to Save Energy*

- *Electric Vehicles*

- *What Every Community Should Do About Solar Access*

- *Energy Conservation Trends*

- *Conservation and Renewable Energy Technologies for Buildings*

For your free copies or more information on the
topic contact: Conservation and Renewable Energy
Inquiry and Referral Service, P.O. Box 3048, Merrifield, VA 22116; 800-523-2929.

Roadside Improvements

Make your neighborhood a cleaner, safer place to live with some help from the Federal Highway Administration.

They publish a variety of brochures, reports, and guides which provide information on highway safety.

Some of the titles include:

- *Roadside Improvements for Local Roads and Streets*

- *Guide to Safety Features for Local Roads and Streets*

- *America On The Move*

- *Fatal and Accident Rates on Public Roads in the United States*

- *Improving Operational Safety on Local Roads and Streets*

For your free copies contact: Federal Highway Administration, Office of Highway Safety (HHS-1), 400 7th St., SW, Washington, DC 20590.

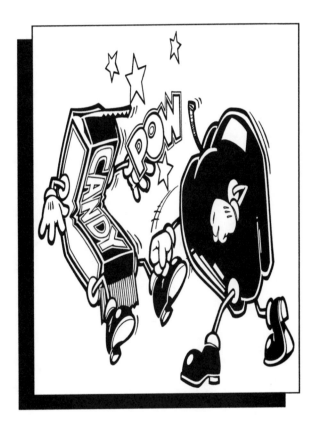

Getting Fit, Losing Fat

Are you struggling with losing weight, and want to know how exercise can help your diet work more effectively? Single copies of a 23-page booklet titled *Obesity and Energy Metabolism*, which explains the relationship between too much food and too little exercise are available free.

Contact: Obesity and Energy Metabolism, Office of Clinical Center Communications, Clinical Center NIH, Building 10, Room 5C305 Bethesda, MD 20892; 301-496-2563.

Anorexia Nervosa and Bulimia

Are you concerned that you or a loved one is suffering from anorexia or bulimia? *Facts About Anorexia Nervosa* explains the causes, symptoms, and treatment for anorexia and bulimia as well as ongoing research efforts at the National Institutes of Health (NIH). This 8-page pamphlet is available free.

Contact: National Institute of Child Health and Human Development, NIH, Building 31, Room 2A32, 9000 Rockville Pike, Bethesda, MD 20892; 301-496-5133.

Some Dinner Reading

For books on nutrition, the Food and Nutrition Information Center offers *Nutri-Topics* which are free brief reading lists designed to help locate information or resources on a given topic.

They are available as separate lists of resources appropriate for one or more user levels: consumer, educator, and health professional. Included are print materials, videos, journal articles, pamphlets, and lists of contacts for further information. Topics include:

- *Diet and Cancer*
- *Food Allergy*
- *Intolerance, and Sensitivity*
- *Food Safety: Ready-Prepared Foods*
- *Nutrition and Cardiovascular Disease*
- *Nutrition and Diabetes*
- *Nutrition and the Elderly*
- *Nutrition and the Handicapped*
- *Nutrition, Learning and Behavior*

- *Sensible Nutrition*

- *Sports Nutrition*

- *Vegetarian Nutrition*

- *Weight Control*

Contact: Food and Nutrition Information Center, U.S. Department of Agriculture, National Agricultural Library, Room 304, 10301 Baltimore Blvd., Beltsville, MD 20705; 301-504-5719.

The Fountain of Food

One of the Food and Drug Administration's (FDA) missions is to protect the safety and wholesomeness of food. They regulate what's termed fresh, what's low fat, and more.

They test samples of food to see if any substances, such as pesticide residues, are present in unacceptable amounts. If contaminants are identified, FDA takes corrective action.

FDA also sets labeling standards to help consumers know what is in the foods they buy. Information is available (for free) on a wide variety of topics including, but not limited to: calcium and other special needs of women, cellulite removal gimmicks, eating disorders, fad diets and diet books, fast food and nutrition, food preparation, nutrition labels, organic foods, saccharin, salt, vitamins.

Contact: Information Office Of Public Affairs, Food and Drug Administration, 5600 Fishers Lane, Rockville, MD 20857; 301-443-3170.

Eating Right To Lower Your Cholesterol and High Blood Pressure

Has your doctor told you that your cholesterol is too high? What about your blood pressure? You may be on medication, or maybe your doctor has suggested a change in life style to help your condition.

The Information Center for the National Heart, Lung, and Blood Institute can answer your questions regarding cholesterol, high blood pressure and heart disease.

They can provide you with free journal articles, and other information on these topics, including several publications dealing with nutrition such as;

- *Check Your Weight and Heart Disease I.Q*

- *Eat Right To Lower Your High Blood Cholesterol*

- *Facts About Blood Cholesterol*

- *Heart Attacks*

- *High Blood Pressure & What You Can Do About It*

- *Nutrition and Your Health: Dietary Guidelines For Americans*

- *Questions About Weight, Salt, and High Blood Pressure*

Contact: Information Center, National Heart, Lung, and Blood Institute, 7200 Wisconsin Ave., P.O. Box 30105, Bethesda, MD 20824; 301-251-1222.

Are the Kids and I Eating Right?

The National Maternal and Child Health Clearinghouse has several free publications concerned with pregnancy and early childhood nutrition:

- *Nutrition During Pregnancy: Weight Gain, Nutrient Supplements*

- *Nutrition and Your Health —* *Dietary Guideline for Americans*

- *Nutritional Disorders of Children: Prevention, Screening, and Follow-up*

- *Nutrition Resources for Early Childhood —* *Resource Guide*

Contact: National Maternal and Child Health Clearinghouse, 8201 Greensboro Dr., Suite 600, McLean, VA 22102; 703-821-8955, Ext. 254.

Information for Community Nutrition Services

The National Clearinghouse for Primary Care Information offers manuals for community health centers, primary care providers, home health services, HMOs, and outpatient clinics on approaches for establishing a nutrition program.

Single copies of a 96-page *Guide for Developing Nutrition Services in Community Health Programs* is available free, and covers the planning, developing, and evaluating of nutrition services as an integral component of community health programs.

Contact: National Clearinghouse for Primary Care Information, 8201 Greensboro Dr., #600, McLean, VA 22102; 703-821-8955.

Know What the Most Informed People Know

The Food and Nutrition Information Center is a great starting place for every nutrition question you could have. They can send you free information, refer you to videos, books, articles, print materials, or other resources on your topic of interest. Some of the materials include:

- *Nutrition Education Printed Materials and Audiovisuals: Grades Preschool through 6*

- *Nutrition Education Printed Materials and Audiovisuals: Grades 7-12*

- *Nutrition Education Resource Guide: An Annotated Bibliography of Educational Materials for the WIC and CSF Programs*

- *Adult/Patient Nutrition Education Materials*

- *Sources of Free or Low-Cost Food and Nutrition Materials*

- *The Idea Book: Sharing Nutrition Education Experiences* (designed for WIC-Women, Infants, and Children)

Contact: Food and Nutrition Information Center, U.S. Department of Agriculture, National Agricultural Library, Room 304, 10301 Baltimore Blvd., Beltsville, MD 20705; 301-504-5719.

Just Can It

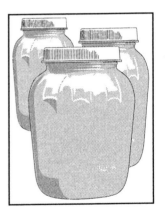

Canning is not a simple task. *Complete Guide to Home Canning* ($2.75) explains the principles on canning techniques. It also discusses canning equipment, and describes the proper use of jars and lids.

For your copy contact: Superintendent of Documents, U.S. Government Printing Office, Washington, DC 20402; 202-783-3238.

What's on a Label?

Cutting down on fat and sodium is going to be much easier with the new labels that are required of food products. Uniform definitions for terms such as light, low-fat and high-fiber have been written to be more helpful for consumers trying to moderate their intake of calories, fat or other nutrients. For an information packet on the new food label, contact the Food Labeling Education Information Center.

Contact: Food Labeling Education Information Center, Food and Nutrition Information Center, National Agricultural Library, Room 304, 10301 Baltimore Blvd., Beltsville, MD 20705; 301-504-5719.

The Road to Good Health

Starts with a good diet. One day you're told to eat carbohydrates, the next day it's fruit. Get the facts from the people who wrote the book on nutrition. The Food and Drug Administration (FDA) has several free publications which can help you eat right and enjoy the good life.

- *Fruit: Something Good That's Not Illegal, Immoral Or Fattening*

- *A Simple Guide To Complex Carbohydrates*

- *Fiber: Something Healthy To Chew On*

- *Primer On Three Nutrients*

- *Dietary Guidelines For Americans*

- *An FDA Guide To Dieting*

For these and other publications on food contact: Food and Drug Administration, Division of Consumer Affairs, HFE-88, 5600 Fishers Lane, Rockville, MD 20857; 301-443-3170.

Talk Turkey

Actually, you can talk about any meat or poultry product with the experts at the U.S. Department of Agriculture's Meat and Poultry Hotline.

They can answer your questions regarding power outages, meat and poultry labels, cooking time, and meat safety.

Some of the publications they have to offer include:

- *Preventing Foodborne Illness*

- *A Quick Consumer Guide to Safe Food Handling*

- *Talking About Turkey*

- *Meat and Poultry Products*

- *Safe Food To Go*

For more information on meat and poultry items contact: Food Safety and Inspection Service, U.S. Department of Agriculture, Washington, DC 20250; 800-535-4555.

Your Food Magazine

Food News for Consumers (quarterly, $5 per year) contains news items pertaining to food safety, food and nutrition research, and more. You can even get the latest information on human nutrition.

For your copy contact: Superintendent of Documents, U.S. Government Printing Office, Washington, DC 20402; 202-783-3238.

Change the Channel

Plug in these videos and turn on a healthy alternative to chips and dip. Discover how to make food taste great without fat, salt, and all the other no-nos.

The Food and Nutrition Information Center has three publications to get you started:

- *Audiovisuals About Low Fat, Low Cholesterol Eating for a Healthy Heart*

- *Audiovisuals About Weight Control*

- *Audiovisuals About Basic Nutrition*

To receive these three publications, send a self-addressed, stamped envelope with 58 cents postage to: Food and Nutrition Information Center, National Agricultural Library, Room 304, 10301 Baltimore Blvd., Beltsviile, MD 20705.

For Your Education

(College Survival Guide)

Crash Course in College Economics

Preparing Your Child for College: A Resource Book for Parents will help you eliminate your fear that you won't be able to afford to send your kids to college.

This free resource book shows that college can really be for everyone.

Contact: Office of Policy and Planning, U.S. Department of Education, 400 Maryland Ave., SW, Washington, DC 20202; 202-401-0590.

Birth Control or Self-Control

The locker room is no place to research contraception, tips on safe sex, or whether college is a good place to start a family. Get the facts on contraception. The Family Life Information Exchange has brochures and pamphlets on family planning, adolescent abstinence, and adoption.

Some of the titles include *Contraceptive Choices* which examines the various birth control methods and *Many Teens Are Saying No (sex)*, which promotes the benefits of abstinence.

Contact: Family Life Information Exchange, P.O. Box 37299, Washington, DC 20013-7299; 301-585-6636.

The GI Bill

If you have served in active duty or in the reserves, you may be eligible for education benefits under the Montgomery GI Bill. The Veterans Benefits Administration publishes two free booklets titled *Summary of Education Benefits Under the Montgomery GI Bill-Active Duty Educational Assistance Program, Chapter 30 of Title 38 U.S. Code* and *Summary of Educational Benefits Under the Montgomery GI Bill-Selected Reserve Educational Assistance Program, Chapter 106 of Title 10 U.S. Code.* Both booklets contain information on eligibility and benefits.

Contact: Veterans Benefits Administration, U.S. Department of Veterans Affairs, 810 Vermont Ave., NW, Washington, DC 20420; 800-827-1000.

What's a Pound Worth?

Does a fad diet seem the only way to chop those excess pounds? Lose weight safely and effectively. *Facts About Weight Loss* is a free publication which helps you avoid deceptive weight loss programs, potentially harmful pills, and phony devices or gadgets.

Contact: Federal Trade Commission, 6th and Pennsylvania Ave., NW, Washington, DC 20580; 202-326-2222.

Speed Trap 101

Caught speeding on your way to school? What about drinking and driving? The report, *Police Traffic Radar*, published in February, 1980, is still accurate and shows that all police radar tracking devices are not accurate all of the time. Such evidence can be helpful in the defense of your case.

This laboratory also has information regarding alcohol breath testing devices, including *Breath Alcohol Sampling Simulator for Qualification Testing of Breath Alcohol Measurement Devices*. Both publications are free.

Contact: Office of Law Enforcement Standards, National Institute of Standards and Technology, Building 225, Room A-323, Gaithersburg, MD 20899; 301-975-2757.

Back to School Zits?

No need to go to the prom with pimples. This Clearinghouse can provide you with a free information packet called "Acne Information".

Contact: National Arthritis and Musculoskeletal and Skin Disease Information Clearinghouse, Box AMS, Bethesda, MD 20892; 301-495-4484.

Majoring In Stress?

The pressure can get to everyone. The National Institute of Mental Health has a publication, *Plain Talk About Stress*, which discusses the three stages of physical and mental stress and how to recognize their symptoms and provides sug-

gestions for dealing with stress. Also available in Spanish.

Contact: Public Inquiries, National Institute of Mental Health, Room 7C-02, 5600 Fishers Lane, Rockville, MD 20857; 301-443-4513.

What's Fair's Fair, Scientifically Speaking

Stumped for a good science project idea? Request a free copy of *Science Fair Projects* which lists references for some interesting projects, including lasers, astronomy, and holograms.

Contact: Science and Technology Division, Library of Congress, Washington, DC 20540; 202-707-5664.

College-Bound and Gagged

Fear of public speaking is nothing to get choked up about, Uncle Sam believes in freedom of speech. The Congressional Research Service has put together several packets of information on speech writing for members of Congress, which you can get for free just by contacting your Representative or Senators.

The reports cover general public speaking information, and provide ideas for all the major national holidays. Some of the reports include:

- *Public Speaking*, Bibliography-in-Brief

- *Speechwriting and Delivery*, Info Pack

- *Speech Material: Fourth of July*, Info Pack

- *Speech Material: Graduation*, Info Pack

- *Speech Material: Martin Luther King's Birthday*, Info Pack.

Contact: Your Congressman, The Capitol, Washington, DC 20510; 202-224-3121.

Native American Programs

The Bureau of Indian Affairs sponsors several programs to promote higher education for Native Americans. They have the Higher Education Grant Program, Special Higher Education Grant Program, Adult Education Program, Summer Law Program and more. A good source of information on Indian education in general is the free annual *Office of Indian Education Programs Education Directory*.

Contact: Office of Indian Education Programs, Bureau of Indian Affairs, U.S. Department of the Interior, 18th and C Sts., NW, Washington, DC 20240; 202-208-4871.

Last-Minute Tans Have a Dark Side

Get a tan before spring break? The Food and Drug Administration (FDA) has information concerning tanning booth use, including the hazards and what you need to do to protect your skin.

You can get a pamphlet and other articles, such as *Tan Now, Pay Later* which discusses the health effects of tanning and information on sun lamps.

Contact: Food and Drug Administration, Division of Consumer Affairs, HFE-88, 5600 Fishers Lane, Rockville, MD 20857; 301-443-3170.

Your Neighborhood College

The convenience, services, and cost make community colleges the way to go for many students. The ERIC Clearinghouse for Community Colleges can provide you with a wealth of information regarding 2-year community and junior college, technical institutes, and 2-year branch university campuses. They have many publications including these free bibliographies:

- *Job Training and Economic Development*

- *Student Personnel Services*

- *General Education*

- *Vocational Education: Goals and Outcomes*

- *Skill Building in the Community College*

Contact: University of California, Los Angeles, ERIC Clearinghouse for Community Colleges, 8118 Math Sciences Building, 405 Hilgard Ave., Los Angeles, CA 90024; 310-825-3931.

Flight Schools

Want to learn how to fly but don't know where to start? The Federal Aviation Administration (FAA) can help you get off the ground, as they have a listing of all the flight schools in the country, including name, address, telephone number, and listing of courses offered.

Contact: Federal Aviation Administration (FAA), Attention: AFS 624, P.O. Box 25082, Oklahoma City, OK 73125; 405-954-4173.

CD-ROM vs. Floppy Disks?

Are you having a hard time trying to decide whether you should buy a CD-ROM or stay with your computer floppy disks? The ERIC Clearinghouse on Information Resources can

send you a number of studies comparing the different types of computer-based media.

Contact: ERIC Clearinghouse on Information Resources, 4-194 Center for Science Technology, Syracuse, NY 13244-4100; 315-443-3640.

I'm Studying Abroad

Want to be part of an exchange program? The U.S. Information Agency can provide you with information on public and private organizations which sponsor international exchange activities.

The free book *Fulbright Grants and Other Grants for Graduate Study Abroad* contains valuable information both on the Fulbright program and on other organizations sponsoring exchanges.

Contact: Office of Public Liaison, United States Information Agency, 301 Fourth St., SW, Room 602, Washington, DC 20547; 202-619-4355.

Free Engineering Degree

Few people know that one way to get an engineering degree — for free — without having to join the military, and without having to be low-income, is through the Merchant Marine Academy in Kings Point, New York. Not only is tuition covered, but so are your books and uniform costs, and you'll receive a monthly stipend for the work you'll be assigned.

Contact: Admissions Officer, U.S. Merchant Marine Academy, Kings Point, NY 11024-1699; 516-773-5000.

SATs Get Tested

Did lousy on the SAT? Maybe it was the SAT's fault, not yours.

From the ERIC Clearinghouse, you can get statistics on how effective the SAT test really is in determining college entrance. Or how the SAT discriminates against certain minority groups. Or how effective they measure aptitude.

Contact: ERIC Clearinghouse on Assessment and Evaluation, Catholic University of America, Education Department, Room 210 O'Boyle Hall, Washington, DC 20064; 202-319-5120.

Pilot Tests

Thinking about taking flying lessons or are you studying for your pilot's test? Uncle Sam can come to your rescue with several publications to help you along.

- *Recreational Pilot and Private Pilot Practical Test Standards* ($4.25) establishes the standards for the recreational pilot certification practical tests for airplanes and rotorcraft.

- *Student Pilot Guide* ($1.25) is for prospective student pilots and for those who are already in flight training. It presents general procedures for obtaining Student, Private, and Recreational Pilot Certificates.

For your copies contact: Superintendent of Documents, U.S. Government Printing Office, Washington, DC 20402; 202-783-3238.

Scholarships and Internships

Millions of dollars are available to students each year in the form of fellowships and scholarships. You just need to know where to look. The Congressional Research Service (CRS) has put together a publication titled, *Internships and Fellowships* (IP0631) Info Pack which lists information to get you started in your search. You must request this free publication through your congressman.

Contact: Your Congressman, U.S. Capitol, Washington, DC 20510; 202-224-3121.

For Your Garden

Plant Facts

Thinking of planting ivies? What about growing orchids? The Horticulture Services Division of the Smithsonian Institution has developed a free series of fact sheets on a variety of plant life.

- *African Violets* fact sheet provides information on how to cultivate the African violet, including potential problems and how to solve them.

- *Tropicals for Indoor Use* provides information about indoor plants native to tropical regions of the world, including background and history, cultivation, fertilization and more.

- *Poinsettias* explains procedures for successfully cultivating this Christmas flower, including saving it from year to year.

There are many other free facts sheets available including ones on grasses, ivies, orchids, ferns, and more.

Contact: Horticulture Services Division, Arts and Industries Building, Room 2282, MRC 420, Attention Laura-ann Mesh, Smithsonian Institution, Washington, DC 20560; 202-357-1926.

Lawn Care Do's

Want the best lawn in the neighborhood? *Lawn Care*, a free environmental fact sheet, lists the do's and don'ts to help you on your way to a healthy, attractive lawn.

Contact: Public Information Center, U.S. Environmental Protection Agency, 401 M St., SW, 3404, Washington, DC 20460; 202-260-7751.

Don't Move Gypsy Moth

Gypsy moths have defoliated up to 13 million acres of trees in one season, so now there is a regulation intended to prevent the interstate spread of this pest. How do you know if you have gypsy moth problems in your area, or what you can do to eradicate this pest which does not have many natural enemies?

Don't Move Gypsy Moth is a free publication which describes the various stages in the life of a gypsy moth, what to look for, and how to prevent their spreading into other neighborhoods.

Contact: Animal and Plant Health Inspection Service, U.S. Department of Agriculture, Room G-195, Federal Building, 6505 Belcrest Road, Hyattsville, MD 20782; 301-436-4478.

Garden Chemical Free

One of the most positive actions a homeowner can take to reduce exposure to pesticides is to cultivate a natural home garden.

There are many simple ways you can reduce or eliminate the need for pesticide use in your garden.

A free *Environmental Fact Sheet: Home Gardening* which explains effective approaches to controlling garden pests.

Another fact sheet *Home Garden Companion Planting* describes how some plants have an ability to repel certain insects and provides a listing of plants that help and hinder each other.

Contact: Public Information Center, U.S. Environmental Protection Agency, 401 M St., SW, 3404, Washington, DC 20460; 202-260-7751.

Don't Plant It Here

Don't waste your money or time trying to grow plants that won't survive the year. *Plant Hardiness Zone Map* ($6.50) shows 10 different zones of the U.S., each of which represents an area of winter hardiness for plants.

It answers questions for horticulturists and home gardeners about any plant they wish to introduce into their growing spaces. It also provides information on day length, radiation, temperature, frost, and more.

For your copy contact: Superintendent of Documents, U.S. Government Printing Office, Washington, DC 20402; 202-783-3238.

The Dirt People

Find out the latest information by going to the source, the U.S. Department of Agriculture (USDA) that is. You can get the *Fact Book of Agriculture* ($4.75) which is published annually and details the mission of the many USDA agencies and provides a plethora of information about agriculture in the United States.

For your copy contact: Superintendent of Documents, U.S. Government Printing Office, Washington, DC 20402; 202-783-3238.

Dig In

Want to grow your own herbs? What about roses? If you need more information on some gardening projects request one of the free reference guides available from the Science and Technology division under the general title, *LC Science Tracer Bullet.*

These guides are designed to help readers locate published material on subjects about which they have only general knowledge. The following is a list of Tracer Bullets dealing with gardening:

- 82-2 *Gardening*
- 82-6 *Biological Control of Insects*
- 83-5 *Plant Exploration and Introduction*
- 85-1 *Herbs and Herb Gardening*
- 85-2 *Landscape Gardening*
- 85-10 *Rose Culture*
- 86-4 *Composite Materials*
- 88-5 *Soil Erosion*

Contact: Science and Technology Division, Reference Section, Library of Congress, Washington, DC 20540; 202-707-5580

Work the Soil

Soil surveys are used not only for conservation purposes but also to identify suitable lands for a wide variety of uses, from maintaining crops to urban uses. Get the scoop on your dirt through some of the free publications available from the Soil Conservation Service (SCS). The titles include:

- *Soil Erosion by Wind*

- *Soil Erosion by Water*

- *Clean Water: Our Conservation Commitment*

Contact: Soil Conservation Service, U.S. Department of Agriculture, P.O. Box 2890, Washington, DC 20013; 202-720-9149.

For Your Grandparents

Jog the Dog

Studies show seniors well into their seventies can benefit from regular exercise, especially lifting weights. Women who pump iron can greatly reduce their risk of osteoporosis, and take care of unwanted overtures from amorous geezers. The National Institute on Aging has an "Exercise Packet" containing articles and other helpful information on the benefits of exercise.

Contact: National Institute on Aging, The Information Center, P.O. Box 8057 - Exercise, Gaithersburg, MD 20898; 800-222-2225.

One Depression Was Enough

Don't let life's roller coaster put you in the dumps. A good attitude is a priceless accomplishment and there are plenty of teachers out there for when you feel lonely or blue. You can get several publications on depression including the free booklet, *Over 65 and Feeling Depressed* which outlines the signs and symptoms of this condition.

Contact: National Institute of Mental Health, 5600 Fishers Lane, Room 7C02, Rockville, MD 20857; 301-443-4513.

Over the Rainbow Coalition

Ellis Island and the Statue of Liberty represents Oz and the Wizard for millions of immigrants following the yellow brick road to freedom. And yes, Dorothy, many eventually made it to Kansas.

12 millions immigrants passed through Ellis Island on their search for freedom. For a free Statute of Liberty pamphlet and a booklet entitled *Ellis Island and Statue of Liberty* describing the importance of these historical sites, contact: Office of Public Inquiries, National Park Service, P.O. Box 37127, Washington, DC 20013-7127; 202-208-4747.

No More Forget-Me-Knots

Tying a piece of string around the finger isn't going to help. Neither is accepting memory loss as a simple fact of aging. Plenty of conditions cause forgetfulness, including stress.

A free Age Page publication called *Confusion and Memory Loss in Old Age: It's Not What You Think* is available from National Institute on Aging, Information Center, P.O. Box 8057, Gaithersburg, MD 20898; 800-222-2225.

Retirement Travel Made Easy

Now that you have time to travel, you better hit the open road. Visit those historic sites you read about long ago or fish in some of the wildlife refuges.

The Golden Age Passport is a free lifetime entrance pass to those national parks, monuments, historic sites, recreation areas and national wildlife refuges administered by the federal government which charge entrance fees.

It is issued to citizens or permanent residents of the U.S. who are 62 or older. It also provides a 50% discount on federal use fees charged for facilities and services such as camping, boat launching, parking, and more.

For application information request the free brochure *Federal Recreation Passport Program* from National Park Service, Office of Public Inquiries, U.S. Department of the Interior, P.O. Box 37127, Washington, DC 20013; 202-208-4747.

Make Their 80th Special

Anyone who lives to be 80 deserves something special. The President will send a special birthday greeting to anyone 80 or over.

All you need to do is send in a special request to The White House Greetings Office, Room 91, 1600 Pennsylvania Ave., NW, Washington, DC 20500.

The Downside of Longevity

Live long enough and you might forget your problems, and just about everything else, too. Uncle Sam has set up an entire medical center devoted to tracking the latest in Alzheimer's research and where to go for the best care and treatment.

They have many free publications including *Alzheimer's Disease Q & A* and *Family Reading List: Caring for Memory Impaired Elders*.

Contact: Alzheimer's Disease Education and Referral Center, P.O. Box 8250, Silver Spring, MD 20907; 800-438-4380.

Smoke Signals

Why kick cigarettes late in life? If you've been smoking for years, the damage has already been done, right? Wrong.

The latest studies show that even after years of tar and nicotine, smokers who quit live longer, healthier, happier lives.

Get a copy of *Good News For Smokers Over 50* from Office on Smoking and Health, Centers for Disease Control, 4770 Buford Highway, NE, MS K-50, Atlanta, GA 30341-3724; 404-488-5705.

Senior Citizen C-Sections?

Cataract surgery has become so common among senior Americans that someone investigated it (and it wasn't 20/20). Guess what they found? Many are unnecessary.

To help you and your doctor decide what is best for you, ask for a free copy of the patient and physician guidelines for cataract surgery titled *Cataract In Adults* from: Agency for Health Care Policy and Research, Publications Clearinghouse, P.O. Box 8547, Silver Spring, MD 20907; 800-358-9295.

Hearing is Believing

There are hearing aids for all types of hearing impairments which is why it is important to learn all you can before making a decision, especially since the Food and Drug Administration required six hearing aid manufacturers to adjust their ads due to incorrect advertising.

For information on hearing and hearing aids and a copy of the free publication *Hearing Loss: Hope Through Research*, contact: National Institute on Deafness and Other Communication Disorders Clearinghouse, P.O. Box 37777, Washington, DC 20013; 800-241-1044, 800-241-1055 (TDD).

Should My Diet Change as I Get Older?

Should I change my diet now that I'm older? You hear so much about salt intake, should I lower mine? The National Institute on Aging can answer these questions and more.

The Institute makes available for free several "Age Pages" which offer tips for senior citizens. Those dealing with nutrition include:

- *Be Sensible About Salt* - discusses the reduction of salt.

- *Constipation* - explains cause and treatment of constipation.

- *Dealing with Diabetes* - explains detection, symptoms, and treatment of diabetes.

- *Dietary Supplements: More Is Not Always Better* - discusses the pros and cons of taking vitamins and minerals.

- *Digestive Do's and Don'ts* - shows steps necessary to keep your digestive system working at its best.

- *Don't Take It Easy—Exercise!* - shows how to design and find an exercise program.

- *Hints For Shopping, Cooking, and Enjoying Meals* - gives shopping and cooking tips.

- *Nutrition: A Lifelong Concern* - explains the major nutrition groups and how to get them into your diet.

Contact: National Institute on Aging, Building 31, Room 5C27, 9000 Rockville Pike, Bethesda, MD 20892; 800-222-2225.

Stronger Medicine

A medicine cabinet full of prescription drugs is an accident waiting to happen. Many elderly patients are forgetful or distracted and drugs in the wrong combination can be fatal.

Out-of-date medications won't control life-threatening conditions such as hypertension or diabetes. The government can tell you how to get organized through a series of free articles called *How To Take Your Medicines*.

Contact: Office of Consumer Affairs, Food and Drug Administration, 5600 Fishers Lane, HFE-88, Rockville, MD 20857; 301-443-3170.

A Special 50th Wedding Anniversary

You can request a special anniversary greeting from the President for your parents' or grandparents' 50th anniversary.

All it takes is a written request to the White House Greetings Office, Room 91, 1600 Pennsylvania Ave., NW, Washington, DC 20500.

Now's the Time

Let the Forest Service inspire you to greater things. The free "Get Inside The Great Outdoors Seniors Poster" can motivate the oldest codger to "Just Do It".

Contact: Forest Service, U.S. Department of Agriculture, Engineering Staff, P.O. Box 96096, Washington, DC 20090-6090; 202-205-1400.

Your Ship Has Come In

If your mom, dad, or grandparents always talk about their Navy stint, you can really bring it back to life with some help from the Cartographic and Architectural Branch of the National Archives. This office compiles the plans of all Navy ships since the Navy was founded. For a copy of a ship plan you must make your request in writing, and provide ship name and designation. Cost for the service is $1.80 per print foot, with the average request costing $7.00.

For more information contact: Cartographic and Architectural Branch, National Archives and Records Administration, Washington, DC 20408; 703-756-6700.

Grandma Getting a Little Shorter?

Bone loss and brittle bones effect as many as 24 million Americans in the form of osteoporosis. The Arthritis and Musculoskeletal and Skin Diseases Clearinghouse has a free "Osteoporosis Information Packet" filled with articles, research reports, resources, and a bibliography.

For your copy contact: Arthritis and Musculoskeletal and Skin Diseases Information Clearinghouse, Box AMS, Bethesda, MD 20892; 301-495-4484.

Your Grandparents' Boat

Did your grandparents come to the country by boat? The National Archives compiles ship passenger arrival records dating from 1820 for most east and gulf coast ports, a few lists dating from 1800 for Philadelphia, and from the 1890's for San Francisco and Seattle. Archives staff can conduct free searches if you know the full name of the passenger, the port of entry, and the approximate date of arrival. If they find your grandparents' name, you can purchase a copy of the log for only $10.

For more information contact: Reference Services Branch, National Archives and Records Administration, 8th St. and Pennsylvania Ave., NW, Washington, DC 20408; 202-501-5400.

When It Is Time To Move

Selecting a nursing home is one of the most important and difficult decisions that you may be asked to make — either for yourself or for a member of your family. A free publication titled, *Guide to Choosing a Nursing Home*, provides information on looking for a nursing home, questions you should ask, payment information, as well as a checklist of things you should look for when visiting a facility.

For your copy write to: Health Care Financing Administration, U.S. Department of Health and Human Services, 6325 Security Blvd., Baltimore, MD 21207.

Medicare Made Easy

It is difficult enough trying to figure out all the doctor bills and insurance forms. What does Medicare cover? Should you get a Medigap policy? What if you have a problem with Medicare paying a claim? The Health Care Financing Administration has put together several free publications which can answer these questions and more. Some of the titles include:

- *Medicare 1993 Handbook*

- *Guide to Health Insurance For People With Medicare*

- *Medicare and Other Health Benefits: Who Pays First?*

- *Medicare and Your Physician's Bill*

- *Medicare Coordinated Care: Q&A*

You can request these publications and more by writing: Health Care Financing Administration, U.S. Department of Health and Human Services, 6325 Security Blvd., Baltimore, MD 21207.

Service Hotline for the Elderly

The Eldercare Locator is a nationwide service designed to help people find needed services for their elderly friends or family members.

Call between 9 am and 8 pm (EST), and you'll be put in touch with thousands of

state and local resources on everything from finding them help, health care, social services, guardianship, and much more.

Contact: Eldercare Locator, Administration on Aging, 1112 16th Street, NW, Suite 100, Washington, DC 20036; 800-677-1116.

For Your Health

Don't Let One Setback Ruin Your Health

You don't have to lose health insurance because of divorce or separation. Under the law, divorced and separated women and their children can continue to receive the same health insurance coverage at the group rate. The only difference is that they have to pay the premium instead of the employer.

For more specific information on this issue, send a self-addressed stamped envelope with a request for a copy of *Health Insurance Continuation*.

Contact: National Displaced Homemakers Network (NDHN), 1625 K St., NW, Suite 300, Department H, Washington, DC 20006.

What Your Children Should Know

AIDS Prevention Guide is written for parents and other adults concerned about young people. It provides ideas to help adults start a conversation about AIDS.

It presents the facts about AIDS, geared to elementary and junior and senior high school students, and offers common questions and accurate answers. It includes handouts for young people aged 10 to 20 years.

Contact: National AIDS Information Clearinghouse, P.O. Box 6003, Rockville, MD 20849; 800-342-2437.

You Can Cure a Cold with Chicken Soup

Before grandma makes you take another spoonful, check out the facts with the Food and Drug Administration (FDA).

There have been no studies done on the benefits of chicken soup, but common sense says that nutritious fluids and rest will help you recuperate.

An FDA consumer article titled *Surviving Cold and Flu Season*, explains the difference between colds and flu, discusses the pros and cons of flu shots, and describes the different types of cold remedies available.

For your free copy contact: Food and Drug Administration, Office of Consumer Affairs (HFE-88), 5600 Fishers Lane, Rockville, MD 20857; 301-443-3170.

Think You Can't Get Pregnant Because You Have Endometriosis?

Think Again. While the pregnancy rates for women with endometriosis remain lower than those of the general population, most women with this condition do not experience fertility problems. It is estimated that between 10 and 20 percent of American women of childbearing age have endometriosis. The National Institute of Child Health and Human Development conducts research to develop an optimal treatment for endometriosis.

For a free booklet, *Facts About Endometriosis*, or for information on current research or other organizations for further assistance, contact: The National Institute of Child Health and Human Development, National Institutes of Health, Bldg. 31, Room 2A32, Bethesda, MD 20892; 301-496-5133.

Lead Poisoning is the Number One Preventable Childhood Disease

Childhood lead poisoning is one of the most common pediatric health problems in the United States today, and it is entirely preventable. New data indicate significant adverse effects of lead exposure in children at blood lead levels previously believed to be safe. For more information on lead poisoning, and a free copy of the Centers for Disease Control's (CDC) *Preventing Lead Poisoning in Young Children*, contact the office listed below.

Contact: Lead Poisoning Prevention Branch, National Center for Environmental Health and Injury Control, Centers for Disease Control (CDC), 1600 Clifton Rd., NE, Atlanta, GA 30333; 404-488-4880.

Down Syndrome, Mental Retardation, and Learning Disabilities

The National Institute of Child Health and Human Development conducts and supports research on the reproductive, developmental, and behavioral processes that determine the health of children, adults, families, and populations.

Research for mothers, children, and families is designed to advance knowledge of fetal development, pregnancy, and birth; to identify the knowledge of fetal development through infancy to adulthood; and to contribute to the prevention and treatment of mental retardation.

Some of the publications include:

- *Facts About Childhood Hyperactivity*

- *Facts About Down Syndrome*

- *Facts About Dyslexia*

- *Learning Disabilities: A Report to the U.S. Congress*

- *Centers of Excellence: The Mental Retardation Centers*

Contact: National Institute of Child Health and Human Development, National Institutes of Health, Building 31, Room 2A32, 9000 Rockville Pike, Bethesda, MD 20892; 301-496-5133.

Help For Handicapped and Gifted Children

ERIC (Educational Resources Information Center) Clearinghouse on Handicapped and Gifted Children gathers and disseminates educational information on all disabilities and giftedness across all age levels.

They have

- publications

- digests (2-4 page summaries of current topics),

- Research Briefs

- Issue Briefs

- Directories of currently funded research

- Topical INFO packets and Flyer Files

- Catalog of products and services available to the Special Educator

They also have database searches and reprints. Two free digests available include *Preschool Services For Children With Handicaps*, which explains early intervention services, and *Educating Exceptional Children* which explains some of the terminology and trends.

Contact: ERIC Clearinghouse on Handicapped and Gifted Children, Council for Exceptional Children, 1920 Association Dr., Reston, VA 22091; 703-264-9474.

Understanding Childhood Immunizations

The Immunization office responds to inquiries and provides free information and publications regarding immunization against vaccine-preventable diseases of young children.

They can provide you with reports of the recommendations of the Immunization Practices Advisory Committee, as well as informational pamphlets on the various vaccines all of our children should receive.

You can receive a free copy of *Parent's Guide To Childhood Immunizations* which explains the vaccines your child should receive, as well as a recommended schedule.

Another free booklet, *Immunization of Adults: A Call To Action*, describes the immunizations adults should have received and their importance.

Contact: Immunization Division, Centers for Disease Control, 1600 Tullie Circle, Atlanta, GA 30333; 404-639-1819.

Sudden Infant Death Hotline

The National Sudden Infant Death Syndrome Clearinghouse was established to provide information
and educational materials on Sudden Infant Death
Syndrome (SIDS), apnea, and other related issues.
The staff responds to information requests from professionals, families with SIDS-related deaths, and
the general public by sending written materials and
making referrals.

The clearinghouse maintains a library of reference
materials and mailing lists of state programs,
groups, and individuals concerned with SIDS. Their
publications include bibliographies on SIDS and
self-help support groups, a publications catalogue,
and a newsletter.

Some of their free publications include:

- *Crib Death* — explains SIDS in easy to read
  booklet.

- *Fact Sheet: Parents and The Grieving
  Process* — defines grief and highlights the
  process.

- *A Guide to Resources in Perinatal
  Bereavement* — offers selected resources.

National Sudden Infant Death Syndrome Clearinghouse, 8201 Greensboro Dr., Suite 600, McLean,
VA 22102; 703-821-8955.

Programs for Children of Alcoholics

The Clearinghouse for Alcohol and Drug Information has a wealth of information regarding children of alcoholics.

Alcohol Alert #9, Children of Alcoholics: Are They Different focuses on various research areas.

Prevention Resource Guide: Children of Alcoholics provides facts and figures that put in perspective the magnitude of the problem of alcoholism and its direct effect on the family. Both are free.

Contact: National Clearinghouse for Alcohol and Drug Information, P.O. Box 2345, Rockville, MD 20847; 800-729-6686.

Caring for Children with AIDS

AIDS is a scary topic, especially when it affects children. The National Maternal and Child Health Clearinghouse has several free publications concerned with AIDS and children.

Some of the titles include:

- *Children with HIV/AIDS: A Sourcebook for Caring*

- *Pediatric AIDS: Abstracts of Active Projects FY 1990 and FY 1991*

- *Questions and Answers about HIV and AIDS in Children*

- *Surgeon General's Workshop on Children with HIV Infection and Their Families Report*

Contact: National Maternal and Child Health Clearinghouse, 8201 Greensboro Dr., Suite 600, McLean, VA 22102; 703-821-8955, ext. 254.

There Is Help for Those Helping Low-Income Mothers

Healthy Mothers, Healthy Babies - A Compendium of Program Ideas for Servicing Low-Income Women provides useful suggestions to health care providers who work with low income populations, and suggests program planning and policy directions for State and national organizations concerned with maternal and infant health.

Contact: National Clearinghouse for Primary Care Information, 8201 Greensboro Dr., Suite 600, McLean, VA 22102; 703-821-8955.

Call For The Answer. . .
The Smoking Hotline

The Smoking Hotline can answer all your questions regarding cigarettes and stop smoking methods.

They can provide fact sheets, pamphlets, posters and other publications, as well as information in response to inquiries.

The Center can access information on the Combined Health Information Database, and its library and reading room are open to the public.

Some of the free publications they have include:

- *Smoking, Tobacco & Health: A Fact Book* - describes health, social and economic aspects of smoking.

- *Out of the Ashes: Choosing a Method To Quit Smoking* - outlines various methods of quitting.

- *Major Local Smoking Ordinances in the United States* - examines smoking ordinances for public places.

- *Smoking In the Americas: At A Glance* - highlights problems of smoking and health.

Contact: Office on Smoking and Health, Centers for Disease Control, 4770 Buford Hwy., Mail Stop K-50, Atlanta, GA 30341-3724; 404-488-5705.

Children and Mental Health

The National Institute of Mental Health (NIMH) conducts research on depression and other mental disorders, distributes information, and conducts demonstration programs for the prevention, treatment, and rehabilitation of the mentally ill. NIMH has several publications which deal with mental health in children. These publications are available at no charge.

Titles include:

- *National Plan for Research on Child and Adolescent Mental Disorders*

- *Working Bibliography on Behavioral and Emotional Disorders*

- *Plain Talk on Adolescence*

- *Assessment Instruments in Mental Retardation*

Contact: National Institute of Mental Health, 5600 Fishers Lane, Room 7C02, Rockville, MD 20857; 301-443-4515.

Parents of Disabled Children Are Not Alone

The National Information Center for Children and Youth with Disabilities helps parents of handicapped children and disabled adults locate services and parent support groups, focusing on the needs of rural areas, culturally diverse populations, and severely handicapped people. This center also provides information on vocational/transitional issues, special education, and legal rights and advocacy.

It provides fact sheets on specific disabilities, including autism, cerebral palsy, hearing impairments, Down syndrome, epilepsy, learning disabilities, mental retardation, physical disabilities, speech and language impairments, spina bifida, and visual impairments.

The materials designed especially for parents include:

- *Parents' Guide to Accessing Programs for Infants, Toddlers, Preschoolers with Handicaps*

- *Parents' Guide to Accessing Parent Programs, Community Services, and Record Keeping*

- *Life After School for Children with Disabilities: Answers to Questions Parents Ask about Employment and Financial Assistance*

- *A Parent's Guide: Accessing the ERIC Resource Collection*

- *A Parent's Guide to Doctors, Disabilities, and the Family*

- *A Parent's Guide: Planning a Move; Mapping Your Strategy*

- *A Parent's Guide: Special Education and Related Services: Communicating Through Letter Writing*

Contact: National Information Center for Children and Youth with Disabilities, P.O. Box 1492, Washington, DC 20013; 800-999-5599.

Does Your Child Have Asthma?

The Asthma Clearinghouse is a new clearinghouse, providing publications, reports, resources, and referrals to experts in the field of asthma. One report, the *Executive Summary: Guidelines for the Diagnosis and Management of Asthma*, explains the diagnosis, therapy, and other considerations for those that suffer from asthma. They can answer your questions or can direct you to those that can. Contact the Clearinghouse for more information.

Contact: National Asthma Education Program, 7200 Wisconsin Ave., P.O. Box 30105, Bethesda, MD 20824; 301-251-1222.

Illegal Drug Use in Youth

The Coordinating Council is a group of 16 Federal agencies who held a workshop to develop inter-agency initiatives to combat the juvenile drug problem.

They produced *Juvenile Alcohol and Other Drug Abuse: A Guide to Federal Initiatives for Prevention, Treatment, and Control* which will serve as a resource for State, local, and private agencies and individuals working to combat juvenile drug and alcohol abuse.

Contact: Office of Juvenile Justice and Delinquency Prevention, P. O. Box 6000, Rockville, MD 20850; 800-638-8736.

A Wealth of Family Planning Information

The Family Life Information Exchange (FLIE) is a service of the Office of Population Affairs, and provides information on family planning, adolescent pregnancy, and adoption.

FLIE's primary audience consists of federally supported service agencies, but it also provides information to family planning service providers, educators, trainers, and consumers throughout the U.S.

A free publications list is available which includes:

- *Information for Men —Your Sterilization Operation*

- *Information for Women—Your Sterilization Operation*

- *Many Teens are Saying "NO"*

- *Family and Adolescent Pregnancy*

- *Your Contraceptive Choices: For Now, For Later*

- *Sexually Transmitted Diseases Treatment Guidelines*

Contact: Family Life Information Exchange, P.O. Box 37299, Washington, DC 20013; 301-585-6636.

Special Health Care Needs

Parents whose children have special health care needs are often overwhelmed and isolated because of their child's condition. But help is just a phone call away. The Clearinghouse has an extensive list of free publications concerned with children with special health care needs.

Two of the publications are resource guides: *Children with Special Health Care Needs - Resource Guide*, and *Circles of Care and Understanding: Support Programs for Fathers of Children with Special Needs*.

Contact: National Maternal and Child Health Clearinghouse, 8201 Greensboro Dr., Suite 600, McLean, VA 22102; 703-821-8955.

What the Experts Say about How to Quit Smoking

Want to stop smoking, but aren't sure how? *Clearing the Air* is a free booklet by the National Cancer Institute that is full of tips for breaking the smoking habit. *Self-Guided Strategies For Smoking Cessation: A Program Planner's Guide* is a free guide to help people who are forming stop-smoking groups or other support groups.

For physicians who are trying to get patients to stop smoking for the sake of their health, *How To Help Patients Stop Smoking: A National Cancer Institute Manual For Physicians* is a free smoking cessation guide for physicians and medical office staff. Give them a call to get you started on the road to good health.

Contact: National Cancer Institute, Bldg. 31, Room 10A18, 9000 Rockville Pike, Bethesda, MD 20892; 800-4-CANCER.

Parent Guides for Alcohol and Drug Information

Are you concerned that your child may have a problem with alcohol or drugs?

Do you want to know what signs to look for?

The National Clearinghouse for Drug and Alcohol Information can help and has the following free publications available, dealing with drug and alcohol use:

- *Parent Training Is Prevention.*
- *Pointers for Parents Card.*
- *Crack Down on Drugs.*
- *Tips for Teens About Alcohol.*
- *High School Senior Drug Use: 1975-1990.*
- *Be Smart! Don't Start!.*
- "Steroids Don't Work Out" (poster).
- *Helping Your Students Say "No" Teacher's Guide.*
- *Too Many Young People Drink and Know Too Little About the Consequences.*

Contact: National Clearinghouse for Alcohol and Drug Information, P.O. Box 2345, Rockville, MD 20847; 800-729-6686.

Mental Health and You

Are you feeling troubled and looking for help? There seem to be more types of therapy than there are breakfast cereals. How do you know what to choose or even look for?

The Consumers Guide to Mental Health Services is a free booklet which explains the different types of services available, questions you should ask, and more.

Contact: National Institute of Mental Health, 5600 Fishers Lane, Room 7C02, Rockville, MD 20857; 301-443-4515.

The Pain People

Find out whether the pain is of the acute or chronic variety, and then get some helpful suggestions on pain reducing strategies.

The National Institute of Neurological Disorders and Stroke has a free publication, *Chronic Pain: Hope Through Research* which describes causes, research, and treatment of pain, as well as where to go for more help and information.

Contact: National Institute of Neurological Disorders and Stroke, P.O. Box 5801, Bethesda, MD 20824; 800-352-9424.

Cerebral Palsy in Children

This center for medical research has information about the latest developments on this disorder as well as a free 26-page pamphlet titled *Cerebral Palsy: Hope Through Research*.

They also can provide you with articles, a bibliography, and other resources on this topic.

Contact: National Institute of Neurological Disorders and Stroke, P.O. Box 5801, Bethesda, MD 20824; 800-352-9424.

Clearinghouse on Disability Information

Wondering if your company complies with the American Disabilities Act? What about trying to find programs to help you?

The Clearinghouse responds to inquiries to a wide range of topics. You can find out about programs serving individuals with disabilities, Federal legislation, and Federal funding for special programs.

Two free publications to get you on your way include:

- *A Summary of Existing Legislation Affecting People With Disabilities* provides a history and description of all relevant Federal laws

- *Pocket Guide to Federal Help* for individuals with disabilities is a summary of benefits and services available to individuals with disabilities.

Contact: National Information Center for Children and Youth with Disabilities, P.O. Box 1492, Washington, DC 20013; 800-999-5599.

Did Your Lifetime Membership Expire when Your Health Spa Closed a Year Later?

Are you having some trouble with your health spa? Do you feel you were ripped off when you joined? The Federal Trade Commission (FTC) has a free publication, *Health Spas: Exercise Your Rights*, which explains things to consider when you join a health spa, as well as what to do when you have a complaint.

The Consumer Protection Division of your State Attorney General's Office can handle complaints against health spas. You can fill out a complaint form and usually within two weeks a representative of the Attorney General's Office will investigate your complaint and hopefully resolve any differences.

Contact: Federal Trade Commission (FTC), 6th & Pennsylvania Ave., NW, Washington, DC 20580; 202-326-2222.

For Your Hobbies

Socks Included

Free photos of the First Family are available. You can get one with or without Hillary, even an 8x10 of First Feline Socks without any of them. Always wanted a picture of the President? On a good day you can kiss it, on a bad day you can throw darts.

All you need to do is send a letter with your request to Presidential Correspondence, White House, Photo Department, Attention Jeff Riley, Old Executive Office Building, Room 94, Washington, DC 20500.

Get Out of the House

Need some inspiration to get you motivated to leave your couch? The Forest Service has a series of free wonderful posters on outdoor activities. They include: "Get Inside The Great Outdoors Biking Poster", "Get Inside The Great Outdoors Water Sports Poster", "Get Inside The Great Outdoors Camping Poster", "Get Inside The Great Outdoors Fishing Poster", "Get Inside The Great Outdoors Hikers Poster", "Get Inside The Great Outdoors Skiing Poster", "Get Inside The Great Outdoors Driving For Pleasure Poster".

Contact: Forest Service, U.S. Department of Agriculture, Engineering Staff, P.O. Box 96096, Washington, DC 20090-6090; 202-205-1400.

Do You Know Someone Who is a Gold Digger?

The Bureau of Mines distributes a free booklet, *How To Mine and Prospect For Gold*, which can get your gold digger started on the right path.

For a free copy contact: Publications Department, Bureau of Mines, U.S. Department of the Interior, 18th and C Sts., NW, Room 2647, Washington, DC 20240; 202-501-9649.

Borrow the Battle

The photography library of the U.S. Park Service will lend you pictures and slides of national parks, monuments, and battlefields. A great resource for Civil War buffs.

Contact: Photo Library, Office of Public Affairs, National Park Service, U.S. Department of Interior, 18th and C Sts., NW, Washington, DC 20240; 202-208-4997.

A Thousand Words

If you need to illuminate a talk or presentation, the National Gallery has a lending library of 50,000 images. There's no catalog, so start a wish list. The images can be borrowed through inter-library loan.

For the *Public Lending Guide* or more information contact: National Gallery of Art, Slide Library, Constitution and 6th St., NW, Washington, DC 20565; 202-842-6100.

For the Would-Be Wine Connoisseur

What exactly does all the writing on a wine bottle mean? *What You Should Know About Grape Wine Labels* is a free brochure which describes the elements written on a label for grape wine and what can be learned from the label.

These include brand, vintage date, variety designations, alcohol content, appellation of origin, viticultural area, name or trade name, and estate bottled. These things are very important in choosing a good bottle of wine, so study hard.

Contact: Distribution Center, Bureau of Alcohol, Tobacco, and Firearms, U.S. Department of Treasury, 7943 Angus Court, Springfield, VA 22153; 703-455-7801.

The Wild, Wild West

The Bureau of Land Management rides herd on over 270 acres of range and has the photos to prove it. It also has hundreds of pictures of cowpokes, prospectors and crusty miners.

No catalog is available, but you can include type of photo, time period, or location in your request.

Contact: Office of Public Affairs, Bureau of Land Management, U.S. Department of the Interior, 1849 C St., NW, Washington, DC 20240; 202-208-7054.

Paint the Chinese Way

"Yani: The Brush of Innocence" is a teachers packet designed for grades 1-5 which provides information on the life of Wang Yani, a young Chinese artist. It also includes activities for students. The Sackler Gallery focuses on Asian art and has a newsletter containing other education materials available to teachers.

Contact: Arthur M. Sackler Gallery, Education Department, MRC 707, Smithsonian Institution, Washington, DC 20560; 202-357-4880.

GOLD Rush

Mining for gold did not end in the 1800's, but continues today. Turn your vacation into a true treasure hunt with the help of some free publications available through the U.S. Geological Survey. *Gold* discusses the nature of gold, and the geologic environments in which it is found. *Prospecting for Gold in the United States* describes various kinds of gold deposits and their locations. *Suggestions for Prospecting* compares modern prospecting techniques with those of earlier years.

Write your request for these publications to U.S. Geological Survey, Map Distribution, Box 25286, Denver, CO 80225.

This Land Is Your Land

A 300,000 photo pictorial survey of the U.S., dating from 1869 to the present, including rivers, volcanoes, and earthquakes, is maintained by the U.S. Geological Service. To obtain information on ordering or purchasing prints, negatives or transparencies, contact the library directly.

Contact: Photographic Library, MS914, U.S. Geological Survey, Box 25046, Federal Center, Denver, CO 80225; 303-236-1010; for the hearing impaired, 303-236-0998 TTY.

Bring The Birds to You

Your favorite food may be Italian and your friend's may be Chinese. Like you, birds have their favorite foods and their favorite types of homes. In order to attract a specific type of bird you need to set the right atmosphere. Some of the free publications available include *Backyard Bird Feeding*, *Build A Birdfeeder For About A Buck*, and *Home For Birds*. These provide all the information necessary to get you started in birding.

Contact: U.S. Fish and Wildlife Service, 4401 N. Fairfax Dr., Arlington, VA 22203; 703-358-1711.

What's the Name of that Bird?

Certain birds seem to prefer certain environments.

To learn more about birds in the U.S., request the free publication *Forest and Rangeland Birds of the U.S.* from the Forest Service. It provides a description

and pictures of birds and discusses their habitats.

Contact: Forest Service, U.S. Department of Agriculture, 12th and Independence, SW, P.O. Box 96090, Washington , DC 20090; 202-205-0957.

An Armchair Walk in the Woods... and Time

The U.S. Forest Service has two entire libraries of photographs and slides dating back to 1890. Topics covered include forestry, timber industry, fish and wildlife, and more.

The Historical Library has images from 1890-1954, with half of the collection on a laser disk. The Current Library can put together photographs or slides based upon your request.

For more ordering or borrowing information contact: Historical Photographs, National Agricultural Library, 10301 Baltimore Blvd., Beltsville, MD 20705; 301-504-5876. Current Library, Forest Service, Office of Public Affairs, U.S. Department of Agriculture, 201 14th St., SW, Washington, DC 20250; 202-205-0963.

Stamp It!

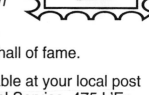

Did the Elvis stamp craze peak your interest? Stamp collecting is the most popular hobby in the world, so join in. The U.S. Postal Service has a pamphlet titled, *Introduction to Stamp Collecting* (pub. 225), which can help get you on your way to the philatelic hall of fame.

This free publication is available at your local post office or by writing U.S. Postal Service, 475 L'Enfant Plaza West, SW, Washington, DC 20260.

What's This?

Get your kids interested in the outdoors by helping them start a rock collection.

Collecting Rocks is a free publication of the U.S. Geological Survey which describes the origin of major rock types and provides suggestions for starting a rock collection and identifying specimens.

Write for your copy to U.S. Geological Survey, Map Distribution, Box 25286, Denver, CO 80225.

Going Fishing without Mosquitoes

A slow day at the fishing hole can lead to lots of ribbing. Take the easy way out and stop at the fish store on the way home, but make sure you keep the fish you buy safe to eat. The Office of Seafood at the Food and Drug Administration has an automated telephone system which can answer your questions regarding seafood storage, cooking, safety, handling, labeling or any problems you may have concerning seafood. Some of the publications include:

- *Seafood Safety Tips*

- *Fishing for Facts*

- *Is Something Fishy Going On?*

- *Seafood Nutrition Information Chart*

- *Ready to Eat Seafood*

For your free publications, or for more information, contact: Seafood Hotline; 800-FDA-4010.

For Your Home

Kung Fu Movers

When it comes to moving companies, you get what you pay for. But if your furniture ends up in pieces or in Peking, there's help from the government. The Interstate Commerce Commission has a publication titled, *Your Rights And Responsibilities When You Move*, which outlines what you need to know regarding moving companies.

Contact: Consumer Assistance Office, Interstate Commerce Commission, 12th St. and Constitution Ave., NW, Washington, DC 20423; 202-927-5500.

Home Shopping Tips for Veterans

Veterans can get an edge on the home buying market through use of a VA loan. The following three free publications can get you started on your house hunt. *Pointers For The Veteran Homeowner* is a guide for veterans whose home mortgage is guaranteed or insured under the GI Bill.

To the Home-buying Veteran is a guide for veterans planning to buy or build homes with a VA loan. *VA-Guaranteed Home Loans for Veterans* helps you understand what the VA can and cannot do for the home purchaser.

Contact: Veterans Assistance Office, U.S. Department of Veterans Affairs, 810 Vermont Ave., NW, Washington, DC 20420; 800-827-1000.

Concerned about Pesticides?

Do you use pesticides on your lawn or in your home? There are concerns about the dangers of pesticide use near people.

The U.S. Environmental Protection Agency (EPA) has several publications which provide the consumer with information concerning pesticides.

Some of the publications include:

- *Citizen's Guide to Pesticides* - An informative brochure describing how to choose and use pesticides, how to pick a pest control company, and what to do in the event of a problem

- *Regulating Pesticides* - which explains EPA's registration process and how they classify pesticides

- *EPA's Pesticide Programs* - pesticide registration and food safety are discussed first, followed by other pesticide programs.

Contact: Public Information Center, 3404, U.S. Environmental Protection Agency, 401 M St., SW, Washington, DC 20460; 202-260-7751.

The Masking Tape Deduction

You can write off many moving expenses if the conditions are politically correct and your motives are pure. You can even deduct expenses of moving back to the United States if you retire while living and working overseas.

Just call the Internal Revenue Service (IRS) and ask for Form 521, *Moving Expenses*, 800-829-3676.

Safe Houses for the 90s

To find a safe little hamlet to raise Junior, you better do some research before you move.

Crime In The U.S., the Federal Bureau of Investigation's (FBI) annual report of violent and property crime, contains statistics for many towns with over 10,000 people, and can provide you with information such as the number of murders, robberies, assaults, burglaries, auto thefts, and more, but they do not rank cities.

Many libraries carry this publication, or you can call the FBI for information on your city.

Contact: Law Enforcement Support Section, Federal Bureau of Investigation, Gallery Row Bldg., Washington, DC 20535; 202-324-5015.

Mortgage Money Guides

You have found your dream house, now what? You need to figure out how to pay for it. It is not as simple as it would seem. The Federal Trade Commission has several free publications dealing with the laws and regulations regarding getting a mortgage, mortgage servicing, mortgage refinancing, and what you need to look for when you are in the process.

The publications include: *Home Financing Primer, Mortgage Money Guide, Mortgage Servicing, Refinancing Your Home, Second Mortgage Financing.*

Contact: Public Reference, Room130, Federal Trade Commission, Washington, DC 20580; 202-326-2222.

Bought Some Swamp Land In Florida?

You are not the first, nor will you be the last victim of a land sale scam. The Federal Trade Commission has a free publication, *Land Sales Scams*, which describes the various scams, regulations and laws pertaining to land sales, as well as information on what you can do to protect yourself.

Contact: Public Reference, Room130, Federal Trade Commission, Washington, DC 20580; 202-326-2222.

Before You Even Start Looking for a House

Real estate brokers are everywhere. How do you know the good from the bad?

A free publication, *Real Estate Brokers*, provides a wealth of information regarding what the law requires for real estate brokers, your rights and responsibilities, as well as what to do when you have been unfairly treated.

Contact: Public Reference, Room130, Federal Trade Commission, Washington, DC 20580; 202-326-2222.

This Old House

Preservation of old homes is not an easy business. Finding weights and pulleys to repair old windows does not involve a simple trip to the hardware store. A free bibliography from the Government Printing Office titled *Public Buildings, Landmarks and Historic Sites of the United States* (SB-140) can get you started on your way to finding good resources for an authentic restoration.

Contact: Superintendent of Documents, Government Printing Office, Washington, DC 20402; 703-783-3238.

Energy Efficiency for You

The U.S. Department of Energy has a wide variety of information available regarding energy efficiency. The have information sheets on automatic and programmable thermostats, solar energy, appliance labeling, fans and ventilation, heat pumps, hot water conservation, insulation, as well as many more.

Two booklets that provide a wealth of information as well as some helpful suggestions include:

- *Tips For Saving Energy In Small Business*

- *Tips For An Energy Efficient Apartment*

All are free. Contact: Public Affairs, U.S. Department of Energy, Washington, DC 20585; 202-586-5575.

Unseen, but Deadly

Heard about the dangers of radon, but need to know more about it? *A Citizen's Guide to Radon* is a free booklet which helps readers understand the radon problem and decide if they need to take action to reduce radon levels in their homes. It explains what radon is, how it is detected, and what the results mean.

Contact: Public Information Center, U.S. Environmental Protection Agency, 401 M St., SW, 3404, Washington, DC 20460; 202-260-7751.

Exactly What's It Going To Cost?

Buying a house can be an overwhelming experience. People are using a language you may never have heard before. Closing costs, mortgage lock-ins, settlement, title search, and more are all terms you need to know and fully understand before you sign on the dotted line.

The Federal Reserve has several free publications which will help you on your way to becoming an informed home buyer.

- *A Consumer's Guide to Mortgage Settlement Costs* discusses closing costs, the title search, title insurance, and government-imposed costs.

- *A Consumer's Guide to Mortgage Lock-Ins* describes various aspects of mortgage lock-ins.

- *A Consumer's Guide to Mortgage Refinancing* explains the process and some of the risks and advantages to mortgage refinancing.

Contact: Federal Reserve System, Board of Governors, Publications Services, MS-138, 20th St. and Constitution Ave., NW, Washington, DC 20551; 202-452-3244.

Let Me Light Your Fire

Do you have a cabin in the woods with a woodstove, or are you thinking of installing one in your new home? Ask the U.S. Environmental Protection Agency (EPA) for some free advice.

Woodstoves can really help lower your heating bill, but you need to be sure that they are safe and effective. The Public Information Center has several free pamphlets on woodstoves including

- *Buying an EPA-Certified Woodstove*

- *Combustion Appliances and Indoor Air Pollution*

- *Noncatalytic Woodstoves: Installation, Operation, and Maintenance*

- *Catalytic Woodstoves: Installation, Operation, and Maintenance.*

Contact: Public Information Center, U.S. Environmental Protection Agency, 3404, 401 M St., SW, Washington, DC 20460; 202-260-7751.

The EPA has a Wood Heater Program which can provide you with a current list of EPA-certified woodstoves as well as provide you with more information about wood burning and EPA's regulations.

They can be contacted at: Wood Heater Program (EN-341W), EPA, 401 M St., SW, Washington, DC 20460; 703-308-8688.

Pesticide Safety

The pests have taken permanent residence in your home, so you reach for some chemical assistance in evicting the little creatures.

- *Pesticide Safety Tips* is a free fact sheet which gives helpful suggestions on pesticide use.

- *Pesticide Labels* discusses the parts of a label and what the information means.

- *Pesticides and Child Safety* lists recommendations for preventing accidental poisoning.

Contact: Public Information Center, U.S. Environmental Protection Agency, 401 M St., SW, 3404, Washington, DC 20460; 202-260-7751.

For a Different Look

Suburbia may not be ready for this, but you could be. *Earth-Shelter Houses* is a free publication from the Conservation and Renewable Energy Inquiry Service, and provides information on different types of earth sheltered houses, their benefits, and information on where to go to learn more about this style of house.

Contact: Conservation and Renewable Energy Inquiry and Referral Service, P.O. Box 3048, Merrifield, VA 22116; 800-523-2929.

Make It as Nature Intended

Many do-it-yourselfers are looking at wood frame houses as a way to build their dream home. The Forest Service has several free publications to get you sawing.

- *The Wood Handbook* discusses different types of wood and their uses.

- *Wood Frame House Construction* takes you through your home's building process.

- *Wood Siding: Installing Finishing, Maintaining* outlines the steps you need to take to protect your home's exterior.

For these free publications contact: Forest Service, U.S. Department of Agriculture, 12th and Independence, SW, P.O. Box 96090, Washington, DC 20090; 202-205-0957.

Counseling for Homebuyers, Homeowners, and Tenants

To help reduce delinquencies, defaults, and foreclosures, the U.S. Department of Housing and Urban Development (HUD) provides free counseling to homeowners and tenants under its programs through HUD-approved counseling agencies.

The counselors advise and assist homeowners with budgeting, money management, and buying and maintaining their homes. This is not just for HUD homes, but for all home buyers and owners. The amount of service available does vary for each counseling agency.

Contact this office or your local HUD office of information for the counseling agency nearest you.

Contact: Single Family Servicing Division, Secretary-Held and Counseling Services, Office of Insured Single Family Housing, U.S. Department of Housing and Urban Development (HUD), Washington, DC 20410-8000; 800-733-3238.

Pest Free Home

Tired of calling the bug man? Worried about the chemicals used to rid your home of pests? The U.S. Environmental Protection Agency has several free environmental fact sheets on pesticide and pesticide safety.

- *Preventing Pests In Your Home* provides tips on general prevention methods and resources for more information.

- *Safety Precautions For Total Release Foggers* gives suggestions on how to use foggers safely to avoid fires and explosions.

Contact: Public Information Center, U.S. Environmental Protection Agency, 401 M St., SW, 3404, Washington, DC 20460; 202-260-7751.

Efficient Houses

Houses are expensive enough. Learn how you can improve the efficiency of your home from the Conservation and Renewable Energy Inquiry and Referral Service (CAREIRS), which covers such topics as active/passive solar, solar thermal, photovoltaics, wind, biomass, alcohol fuels, hydroelectric, geothermal, and ocean thermal energy.

Some of the free publications include:

- *Solar Energy Systems, Consumer Tips*

- *Passive Solar Heating*

- *Efficient Air Conditioning*

- *Buying an Energy Efficient House*

- *Home Energy Audits*

- *Converting A Home To Solar*

- *Heat Pumps*

- *Insulation*

For these publications and information on others available contact: Conservation and Renewable Energy Inquiry and Referral Service, P.O. Box 3048, Merrifield, VA 22116; 800-523-2929.

For Your Investments

Your Own Investment Counselor

The Securities and Exchange Commission are the guys who write the rules and regulations and provide protection for investors, making sure that the securities markets are safe and honest.

They have a free publication, *Consumer's Financial Guide*, which contains basic information on choosing investments and keeping them safe, trading securities, and different protections guaranteed by law.

Contact: Publications Section, Printing Branch, Stop C-11, Securities and Exchange Commission, 450 5th St., NW, Washington, DC 20549; 202-272-7040.

Credit Handbook

Worried about your credit rating? Need some advice about restoring your credit rating? *The Consumer Handbook To Credit Protection Laws*, can help you understand how the credit protection laws can help you, and is available free from this office.

Contact: Publications Services, MS-138, Board of Governors, Federal Reserve System, Washington, DC 20551; 202-452-3244.

ith Savings Bonds

Trying to save for your kids' education? *Buyer's Guide* (SBD 2085) describes the information you need to purchase savings bonds, such as available series and denominations, interest rates, where to buy, registration, annual limitation on purchases, redemption, tax status, exchange of series HH bonds, and safety features.

Contact: Office of Public Affairs, U.S. Savings Bonds Division, U.S. Department of the Treasury, 800 K St., NW, Washington, DC 20226; 202-377-7716.

Save For The Future With Futures

Thinking of moving into the futures market? What things to do you need to know before you invest? The Commodity Futures Trading Commission (CFTC) can provides studies of the function of futures markets. They also have free reports and publications about the Commission, as well as information on commodities futures trading. Some of the free information includes: *CFTC Annual Report*, and *Economic Purposes of Futures Trading*.

Contact: Office of Communication and Education Services, Commodity Futures Trading Commission (CFTC), 2033 K St., NW, Washington, DC 20581; 202-254-8630.

Commemorative Coins Bring Big Bucks

Commemorative coins have become a way to raise money for a particular national cause. The 1986 Statue of Liberty coins raised 83 million for the national cause. These are just a few of the facts available in *A Brief History of the United States Mint.*

For your free copy contact: United States Mint, 633 Third St., NW, Washington, DC 20220; 202-874-6450.

Minerals into Money

The Bureau of Mines conducts research in the areas of mining, processing, and materials technology, with an emphasis on health and safety, mining efficiency, environmental concerns, and energy and materials conservation. There is information available on all the different minerals, as well as a publication called *Mineral Commodity Summaries* which comes out annually and has interesting facts about different commodities.

Call or write for any of the free publications: U.S. Department of the Interior, Bureau of Mines, 810 Seventh St., NW, Washington, DC 20241; 202-501-9649.

Get Rich Quick Schemes

How quick can you get rich investing in a pyramid scheme? How quickly can you lose your shirt? The Securities and Exchange Commission can send you the following free publications on various fraudulent investment scams:

- *How to Avoid Ponzi and Pyramid Schemes*

- *Applicability of Securities Laws to Pyramid Schemes*

- *Warning to Investors About Get Rich Quick Schemes*

Contact: Publications Section, Printing Branch, U.S. Securities and Exchange Commission, 450 6th St., NW, Room 3C48, Washington, DC 20549; 202-272-7460.

Van Gogh for $1,000?

A friend of a friend knows where you can get an original Van Gogh for $1,000, and he swears he found it in his grandmother's attic. How can you be sure it's for real? The FBI will run a check of the National Stolen Art File, a computer list of all the currently missing works of art reported as stolen in the U.S., and let you know if the painting is hot or not.

Contact: National Stolen Art File, Federal Bureau of Investigation, U.S. Department of Justice, Washington, DC 20535; 202-324-4192.

Did Your Broker Make You Broke?

Are you having some problems with your brokerage firm regarding fees or money? *Arbitration Procedures* is a free publication which discusses procedures for disputes with brokerage firms involving financial claims.

Contact: Publications Section, Printing Branch, Stop C-11, U.S. Securities and Exchange Commission, Washington, DC 20549; 202-272-7040.

For Your Kids

Why Do Leaves Change Colors?

Kids ask the best questions.

Why Leaves Change Color can be used to learn why leaves change to yellow, orange, and red each fall. It also contains instructions on how to copy leaves with crayons and how to make leaf prints with a stamp pad.

Contact: Forest Service, U.S. Department of Agriculture, 12th and Independence, SW, P.O. Box 96090, Washington, DC 20090; 202-205-0957.

For a Clean Environment

Learn the importance of keeping the environment clean with everyone's favorite comic strip, Mark Trail.

A free loan video is available titled, "Take Pride in America with Mark Trail", which explains how pollution destroys the environment.

Contact: Bureau of Mines, U.S. Department of the Interior, Cochrans Mill Rd., P.O. Box 18070, Pittsburgh, PA 15236; 412-892-6846.

Shake It Up Baby!

Are earthquakes your thing? Contact the U.S. Geological Survey for free publications, such as, *Earthquakes, Safety and Survival in an Earthquake*, and *The San Andreas Fault*, all of which are free and provide a wealth of information on a very shaky subject.

You can learn how earthquakes start, what to do when one occurs, and what area of the country is most likely to experience tremors.

Contact: U.S. Geological Survey, P.O. Box 25286, Denver, CO 80225.

Step Out of the Way

Volcanoes can erupt at any time. Remember Mount St. Helens? The U.S. Geological Survey has two free publications that explain how volcanoes are formed, why they erupt and more.

Request *Volcanic Hazards at Mount Shasta, California* and *Volcanoes* by writing U.S. Geological Survey, P.O. Box 25286, Denver, CO 80225.

What Does the Coast Guard Do?

Our Day With the Coast Guard provides a fun way to learn about the U.S. Coast Guard. This coloring book allows you to learn what it's like to be in the Coast Guard. It includes activities such as a maze and connect-the-dots.

Contact: Public Affairs, U.S. Coast Guard, U.S. Department of Transportation, Washington, DC 20593; 202-267-2596.

How Do Things Grow?

The poster "How A Tree Grows" teaches about photosynthesis, enzymes, and the various parts of a tree. There is also a booklet that goes along with the poster that explains more about a tree's growth.

Contact: Forest Service, U.S. Department of Agriculture, 12th and Independence, SW, P.O. Box 96090, Washington, DC 20090; 202-205-0957.

Do You Dream of Flying High in the Sky?

How We Made The First Flight is a free publication about the Wright brothers experiences.

Written in Orville Wright's own words, it is a description of his and Wilbur's first flights.

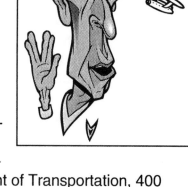

Contact: Aviation Education Division/AHT-100, Federal Aviation Administration, U.S. Department of Transportation, 400 7th Ave., SW, Room PL-100, Washington, DC 20590; 202-366-7018.

Let the Sun Shine In

People are trying to find new ways to heat their homes, factories, offices and schools without using so much expensive oil and gas. *Solar Energy and You* helps teach you about solar energy and solar heat. They also have other publications for kids dealing with alternative energy sources.

Contact: Conservation and Renewable Energy Inquiry and Referral Service (CAREIRS), P.O. Box 3048, Merrifield, VA 22116; 800-523-2929.

Learn Fire Safety with Big Bird

The Sesame Street Fire Safety Book contains Muppet skits and activities that teach thousands of children about fire safety. Each book is accompanied by a cassette tape that contains five songs.

Write: Attention: Sesame Street Fire Safety, Federal Emergency Management Agency, P.O. Box 70274, Washington, DC 20024.

Money, Money, Money

Did you know that 95% of the notes printed each year are used to replace notes already in circulation; that 48% of the notes printed are $1 notes?

You can learn a lot about your money from the Bureau of Engraving and Printing. Some information sheets available include:

- *Changes in $1 From July 1929*, which describes the value of $1.

- *Engravers and Engraving*, which gives the history of the printed dollar.

- *Fun Facts about Dollars*, on money trivia.

- *The Story of Money.*

Contact: Bureau of Engraving and Printing, U.S. Department of the Treasury, 14th and C Sts., SW, Washington, DC 20228; 202-874-3019.

Water

We all drink it, but what exactly is it? The U.S. Geological Survey can provide you with many free publications that explain water, water usage, and water contamination. Some of the titles include:

- *What is Water?*

- *The Water of the World*

- *How Much Water in a 12-ounce Can?*

- *Why is the Ocean Salty?*

Contact: U.S. Geological Survey, P.O. Box 25286, Denver, CO 80225.

Do You Like to Second Guess the Weather Channel?

The National Oceanic and Atmospheric Administration can provide you with information on keeping a weather log, weather warnings and more. Some of the free publications they have include *The Amateur Weather Forecaster*, which shows what you need to look for in predicting the weather, and *Watch Out...Storms Ahead! Owlie Skywarn's Weather Book*, a fun book describing different weather conditions.

Contact: Educational Programs Branch, National Oceanic and Atmospheric Administration, 1825 Connecticut Ave., NW, Washington, DC 20235; 202-606-4380.

Want to Learn about the Capitol?

The United States Capitol contains a wealth of architectural history.

They have publications that teach you about the Capitol's history and architecture.

Some of the publications include:

- *Architects of the Capitol*, which gives names and biographies of people who designed the capitol.

- *Statue of Freedom*, which describes the Statue.

- *The United States Capitol*, which provides a history of the Capitol.

- *Flags over the East and West Central Front of the U.S. Capitol*, which explains about the various flags and their symbolism.

Contact: Architect of the Capitol, Washington, DC 20515; 202-225-1222.

Do You Know Who the World's First Black Pilot Was?

August Martin. *The August Martin Activities Book* is a great way to learn about the world's first black airline pilot.

Contact: Aviation Education Division/AHT-100, Federal Aviation Administration, U.S. Department of Transportation, 400 7th Ave., SW, Room PL-100, Washington, DC 20590; 202-366-7018.

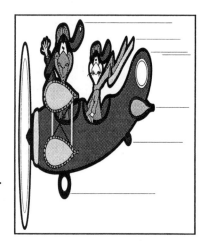

Having Trouble Breathing?

You can learn about air pollution through the coloring book *Airy Canary Learns to Fly*. It is about a bird who is having difficulty learning to fly because of the presence of Nasty Nitrogen Dioxide, Otto Ozone the Air Pollutant, and Sully Sulfur Dioxide.

Contact: Department of Air Pollution Control, Commonwealth of Virginia, P.O. Box 10089, Richmond, VA 23240; 804-786-2378.

Give a Hoot! Don't Pollute!

Woodsy Owl's 1992-93 Campaign Catalog is filled with dozens of items you can use (such as bike stickers, bookmarks, name tags, balloons, pens, and more) that have the Woodsy Owl logo on them.

Contact the office for your free catalog: Forest Service, U.S. Department of Agriculture, 12th and Independence, SW, P.O. Box 96090, Washington, DC 20090; 202-205-0957.

Help Your Kids to Read and Write a Fun Way

Kids love getting a letter addressed to themselves at home. Carry that excitement over to school!

The U.S. Postal Service offers a free starter kit called "Wee Deliver", which is designed to help them set up an in-school post office.

Kids can design stamps, pick a postmaster, and even write letters to each other. The starter kit includes information and a video to get you mailing.

Write: Corporate Relations, U.S. Postal Service, 475 L'Enfant Plaza, SW, Room 10541, Washington, DC 20260-3100.

Help Your Kids Hit the Books

Every child learns in his or her own way. To help encourage children to excel in school, the U.S. Department of Education has developed the *Help Your Child* series, to teach parents strategies they can use every day to teach their children to

read, learn geography, even to use the library.

The free series include:

- *Help Your Child Become a Good Reader*

- *Help Your Child Do Better in School*

- *Help Your Child Learn to Write Well*

- *Help Your Child Learn Geography*

- *Help Your Child Learn Science*

- *Help Your Child Use the Library*

- *Help Your Child Get Ready for School*

- *Help Your Child Learn Math*

Contact: U.S. Department of Education, Office of Educational Research and Improvement, 555 New Jersey Ave., NW, Washington, DC 20208; 800-424-1616.

Listen To Your Elders

Words of wisdom make more of impression when you get them directly from the source. *The Grand Generation: Interviewing Guide and Questionnaire* ($4.50) lists guidelines for collecting folklore and oral history from older tradition-bearers.

It includes a general guide to conducting interviews, a list of sample questions, and examples of ways to preserve and present findings.

Family Folklore Interviewing Guide and Questionnaire ($4.75) is a guide to collecting family folklore, including background information on the importance of recording it, details on techniques and presentation, and a sample questionnaire.

Contact: Smithsonian Institution Traveling Exhibition Service (SITES), Publications Department, Department 0564, Washington, DC 20073; 202-357-1338.

How Old Is the Tree Out Front?

Tree Rings: Timekeepers of the Past explains how past environmental conditions have been recorded in tree rings and how scientists interpret this information.

Contact: U.S. Geological Survey, P.O. Box 25286, Denver, CO 80225.

Safety First

Kids love to go to the park, but often forget safety rules while there. *Little Big Kids* (for ages 3-5) assists children in learning safe play habits on the playground and reinforces those lessons.

Write: U.S. Consumer Product Safety Commission, Office of Information and Public Affairs, Washington, DC 20207.

Swim with the Sharks

But you better swim fast. Learn what you are up against before you dive in. You can get a free educational "Shark Kit", which includes shark teeth, shark jaws, skin, freeze dried sharks, stickers, shark stamp, a video, manuals, books, and more with you paying for return shipping.

For more information call: Robert Shallcross, Natural History Museum, Office of Education, MRC 158, 10th St. and Constitution Ave., NW, Washington, DC 20560, 202-357-3045.

Get in Shape a Fun Way

The kids need to get off the couch and get outside. *Get Fit! A Handbook for Youth Ages 6-17* will help you become as physically fit as you can be.

Contact: Physical Fitness Award Program, President's Council on Physical Fitness and Sports, 450 5th St., NW, Washington, DC 20001; 202-272-3421.

Read Me a Story

Reading Is Fundamental is a program designed to encourage children of all ages to read and to help distribute books to those who can't afford them. They have developed a series of brochures (50 cents each) which deal with a variety of reading topics. Some of these include

- *Building a Family Library*

- *Choosing Good Books For Your Children*

- *Encouraging Soon-to-Be Readers*

- *Reading Aloud to Your Children*

- *Summertime Reading*

- *Upbeat and Offbeat Activities to Encourage Reading.*

To order these and to find out about other information available contact the Reading Is Fundamental program.

Contact: Reading Is Fundamental, Publications Department, 600 Maryland Ave., SW, Suite 500, Washington, DC 20024; 202-287-3371.

Creatures Great and Small

Kids love to learn about animals of all kinds. The Department of Vertebrate Zoology has several free bibliographies and booklets on a wide variety of species.

- *Endangered, Threatened, and Recently Extinct Vertebrates* is a bibliography which provides background information and other resources for these vertebrates.

- *Giant Panda* is two page bibliography on resources to learn more about the panda.

- *Loch Ness Monster* is a bibliography outlining resources to clues on whether or not this monster does exist.

For your copies of these and other bibliographies contact: National Museum of Natural History, Department of Vertebrate Zoology, Room 369, MRC 109, Smithsonian Institution, Washington, DC 20560; 202-357-2740.

For Your Little Scout

The President always likes a good cause. Girl Scouts and Boy Scouts are worthy of notice, so let the White House know of your special Scout and President Bill will send a certificate.

Contact: White House, Greetings Office, 1600 Pennsylvania Ave., NW, Washington, DC 20500; 202-456-2724.

The School Bus Is Not A Zoo

Get thirty kids together in a confined space, and a circus can occur at the drop of a hat. Teach your kids important bus safety rules through a free fact sheet titled *School Bus Safety*. Your kids spend a lot of time on the bus, so make sure they arrive at school and home safely by reviewing the rules. Your bus driver will thank you.

Contact: National Highway Traffic Safety Administration, Auto Safety Hotline NEF-11.2HL, 400 Seventh St., SW, Washington, DC 20590; 800-424-9393.

De-Video the Kids

Help your kids move away from the T.V. set, and into the outdoors. You can get some free help from the Forest Service as they have a free "Get Inside The Great Outdoors Kids" poster to show your kids there is something more than Nintendo.

Contact: Forest Service, U.S. Department of Agriculture, Engineering Staff, P.O. Box 96096, Washington, DC 20090-6090; 202-205-1400.

Pueblos in Pittsburgh

Jazz up your geography lesson or teach your kid about the great Southwest. *The Children's Activity Book* ($2) contains a variety of activities from New Mexico, including building adobe architecture, tin-working, preparation of special foods, and designing Native American pottery and Rio Grande blankets.

Contact: Center for Folklife Programs and Cultural Studies, 955 L'Enfant Plaza, SW, Room 2600, Smithsonian Institution, Washington, DC 20560; 202-287-3424.

Send Your Kids to the Moon

Looking for an interesting way for your kids to spend summer vacation? Space Camp is a way for your kids to learn about science, planets, rocketry, and more at the Space and Rocket Center. It does cost to send your kids to camp, but a scholarship program is available where kids can go for free.

To apply for this program kids need to complete an application, write a one-page essay, and have a teacher recommendation.

For an information packet on Space Camp and a scholarship application contact: Space and Rocket Center, One Tranquillity Base, Huntsville, AL 35807; 800-63-SPACE.

Images for Space

National Aeronautics and Space Administration (NASA) offers incredible posters free of charge. The posters include: "The Descent of an Orbiter", "The Search for Black Holes", "Images from Space", and much, much more.

Call or write for posters to: National Aeronautics and Space Administration, Publication Center, 300 E St., SW, Washington, DC 20546; 202-453-1287.

A View from Above

Show your kids the real thing when they ask about space. Free pictures with a synopsis on the back are great teaching tools for children or that obsessive Space person. Stickers are also available for various Space Shuttles.

Some of the pictures include your favorite space shuttle mission and:

- The First "Solo" in Space

- The Endeavor

- Apollo 17's View of Earth

Don't miss out. Call or write for pictures to: National Aeronautics and Space Administration, Publication Center, 300 E St., SW, Washington, DC 20546; 202-453-1287.

Shopping Made Safe

Toys are suppose to be fun, not dangerous. The U.S. Consumer Product Safety Commission's mission is to protect the public from unreasonable risks of injury and death associated with consumer products. They have published a series of publications dealing with toy safety including:

- *Toy Boxes and Toy Chests Fact Sheet*
- *Baby Rattles Fact Sheet*
- *For Kids Sake, Think Toy Safety Pamphlet*
- *Toy Safety Coloring Book*

For your free copies or a complete publications list write: Publication Request, Office of Information and Public Affairs, U.S. Consumer Product Safety Commission, Washington, DC 20207.

Help Them To Read

In order to help their children succeed, parents need to encourage and help their kids become good readers. The ERIC Clearinghouse on Reading and Communication Skills provides information in the fields of reading, writing, English, literacy, and more. They publish a series of parent booklets to encourage family involvement, which include:

- *You Can Encourage Your High School Student to Read* ($1.75)
- *Helping Your Child Become a Reader* ($1.75)

- *Beginning Literacy and Your Child* ($1.75)

- *How Can I Prepare My Young Child For Reading?* ($1.75)

- *Creating Readers and Writers* ($1.75)

For a complete list of publications and more information contact: ERIC Clearinghouse on Reading and Communication Skills, Indiana University, Smith Research Center, Suite 150, 1805 East 10th St., Bloomington, IN 47408; 812-855-5847.

Get Out the Crayons

Teach your kids about the environment in a fun way. The U.S. Environmental Protection Agency has two coloring books to help you increase your child's awareness of the Earth.

- *Once There Lived A Wicked Dragon* shows how pollution and chemicals effect a town.

- *Chessie: A Chesapeake Bay Story* shows how the Bay supports fish and wildlife.

For your free copies contact: U.S. Environmental Protection Agency, Information Access Branch, Public Information Center, 401 M St., SW, 3404, Washington, DC 20460; 202-260-7751.

Ready for Kindergarten?

Raising kids is no easy job, but there is some help available through the ERIC Clearinghouse for Elementary and Early Childhood Education.

This Clearinghouse encompasses the physical, social, and educational development of children from birth through early adolescence. They publish a free newsletter which describes the latest research in the field and other related information.

The Clearinghouse also makes available *ERIC Digests* which are concise reports on timely issues. These are free, but please include a self-addressed stamped envelope. Some of the titles include:

- *Readiness: Children and Schools*

- *Infant Child Care*

- *Approaches to School-Age Child Care*

- *Measuring Kindergartners' Social Competence*

- *Positive Discipline*

For these and other information contact: ERIC Clearinghouse for Elementary and Early Childhood Education, University of Illinois, College of Education, 805 West Pennsylvania Ave., Urbana, IL 61801; 217-333-1386.

Helmets are the Rule

It is such a thrill to learn how to ride a bike without training wheels, but bikes are involved in over 500,000 injuries. Teach your kids to ride safely through two free publications available from the U.S. Consumer Product Safety Commission. *Sprocketman Comic Book* and *Ten Smart Routes to Bike Safety* can both help your kids have a great and safe time bicycling.

For your free copies write: Publication Request, Office of Information and Public Affairs, U.S. Consumer Product Safety Commission, Washington, DC 20207.

Solar System Puzzle

Want to help your child build a solar system? "Solar System Puzzle Kit" is an activity for parents and children which includes patterns and supplemental materials. Kids are asked to assemble and eight-cube paper puzzle, and when solved, they can create a miniature solar system.

Free from: National Aeronautics and Space Administration Educational Publications, Code FEP, Washington, DC 20546; 202-453-1287.

Right to the Moon

Astronaut Fact Book is an absolute must for any space program enthusiast, with biographical sketches that include the graduate and postgraduate education of current, former and deceased astronauts. This is a great resource for any astrophile. "Networking" possibilities with astronauts in your area are made possible with information about where and for whom they work.

Free from: National Aeronautics and Space Administration Educational Publications, Code FEP, Washington, DC 20546; 202-453-1287.

Color Me

Teach your kids about the world around them with two great coloring books. *My Wetland Coloring Book* ($2.25) introduces children to drawings of swamps, marshes, bogs, and other kinds of wetlands. *Endangered Species Coloring Book: Save Our Species* ($1.75) contains more than 23 drawings illustrating endangered species in their natural habitat.

For your copies contact: Superintendent of Documents, U.S. Government Printing Office, Washington, DC 20402; 202-783-3238.

For Your Love Life

The Marriage-Go-Round

Check out the singles scene anywhere in the country by contacting the Bureau of the Census, which keeps some interesting figures regarding the population, such as the ratio of total number of single men to single women in metro areas.

Give them a call to find out what areas of the country will improve your chances of finding that special someone.

Contact: Marriage and Family Statistics, Population Division, Bureau of the Census, Bldg. 3, Room 231, Washington, DC 20233; 301-763-7987.

Keep Up with the Joneses

Neighbors are always keeping tabs on each other, so why should sex be any different? What do they know that you don't?

Want to know how many people and what type of person uses a certain kind of birth control? It's all in a free report entitled, *Contraceptive Use In The United States.* Find the trend, so you can be a member of the group.

Contact: National Center for Health Statistics, 6525 Belcrest Rd., Hyattsville, MD 20782; 301-436-8500.

Impotence...
When Love's a Letdown

Many types of sexual dysfunction can now be treated.

Some 10 million men suffer from impotence, so the National Kidney and Urologic Diseases Information Clearinghouse has developed a free "Impotence Information" packet, which includes articles and literature searches on the causes and cures for impotence and examines the pros and cons of different types of penile implants.

Contact: National Kidney and Urologic Diseases Information Clearinghouse, P.O. Box NKUDIC, Bethesda, MD 20892; 301-468-6345.

The Top Nine

The Food and Drug Administration (FDA) regulates drugs and medical devices to ensure that they are safe and effective. They publish *Comparing Contraceptives*, which discusses the possible side effects and effectiveness of nine different types of birth control. Another free publication is *Cervical Cap? Newest Control Device* which explains the cap.

Contact: Office of Consumer Affairs, Food and Drug Administration, 5600 Fishers Lane, HFE-88, Rockville, MD 20857; 301-443-3170.

The Condom People

The Food and Drug Administration regulates condoms to make sure they are both safe and effective.

The Consumer Affairs Office can provide you with information on the effectiveness of condoms in the prevention of the spread of AIDS and more. Some of their free publications include:

- *Condoms and Sexually Transmitted Diseases... Especially AIDS*

- *Condoms for Prevention of Sexually Transmitted Diseases*

- *Letter to: All U.S. Condom Manufacturers, Importers and Repackagers of Condoms*

Contact: Division of Consumer Affairs, Center for Devices and Radiological Health, 5600 Fishers Lane, HFZ-210, Rockville, MD 20857; 301-443-4190.

Bigger Breasts: Sure, but How Safe?

Seems like each week the newspaper runs some story regarding the dangers of silicone gel-filled breast implants.

To get the facts on these implants and under what conditions implants are still permitted contact the Food and Drug Administration's Breast Implant Hotline.

You can request a free "Breast Implants Information" packet, which includes information on clinical trials and regulations concerning breast implants.

Contact: Center for Devices and Radiological Health, Food and Drug Administration, 5600 Fishers Lane, Rockville, MD 20857; 800-532-4440.

AIDS: Changing Sex in the Nineties

Are you concerned about AIDS? What risks are you taking in having sex? There is so much information out there regarding AIDS, how do you know what is true?

The AIDS Clearinghouse can answer all your questions, refer you to testing centers, link you with support groups, send you publications, reports, posters, and more. Some of the free publications include:

- *Voluntary HIV Counseling and Testing: Facts, Issues, and Answers*

- *Surgeon General's Report on Acquired Immune Deficiency Syndrome*

- *Information about the AIDS Clinical Trials Information Service*

Contact: National AIDS Information Clearinghouse, P.O. Box 6003, Rockville, MD 20849; 800-458-5231.

Are Your Hot Flashes Getting Hotter?

Menopause doesn't have to be the hormonal hurricane women faced in the past.

Taking estrogen and progesterone can help relieve the problems of menopause, although they are not without problems of their own.

A free booklet entitled, *Menopause*, can answer many of your questions and outlines different forms of treatment.

Contact: National Institute on Aging, P.O. Box 8057, Gaithersburg, MD 20898; 800-222-2225.

Free Condoms!

Now there is no excuse. Title X Family Planning Clinics will provide free condoms and other birth control devices to people who meet certain income level requirements.

These clinics will also provide physical examinations (including testing for cancer and sexually transmitted diseases), infertility services, services for adolescents, pregnancy tests, periodic follow-up examinations, referral to and from other social and medical services agencies, and ancillary services.

To locate a clinic near you contact: Family Life Information Exchange, P.O. Box 37299, Washington, DC 20013; 301-585-6636.

Norplant – The Latest Thing

This Center can provide you with free reports and information regarding the new contraceptive called Norplant. Reports include information on patient labeling, prescribing, usage, warnings, and Food and Drug Administration (FDA) statements regarding Norplant. There is a free FDA consumer article detailing the pros and cons of Norplant.

Contact: Center for Drug Evaluation and Research, HFD-8, Food and Drug Administration, 5600 Fishers Lane, Rockville, MD 20857; 301-594-1012.

Contraceptive Risk and Effectiveness – Get the Facts

The National Institute of Child Health and Human Development distributes pamphlets and reports on various methods of contraception, as well as medical updates on the risks and/or effectiveness of new forms of birth control.

Two of their free publications include:

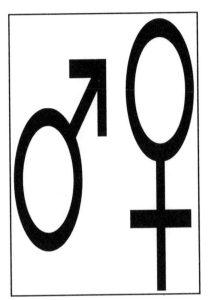

- *Facts About Oral Contraceptives* which describes different forms of contraception, and

- *Facts About Vasectomy Safety* which describes vasectomies. Contact the Institute for more information on contraception.

Contact: National Institute of Child Health and Human Development, National Institutes of Health (NIH), Building 31, Room 2A32, 9000 Rockville Pike, Bethesda, MD 20892; 301-496-5133.

Fearless Sex Hotline

Sexually transmitted diseases (STD) are nothing new. From Casanova to Sigmund Freud, some of the greatest lovers of all times had to pay for not being careful. The Sexually Transmitted Diseases hotline can give you the latest information on a wide range of STDs and how to protect yourself. Some of the free publications include;

- *Condoms, Contraceptives and Sexually Transmitted Diseases* - discusses how some forms of birth control protect against STDs.

- *Protect Yourself and Your Baby From Sexually Transmitted Disease* - explains the dangers of STDs for unborn babies.

- *Questions: STD/VD* - answers some basic questions on STDs.

Contact: National Sexually Transmitted Diseases Hotline, P.O. Box 13827, Research Triangle Park, NC 27709; 800-227-8922.

The Way to a Man's Heart Is through His Stomach

If this is true, let's find out what he eats, so we can dish it up.

According to the Nationwide Food Consumption Survey, men in the marrying age range seem to prefer beef, beer, and bagels, so hold the tofu and wine spritzers. This survey provides a wealth of information on what men  and women in various age groups like to eat and drink.

For your free copy contact: Human Nutrition Information Service, U.S. Department of Agriculture, 6505 Belcrest Rd., Hyattsville, MD 20782; 301-436-5825.

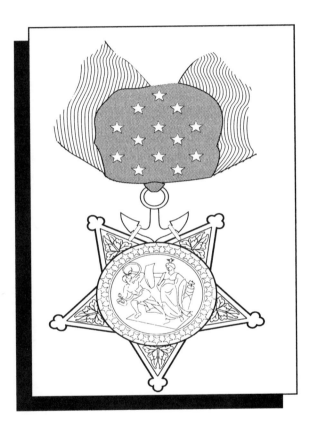

Superheros, For Real

The Congressional Medal of Honor is awarded to those members of the Armed Services whose actions against the enemy go above and beyond the call of duty. Past winners include Buffalo Bill Cody, and Dr. Mary Walker, who was a Civil War surgeon and the first and only female to receive the award.

For information concerning this and other medals and decoration of the Armed Forces contact: Public Affairs, attn. Gerri Taylor, U.S. Department of Defense, Room 2E777, The Pentagon, Washington, DC 20301-1400; 703-697-5737.

And the Emmy for Exports Goes to....

Superpowers these days fight over commodities and trade barriers, armed with fax, phone, and the latest figures. The President's "E" Award and the "E Star" Award for Excellence in Exporting is designed to honor American exporters, who demonstrate breakthroughs in competitive markets and the overcoming of export problems. Some past winners include Karsten Manufacturing Corp. for Ping Golf Clubs, Coleman Company, and Frymaster Corporation.

For more information contact: "E" Award Program Officer, Office of Domestic Operation, U.S. and Foreign Commercial Service, ITA, U.S. Department of Commerce, Room 3810, Washington, DC 20230; 202-482-1289.

When The Little Guy Sees Big

While corporate giants are downsizing to beat the band, scores of dynamic small businesses are busy building America's tomorrow. If you know of an innovative small business owner in your state, then nominate them for The Small Business Person of the Year award. Other categories include minority, women, or veterans small business, exporter, young entrepreneur, and even for Federal government contractor or subcontractor of the year.

For more information on these awards contact: Your local SBA office, or the Answer Desk, U.S. Small Business Administration, 409 3rd. St., SW, Washington, DC 20416; 800-U-ASK-SBA.

Physics Fun

Unlike the universe, science and math didn't just happen. The Presidential Awards For Excellence In Science And Mathematics Teaching recognizes this, and is open to teachers in grades kindergarten through 12th grade. This award includes a $7,500 grant to the awardee's school and a free trip to Washington.

For more information contact: Presidential Awards For Excellence In Science And Mathematics Teaching, National Science Teachers Association, 1840 Wilson Blvd., Arlington, VA 22201-3000; 703-243-7100.

Bringing Technology to the Common Man

Which came first, the popsicle or the stick? Inventors may come up with great ideas, but getting them to market takes technical know-how. National Medal of Technology is given to a U.S. citizen or company which excels in the commercialization of technology. Past winners include Del Meyer, the man who brought us polyester, and Bill Gates from Microsoft.

For an application contact: U.S. Department of Commerce, Technology Administration, Dr. Paul Braden, National Medal of Technology, Room 4418, 14th St. and Constitution Ave., NW, Washington, DC 20230; 202-482-5572.

Be True to Your School

The Blue Ribbon School Award is given by the U.S. Department of Education to award schools that excel in educational leadership, instruction, organization, and parental and community involvement. Schools are asked to report their progress toward achieving the National Education Goals and to describe in detail the school program.

For more information contact: U.S. Department of Education, Blue Ribbon Schools Program, 555 New Jersey Ave., NW, Washington, DC 20208-5645; 202-219-2149.

Beam Me Up, Scotty

Space holds a special fascination for kids and there are several special award programs to keep that interest on the front burner.

Both NASA and the National Science Teachers Association sponsor competitions for would-be skywalkers.

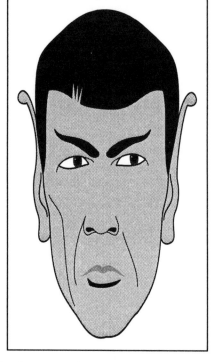

- The Interplanetary Art Competition (grades 3-12) is for students who have a vision of interplanetary space, including a description.

- Future Aircraft/Spacecraft Design (grades 3-5) encourages students working in teams to design aircraft.

For guidelines, information, and application procedures contact: National Science Teachers Association, 1742 Connecticut Ave., NW, Washington, DC 20009; 202-328-5800.

It's Just Gas

Come up with a novel way to expand U.S. fossil fuel reserves without stepping on Mrs. Nature's toes and everyone wins but the Iraqis.

The Lowry Award winners work to find ways to expand the U.S.'s finite gas, coal and oil reserves in an environmentally responsible manner with winners receiving a gold medal, citation, and $10,000.

For nominations procedures contact: Awards Officer, FE-72, Office of Fossil Energy, Attn: Fred Glaser, U.S. Department of Energy, Washington, DC 20585; 301-903-2786.

Honors for a Class Act

Getting kids to think creatively and critically is something we all want to encourage.

The Quigg Excellence in Education Award is presented to teachers, students, parents, or others that encourage this kind of analytical thinking in America's youth. You can win for a single specific event or for a series of activities which get America's youth inventing.

Contact: Project XL, Office of Public Affairs, The Patent and Trademark Office, Washington, DC 20231.

Uncle Sam's Star Awards

Space Science Student Involvement Program (SSIP) is an annual program that involves students in creating experiments, art, and writing in areas of interest to NASA.

- Mission To Planet Earth (grades 6-8) allows teams to develop a project that uses satellites to determine effect of human activity on Earth.

- Mars Science Experiment Project (grades 9-12) asks students to design an expedition to Mars.

- Aerospace Internship Competition (grades 9-12) requires students to design experiments that could be theoretically performed in a NASA center.

For guidelines, information, and application procedures contact: National Science Teachers Association, 1742 Connecticut Ave., NW, Washington, DC 20009; 202-328-5800.

Grade the Principal

To reward people who have devoted their careers to other people's children, the U.S. Department of Education and the National Association of Elementary School Principals (NAESP) present awards to National Distinguished Principals. The guidelines include nomination and selection by peers, demonstrated commitment to excellence, evidence of support, high standards and expectations for students and staff, and service as a principal for at least five years.

For more information contact: National Association of Elementary School Principals, 1615 Duke St., Alexandria, VA 22314; 703-684-3345.

Start by Jogging Your Dog

Not everyone has time to become an Olympic-class athlete, but that doesn't mean you can't compete. Take the President's Challenge, which is a physical fitness testing program of the President's Council on Physical Fitness and Sports with schools nationwide participating in the program. Anyone age 6 to 96 can also earn the Presidential Sports Award in any one of 68 activities, and there is even a Family Fitness Award.

To learn how to be a winner contact: The President's Council on Physical Fitness and Sports, 701 Pennsylvania Ave., NW, Suite 250, Washington, DC 20004; 202-272-3430.

Intellectual Athletics

Some students would rather compete on the black-board than on the grid iron, but that doesn't make them geeks. It makes them tomorrow's Oxford scholars and possible presidential material. The White House and the U.S. Department of Education recognize these students through the Presidential Scholars awards program for both academic and art scholars.

For more information contact: The White House, Commission on Presidential Scholars, Room 2189, 400 Maryland Ave., SW, Washington, DC 20202; 202-401-2910.

Top Ten Quality Control Freaks

Think your company is tops when it comes to quality? For quality awareness and strategies, the Malcolm Baldrige National Quality Award may be given annually in each of three categories: manufacturing, service, and small business. Applicants must undergo a rigorous evaluation by an independent board and be judged in many different areas. In fact, many executives use the Baldrige criteria to establish quality improvement programs in their companies. Past winners include AT&T Network Systems Group, The Ritz-Carlton Hotel Co., and Federal Express Corp.

For more information contact: Malcolm Baldrige National Quality Award Office, A537 Administration Building, National Institute of Standards and Technology, Gaithersburg, MD 20899; 301-975-2036.

For Your Mind

News of the Day

Is this a good time to open your dream restaurant, Cafe, Tea, and Me? What about building your country house? This U.S. Department of Commerce recorded message provides you with the latest numbers on monthly housing completions, composite indexes, leading economic indicators, wholesale and retail sales and more.

Call: Commerce Department News; 202-393-1847.

All Aboard

Kids love to watch planes, trains, and ships. You can call this recorded message to find which ships and barges are coming and going, as well as their departure times.

Call: St. Lawrence Seaway Ship Arrival Message Line; 315-769-2422.

How Much Is too Much?

Uncle Sam goes shopping each month and you can find out how much we spend on everything from cupcakes to satellite dishes. It's a goldmine for comparison shoppers and entrepreneurs looking for the next super market. Call for the latest U.S. Department of Labor figures.

Call: Consumer Price Index; 202-606-7828.

Labor Pains

Out of work or looking for a new job? You can take comfort in the numbers while tracking the latest employment trends and opportunities. The U.S. Department of Labor provides information on employment levels, labor indicators, consumer and producer prices as well as information on available publications on this recorded message.

Call: Current Labor Statistics; 202-606-7828.

A Raise is a Raise

By any other name, it still smells sweet. You can find out if everyone's getting a raise but you. Or, if your benefits are keeping up with the Joneses.

Call the Employment Cost Index Information recorded message at the U.S. Department of Labor; 202-606-7828.

Time for a Sale?

Is no one buying your product? Are your investments in a slump?

Find out how everyone else is doing by calling the Merchandise, Trade, and Equipment Transactions message line from the U.S. Department of Commerce to get current information on merchandise trade balance, investment income, goods and services and more.

Call: Merchandise, Trade, and Equipment Transactions Message Line; 202-898-2453.

Pick a Job, Any Job

Looking for a career with the lowest current unemployment rate? Are your prospects of getting off unemployment improving?

Call the U.S. Department of Labor Employment Situation Information recorded message line for current information on the unemployment rate, unemployment rate of major worker groups, and other labor market activity.

Call: Employment Situation Information; 202-606-7828.

Just the Facts, Ma'am

Get the numbers on the numbers. For the latest figures from the U.S. Department of Commerce on what makes up the Gross National Product (GNP), from quarterly gross domestic profits to import/export figures and indicators in between, call: Gross National Product message line; 202-898-2451.

Be Your Own Economist

Put your finger on the economic pulse of the nation. Call this U.S. Department of Commerce message line for monthly numbers on building permits, orders for plants and equipment, unemployment insurance claims, and other economic forecasters.

Call: Leading Economic Indicators Message Line; 202-898-2450.

How Much Can You Really Take with You?

This Pension Benefit Guaranty Corporation message provides you with interest rates for valuing benefits and pension plans, so you can plan your retirement in style.

Call: Pension Plans and Interest Rates Message Line; 202-778-8899.

What Comes in Goes Out

Are you due for a raise? Would you like to know how the whole country is doing? What about wages and salaries?

Call to get month by month personal income and outlays, total wages and salaries, proprietors' income, interest and dividend income, and more from the U.S. Department of Commerce.

Call: Personal Income and Outlays Message Line; 202-898-2452.

Bills, Bills, Bills

The bond market is where the economy stretches its legs. Find out whether to invest in a T-bill or a T-bird, or whether savings bonds are still great graduation gifts.

The U.S. Department of Treasury will tell you all you need to know about Treasury bills, notes, and bonds, as well as auction results, and more.

Call: Treasury Bills Hotline; 202-874-4000.

Who Do You Believe?

Did the product you bought to grow hair on your head actually just color your scalp? Did you buy a "Made In America" product only to find "Made in Taiwan" stamped on the bottom?

The Federal Trade Commission deals with unfair methods of competition and unfair or deceptive acts or practices. You can call this message line for weekly Commission information on topics for meetings, hearings, and speeches.

Call: Federal Trade Commission Meetings Message Line; 202-326-2711.

An ARM and a Leg

Keep a step ahead of the bank if you have an adjustable rate mortgage by tracking fluctuation in interest rates. Remember, it's your pound of flesh. Call the Office of Thrift Supervision to hear a recorded message on the current data that is used by many financial institutions as a basis for computing their adjustable rate mortgages.

Call: Office of Thrift Supervision; 202-906-6988.

The Latest Dirt

Should you plant sunflowers or soybeans? Should you invest in pork bellies or potatoes? Is the local grocery chain inflating its prices? The U.S. Department of Agriculture newsline will tell you more than you ever will need to know. And depending upon when you call, you can also keep up on political appointments and the latest agricultural techniques and discoveries.

Call: Agriculture Department News Hotline; 202-488-8358.

Invitation Lost in the Mail?

Don't let Bill and Hillary have all the fun. When you come to our Nation's capitol, find out what fun events are happening on Pennsylvania Avenue just by listening to this recorded message of the Pennsylvania Avenue Development Corporation.

Call: Nation's Capitol Events Hotline; 202-PA4-0009.

Better than a Rolex

Tired of being late? Did your grandmother teach you that punctuality is a virtue? Set your watch to the exact time of the Atomic Clock at the Naval Observatory, and see how you do.

Call: Time (within milliseconds); 202-653-1800.

Project Blue Book

In 1969 the government undertook a huge investigation of UFO sightings called Project Blue Book.

The case is now closed and all the findings are available to the public at the National Archives on 95 rolls of microfilm containing over 2.3 million pages. They will send you a 10-page index on microfilm free of charge, but more detailed index is $23. You can also get up to 10 pages of an individual sighting report from the Project copied and sent to you free of charge.

Contact: National Archives and Records Administration, Modern Military Reference Branch, Washington, DC 20408; 202-501-5385.

Flowerpower Plus

Get green-thumb advice from the bonsai samurai staffers at the U.S. Botanic Garden in Washington, DC. Listen to the nation's Gardeners of Eden and learn about free on-site classes for visitors and expert analysis of your own gardening problems by phone.

Call: Botanic Garden Upcoming Events Hotline; 202-225-7099.

Ready to Hit the Open Road?

This message system of the Office of Personnel Management is set up to provide information to current or retired federal employees or survivors, regarding retirement benefits, forms necessary, as well as directing you to the appropriate sources for more information.

Call: Federal Employees Retirement Information Hotline; 202-606-0400.

Recall Their Bluff

You can become a grassroots pain in the pocketbook for manufacturers of shoddy products. The U.S. Consumer Product Safety Commission Investigations hotline will tell you how to make your complaints heard and also tell you about available publications and tips on purchasing products.

Call: Consumer Product Safety Commission Hotline; 800-638-CPSC.

How Much?

Let Uncle Sam set your prices for you. The government tracks the prices of specific products each month and then releases the price changes in the form of the producer price index. All you need to do is follow the trend of the U.S. Department of Labor.

Call: Producer Price Index Message Line; 202-606-7828.

Does Money Grow on Trees?

You can see money being made by the billions during your tour of the Bureau of Engraving and Printing. Call this message line for information concerning tour hours, directions, and best places to park. You shouldn't leave your wallet at home, as they have a great gift shop too.

Call: Engraving and Printing Message Line; 202-874-3188.

A Job Bank for Globetrotters

Throw out the classifieds. Uncle Sam is always hiring bright people like yourself, not just here but all over the world.

This Career America hotline, sponsored by the U.S. Office of Personnel Management, will help you find out exactly what government jobs are available in your area, what the qualifications are, and to whom you need to talk to get you started on the payroll.

Call: Career America Hotline; 912-757-3000.

Share the Wealth

Tired of sitting back and watching third world countries fall apart before your eyes? You can become a Peace Corps volunteer and use your special talents to improve life.

Call: Peace Corps; 800-424-8580.

Televidiots, Fight Back

Tired of being pushed around by the obnoxious cable companies? Mysterious 900 charge on your phone bill?

Don't get mad as heck, get even. File a complaint. You can learn about the

process and also get free facts and publications by calling the U.S. Federal Communications Commission Hotline.

Call: Federal Communications Commission Hotline; 202-632-7000.

Let Your Fingers Do The Walking

Just sit back, relax, and dial up a job for yourself. The Federal Job Information Center of the Office of Personnel Management can provide you with information on the application process, job availability, testing centers, and more. Just give a call and get your career jump started.

Call: Federal Job Information Center Hotline; 202-606-2700.

Better than Sitting Home

Are you retired, and love the outdoors? Want to volunteer? Give some time to the U.S. Geological Survey (USGS). You can get a comprehensive listing of all USGS departments, phone numbers, and division coordinators.

Call: Geological Survey Volunteers Hotline; 703-648-7440.

Legal or Not?

Is getting your green card turning you red? The Immigration and Naturalization Service has set up a message line to provide information on forms, nearest offices, passports, green cards, citizenship, work visas, foreign adoption, bringing your family to the U.S., and more.

Call: Immigration and Naturalization Message Line; 202-307-1501.

Plan Ahead

Is your child another Einstein? Then you better start saving now for college. Call the Savings Bond hotline of the U.S. Department of Treasury to receive information on the market base interest rate of bonds, and to find out about the education savings bond program.

Call: Savings Bonds Hotline; 202-447-1775.

Uncle Sam's Poor Box

Want to help Uncle Sam pay off his charge account? Just call this number sponsored by the U.S. Department of Treasury's Bureau of the Public Debt and hear who you need to make the check out to and do your part.

Call: Public Debt Information Line; 202-874-4000.

Your Travel Agent

Plan ahead for your trip to the nation's capitol. This message provides you with information on what is happening at the thirteen Smithsonian museums, including hours of operation and special exhibits.

Call: Smithsonian Dial-A-Museum; 202-357-2020.

Stars in Your Eyes

Are you a star gazer? Want to impress your date with your terrestrial knowledge? Just call the Skywatchers Report to learn what the most prominent stars and planets are in the sky this month, and
maybe your date will start gazing into your eyes.

Call: Smithsonian Skywatchers Report; 202-357-2000.

Aye and Nay

Have your Senators been busy? Just give a call and see what they've been doing. This message provides you with information regarding when the Senate was in session, bills voted on, and their outcomes.

Call: U.S. Senate Floor Votes: Democratic Cloakroom; 202-224-8541. Republican Cloakroom; 202-224-8601.

UFOs

Where do you get information on Unidentified Flying Objects (UFOs)? The Air Force will send you a free *UFO Fact Sheet* that lists key resources, both government and private, to get you started in your search for extraterrestrial life.

Contact: U.S. Air Force, Office of Public Affairs, Resource Library, 1690 Air Force Pentagon, Washington, DC 20330-1690; 703-697-4100.

Disappearing Towns

Your map is brand new, but you can't find the town where your grandmother says she was born. Before you write your grandmother off as crazy, there's free help. The U.S. Geological Survey can search their Geographic Names database for you to find out if it still exists, or if it doesn't, the exact longitude and latitude of where it used to be.

Contact: Geographic Names Information, Branch of Geographic Names, U.S. Geologic Survey, 12201 Sunrise Valley Dr., Mail Stop 523, Reston, VA 22092; 703-648-4547.

Tally Up

Want to know how your guy voted? Have you been following a particular bill? This message provides you with information regarding when the House was in session, bills 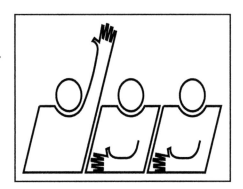 voted on, and their outcomes.

Call: U.S. House of Representatives Floor Votes: Democratic Cloakroom; 202-225-7400. Republican Cloakroom; 202-225-7430.

Cost of Illegal Drugs

Just how much is the illegal traffic of drugs costing the country? The Drugs and Crime Date Center and Clearinghouse has the most current data on drugs and crime, and will do free searches of their database for you on specific topics.

Contact: Drugs and Crime Data Center and Clearinghouse, 1600 Research Blvd., Rockville, MD 20850; 800-666-3332, or 301-251-5140 (in DC metro area).

Television Interference Problems

Is your favorite T.V. show ruined by interference from a local radio station? Does your cordless phone pick up radio signals? *Something About Interference* and the *Interference Handbook* are two free publications from the Federal Communications Commission (FCC) on your interference problems.

Contact: Consumer Assistance, Federal Communications Commission, 1919 M St., NW, Room 725, Washington, DC 20554; 202-632-7000.

How Schools Spend Your Tax Money

Frustrated with the way your local public schools are spending your tax dollars? The free publication, *Making Sense of School Budgets: A Citizen's Guide to Local Public Education Spending*, will help you better understand and control how your money is used.

Contact: Education Information Branch, Office of Educational Research Improvement, U.S. Department of Education, Capitol Plaza Building, Suite 300, 555 New Jersey Ave., NW, Washington, DC 20208-5641; 800-424-1616.

April 15th Seems to Come Earlier Each Year

The Internal Revenue Service has the hottest lines in town. Their Information Line answers all your tax questions. Their Tele-Tax Line provides pre-recorded tax information. And the Forms Line will send you those special tax forms we all love.

Call: Information Line; 800-829-1040, Tele-Tax Line; 800-829-4477, Forms Line; 800-829-3676.

Social Security: Just Another Wrong Number?

Everyone complains about how little they get each month from Social Security, but if their check is late, look out.

Need to get another copy of your Social Security card? Moved? Want to know how much you will get from Social Security if you retired today? Just give this hotline a call, and don't forget your special number.

Call: Social Security Hotline; 800-772-1213.

The Economic Outlook

The Congressional Budget Office has a report available called *The Economic and Budget Outlook* which is an analysis of the economic outlook.

Information included are projections of the Federal deficit and debt by fiscal year developments in the labor market and much more.

For your copy contact: Congressional Budget Office, Second and D St., SW, Washington, DC 20515; 202-226-2621.

Don't Be A Broke Bookworm

Money's tight everywhere, but Uncle Sam can help you pay for school. The Federal Student Aid Information Center can help would-be college and trade school students learn about financial aid programs, understand eligibility requirements and even complete financial aid applications.

Call: Federal Student Aid Information Center; 800-4-FED-AID.

A Big Number for Small Business

You ask it; they answer it. The U.S. Small Business Administration (SBA) provides you with a wealth of information for all your small business needs, including publications, videos, local SBA offices, referrals, and more.

Call: SBA Answer Desk; 800-8-ASK-SBA.

The Safe Sex Buzz

You can find out the latest information on AIDS, such as: locations of testing centers near you, treatment and referral options, and answers to questions like can you get AIDS if you use a condom?

Call: The Centers for Disease Control-National AIDS Hotline; 800-342-AIDS.

Understanding Lemons, Roadkills, Grouchy Drivers

Learn about safety problems in motor vehicles, tires, and automotive equipment.

Get even with your manufacturer by having the defective product recalled. If a safety-related defect exists, the manufacturer has to fix it at no cost to the owner.

Call: Auto Safety Hotline; 800-424-9393.

Cancer Answers

Each day the newspaper seems to carry a story on a new cancer treatment, cure, or prevention method. Who do you believe?

The Cancer Information Service is the place to call for the latest information on detection, treatment, rehab, and financial assistance for those concerned about cancer.

Call: Cancer Information Service; 800-4-CANCER.

Medicare Madness... Keep Tabs on Benefit Erosion

How do you apply for Medicare benefits?

What is and is not covered? What about supplemental insurance?

The Medicare Hotline will help you maneuver through the forms and filing maze to get what you deserve.

Call: Medicare Hotline; 800-638-6833.

When Meat's a Mystery, Call Uncle Sam

Worried about that special recipe Uncle Bob has for cooking the Thanksgiving bird?

What about the smoked turkey your grandma sent through the mail?

The Meat and Poultry Hotline answers questions related to food safety, preparation tips, power failures, and food labels.

Call: Meat and Poultry Hotline; 800-535-4555.

Loose Lips Save Ships

No need to stay on a sinking ship if you plan ahead. Call for information on boating safety recalls, consumer complaints about boat defects, and even boating classes.

Call: Boating Safety Hotline; 800-368-5647.

The Dump Snitchline

Does your dump have a very funny odor? Want to start recycling? Wondering what can be dumped in your dump?

The Resource Conservation and Recovery Act (RCRA)/Superfund Hotline will answer these questions and more, including hazardous waste disposal, used oil, and land disposal restrictions.

Call: RCRA/Superfund Hotline; 800-424-9346.

Spreading the Clean (and Sober) Word

Are drugs or alcohol taking over your life? What about someone you love? Want to help keep your kids off drugs? Call this number and receive publications, posters, videos, and even treatment and referral information.

Call: National Clearinghouse for Alcohol and Drug Information; 800-729-6686.

Confessed Under Hypnosis?

Did the police make you confess to a crime you didn't commit because they put you under hypnosis? Find out how they did it, and how valid confessions gotten under hypnosis are in the court-room, from the free publication, *Forensic Use of Hypnosis.*

Contact: National Victims Resource Center, Box 6000-AIQ, Rockville, MD 20850; 800-627-6872, 301-251-5525 (DC metro).

For Your Nonprofit

Tons of Free Books

Need to raise a little cash? Hold a book sale.

Thousands of surplus books from the Copyright Division and private gifts in a variety of subject areas are available to non-profit organizations from the Library of Congress.

All you need is a letter from your non-profit which includes the name of the person coming to select books and the name of the organization, but you must pay for shipping and handling.

Or you can bring a letter from your Congressman's office. Their office will have the option of paying for the shipping with franks (postage for which their office will pay).

Contact: Exchange and Gift Division, Library of Congress, Madison Bldg., 101 Independence Ave., SE, Room B03, Washington, DC 20540; 202-707-5243.

Learn the Ropes

Don't let the IRS rain on your parade. Get all your ducks in a row before there are any unpleasant surprises. Contact the Internal Revenue Service for a guidebook *Tax-Exempt Status For Your Organization* (Publication 557) on tax-exempt nonprofits. It explains the procedures you must follow to obtain an appropriate ruling or a determination letter recognizing such exemption, as well as certain other information that applies generally to all exempt organizations.

Contact: The Internal Revenue Service Forms Line; 800-829-3676.

Giveaway Wish List

Need some desks, chairs, even hospital beds for your non-profit? Nonprofits, which include medical institutions, clinics, schools, museums, libraries and more, can receive free furniture, clothing, and equipment from Uncle Sam through their State surplus property agency which receives items for distribution from the Federal Government.

To find out about the office near you, request the brochure *Federal Surplus Personal Property Donation Programs* from Property Management, Federal Supply Service, General Services Administration, Washington, DC 20406; 703-305-7240.

Step Inside the Loop

So who's getting all that money Congress spends each year in grants?

Find out in a free Congressional Research Service report *Grants And Foundation Support* (IP50G), which helps the grantseeker find sources of funding, both government and private, and grant proposal development.

Request the publication through Your Congressmen's Office, U.S. Congress, Washington, DC 20515; 202-224-3121.

Strike Up the Band

Your parade can get a little noisier and more colorful with a band and color guard supplied by some local Defense Department installations.

Most installations have community relations officers who handle requests from nonprofit organizations for these services and more, so contact them for information on availability and restrictions.

If you would like an aerial flyover from the Blue Angels or the Thunderbirds, or a parachute show from the Golden Knights (there are some costs involved), you must put your request in writing to: OASD (PA) DCR, The Pentagon, Room 1E776, Washington, DC 20301-1400.

A Home for the Holidays

If you are part of a non-profit organization ministering to the homeless, the government is taking applications for eligible groups to receive excess or unused federal buildings or land for homeless people.

The program is administered by a combination of the U.S. Department of Housing and Urban Development (HUD), which screens applications, the General Services Administration (GSA), which makes the properties available, and the U.S. Department of Health and Human Services (HHS), which reviews applications. In accordance with Title V of the McKinney Homeless Assistance Act, HUD publishes a list of properties available in the *Federal Register*.

Additional information regarding the properties, as well as the Title V process can be obtained by call 800-927-7588, a toll-free number established by HUD. After a property is published, homeless providers must submit expressions of interest by providing a written notice to the Division of Health Facilities Planning at HHS within 60 days of publication. You will then receive an application packet containing complete instructions on how to apply for the property.

You can also request the following publications: *How To Acquire Federal Surplus Real Property for Public Health Purposes*, *Obtaining Federal Property for the Homeless*, *Questions and Answers*

About Federal Property Programs, and HHS/HUD/GSA joint regulation covering specific information on Title V process.

Contact: Division of Health Facilities Planning, Public Health Service, U.S. Department of Health and Human Services, Room 17A-10, Parklawn Building, 5600 Fishers Lane, Rockville, MD 20857; 301-443-0084.

Soup's On

Does your non-profit offer meals or food to those in need? Through the Food Distribution Program, the U.S. Department of Agriculture (USDA) distributes foods to State agencies for use by eligible local agencies.

USDA purchases foods from U.S. markets under surplus removal and price support programs. The foods go to schools and institutions participating in the child nutrition programs, to nutrition programs for the elderly, to needy families on Indian reservations and to food banks, soup kitchens, hospitals, and prisons.

The foods are also used to help victims of natural disasters and situations of distress. For a free copy of *Food Distribution - State Distributing Agencies Directory*, contact the address listed below.

Contact: Food Distribution Division, Food and Nutrition Service, U.S. Department of Agriculture, 3101 Park Ctr. Dr., Room 502, Alexandria, VA 22302; 703-305-2660.

Pledge Drive Propaganda

Overcome contribution jitters by handing out a copy of Publication 526 titled *Charitable Contributions*, which explains the contributions you can deduct and the types of organizations that qualify.

Contact: The Internal Revenue Service Forms Line, 800-829-3676.

For Your Pets

And You Thought They Were Just Cute

They are more than Snoopy's cousins; beagles have now been put to work. *USDA's Beagle Brigade* is a free booklet which explains the background, training, care and feeding of a group of detector dogs that work in international airports throughout the United States keeping a lookout for agricultural contraband. *Beagle Trivia* is another free booklet which provides information on the origin characteristics and myths about beagles.

Contact: Animal and Plant Health Inspection Service, U.S. Department of Agriculture (USDA), Room G-195, Federal Building, 6505 Belcrest Road, Hyattsville, MD 20782; 301-436-4478.

It Was Love at First Sight

You were strolling along an idyllic river in France when you stumbled upon an injured ferret. You nursed it back to health and now you want to bring it home with you.

Pets and Wildlife is a free publication that describes the rules regarding bringing pets and wildlife into the U.S., and the quarantine procedures, as well as a list of prohibited species.

For your free copy write: U.S. Customs Service, P.O. Box 7407, Washington, DC 20044; 202-927-6724.

Mommy, Mommy, May I PLEASE Have a Dog?

Kids beg their parents every day for a family dog, but few know what is involved, such as the care and feeding of a household pet.

The office below has several fact sheets which parents can use to teach their children how to care for pets properly.

Some of the free fact sheets include

- *Dog Ownership Self-Test* - for people who are considering adopting a dog

- *Facts and Fallacies About Canine Parasites* - which provides information on your dog's health.

Contact: Center for Veterinary Medicine, Food and Drug Administration, U.S. Department of Health and Human Services, 7500 Standish Place, Rockville, MD 20855; 301-295-8755.

Take Good Care of Fido

Do you run an animal lab or breeding enterprise and want to train your staff? What about animal husbandry? The Animal Welfare Information Center has a free publication titled *Audio-Visuals Relating to Animal Care, Use, and Welfare*, which lists videos they have available for free interlibrary loan. These videos cover topics such as livestock, household pets, lab animals, rabbits, guinea pigs, husbandry, and more.

For your copy contact: Animal Welfare Information Center, National Agricultural Library, 10301 Baltimore Blvd., Beltsville, MD 20705; 301-504-6212.

Vet Speak

Your vet tells you your dog has parvo, but what does that mean? The Food and Drug Administration (FDA) Center for Veterinary Medicine has a free publication, *When Your Vet Says...*, which explains some of the more common terms used by veterinarians when discussing cats or dogs.

The Center also has three free publications dealing with pet food, including:

- *Food Fit for a Fido*

- *Pet Cuisine*

- *Selecting Nutritious Pet Foods*
Contact: Center for Veterinary Medicine, Food and Drug Administration, U.S. Department of Health and Human Services, 7500 Standish Place, Rockville, MD 20855; 301-295-8755.

America's Most Wanted

Recognize your neighbor among the mug shots at the post office?

You could be in line for a reward. The Federal Bureau of Investigation (FBI) sometimes pays cold cash for information which leads to an arrest and conviction. All rewards are given on a case by case and cash on delivery basis.

To discuss the specifics, contact: Your local FBI office or, Federal Bureau of Investigation, J.E.H. Building, 10th and Pennsylvania Ave., NW, Washington, DC 20535; 202-324-3000.

Mileage Meter Mess

If you suspect someone's monkeyed with the mileage on that second-hand station wagon you just bought, it's time to squeal. As a victim, you can receive an award up to $1500 or three times the amount of damages, whichever is greater, plus court costs and reasonable attorney fees. The state attorney may even bring civil actions on behalf of consumers.

For more information contact: Auto Safety Hotline, National Highway Traffic Safety Administration, NEF-20, 400 Seventh St., SW Washington, DC 20590; 202-366-0123; 800-424-9393.

Mother Nature's Watchdogs

You can become the first environmental vigilante on your block and get paid by the U.S. Environmental Protection Agency (EPA) for every littering creep you nab. The Comprehensive Environmental Response Compensation and Liability Act authorizes the EPA at its discretion to pay up to $10,000 for information leading to the arrest and conviction of persons who engage in unreported dumping of hazardous substances.

For more information contact: U.S. Environmental Protection Agency, Office of Criminal Enforcement, 401 M St., SW, 2232, Washington, DC 20460; 202-260-9660.

Don't Get Mad, Get Even

If you suspect someone is cheating on their taxes, tell the Internal Revenue Service (IRS) and receive 10 percent of every dime in back taxes the feds collect. As with everything with the IRS, you must fill out the appropriate form in order to be eligible. Request Form 211, *Application For Reward For Original Information.*

Call: The Internal Revenue Service; 800-829-3676.

And That $60,000 Toilet

Sometimes it seems like there just isn't enough golden fleece to go around. If you know of a case of obvious contractor fraud, you might be eligible for 15-25 percent of the money recovered. You can file a complaint in the US District Courts using the Qui Tam Provisions of the False Claims Act. Your complaint will remain sealed for 60 days during which time the government will investigate to determine if they wish to take over your case. Even if they don't take your case, you can still take your case to trial and if you win you are still eligible for the 15-25%.

For more information contact: U.S. Department of Justice, 10th and Constitution Ave., NW, Washington, DC 20530; 202-514-7179.

Ton 'O Trash Ahoy

The next time you take a cruise, don't forget your video camera. Several resourceful cruise takers have caught ship employees dumping large amounts of trash into the ocean, and have won big bucks in court. If you witness or produce evidence of illegal ocean dumping, report it to the Coast Guard. If the case goes to trial and is won, you can receive 50% of the penalty assessed.

For more information contact: Office of Marine Safety, Security and Environmental Protection, U.S. Coast Guard, 2100 2nd St., SW, Washington, DC 20593; 202-267-6714 (working hours); 800-424-8802 (24 hours).

Lassie, Call Flipper

Kids turning sea tur-
tles on their backs?
Tuna nets killing
dolphins? There
are thousands of
miles of shoreline
and not nearly
enough eyes to pro-
tect our marine
friends. The
National Marine
Fisheries Service of-
fers rewards for in-
formation on the
disturbance of
marine animals.

They are determined on a case by case basis and
range from $1500-2500.

For more information contact: Your regional Na-
tional Marine Fisheries Service or National Marine
Fisheries Service, 1335 East West Highway, Silver
Spring, MD 20910.

Bowling For Drug Kingpins

If suspicious boats, low flying aircraft, even strange
activity at the neighbors makes you think that drug
activity is taking place, you should report it to your
local Drug Enforcement Administration. They give
rewards on a case by case basis for information
leading to the arrest of individuals involved in drug
related crimes.

For more information contact: The Drug Enforcement Administration field division in your area, or to locate that office contact Office of Public Affairs, Drug Enforcement Administration, Washington, DC 20537; 202-307-7977.

Me and My Bogus Kalvins

If you're streetwise, you know what most vendors already know: there's more money in counterfeit blue-jeans than in greenbacks. From fake Gucci bags to phony Pac-Man cassettes, the Customs Service will pay for bonafide tips. They pay rewards to people who provide Customs with original information which results in a seizure, arrest, or indictment, with a maximum reward of $2500.

Contact: U.S. Customs Service, 1301 Constitution Ave., NW, Washington, DC 20229; 800-BE-ALERT.

Double-Dipping Doctors

If you can figure out your Medicare bill, you may find some charges that don't make sense. Take the time to look a little deeper, and if you discover some instances of Medicare fraud, file your complaint with the US District Courts using the Qui Tam Provisions of the False Claims Act. The U.S. Department of Justice will investigate, and if they take the case and win, you can receive 15-25% of the money.

For more information contact: U.S. Department of Justice, 10th and Constitution Ave., NW, Washington, DC 20530; 202-514-7179.

Free Muggers Money

The Victims of Crime Act of 1984 created a Crime Victims Fund in the U.S. Treasury to provide Federal financial assistance to State governments to compensate and assist victims of crime.

Victims are compensated for expenses such as medical costs resulting from victimization. To get additional information you should contact your local police department or the Office of Justice Programs.

Contact: Office of Congressional and Public Affairs, Office of Justice Programs, U.S. Department of Justice, 633 Indiana Ave., NW, Washington, DC 20531; 202-307-0781.

For Your Pleasure

Turn on the Ocean Blue

Change the channel from Bowling for Dollars to a wonderful film or video on fish and wildlife, which are available for free loan through the Fish and Wildlife Service regional offices. Some of the topic areas covered include current research and environmental issues, wetland, fisheries and more, and sev-

eral even come with teacher's guides. Here is a sampling of the more popular videos:

- "America's Wetlands"

- "A Home For Pearl"

- "In Celebration of America's Wildlife"

- "Parrots of Luquillo"

- "Striper! Restoring Coastal Striped Bass"

Contact: Your regional office for a free catalog, or you may contact the Office of Public Affairs for information regarding the Office nearest you: Office of Public Affairs, Fish and Wildlife Service, U.S. Department of Interior, Washington DC 20240; 202-208-5611.

Science and You

The National Science Foundation (NSF) produces a limited number of films and videos each year to report the progress of scientific research and its applications to the public. A few of these productions document research results for a more narrowly focused, technical audience. All of them reflect important research and cover a large array of scientific disciplines supported by the Foundation. NSF audiovisuals are available directly from the distributors and information is provided on the types of services offered (rental/sale/free loan).

For your free *Film and Video Catalog* contact: National Science Foundation, 1800 G St., NW, Washington, DC 20550; 202-357-9498.

Up, Up, and Away

The Federal Aviation Administration (FAA) is responsible for the fostering the growth and regulating the safety of civil aviation. The FAA has films and videos available through free-loan to schools, community groups, and others which describe the kinds of programs and measures that can be taken to increase safety, capacity, and efficiency of air travel. Some of the titles include:

- "General Aviation - Fact or Fiction"
- "How Airplanes Fly"
- "In Celebration of Flight"

- "Where Airports Begin"

- "Cleared For Takeoff"

For a copy of a catalog, contact: Public Inquiry, Federal Aviation Administration, U.S. Department of Transportation, Washington, DC 20591; 202-267-3476.

Outer Space in Omaha

Actually, the National Aeronautics and Space Administration (NASA) through their Aerospace Education Services Program will send people anywhere in the U.S. to discuss NASA history, rocketry, living and working in space, aeronautics, and more. They can conduct assemblies, classroom visits, teachers workshops, and hands-on activities. The visits are scheduled by eight NASA field centers.

If you do not know the field center near you, contact: Elementary and Secondary Programs Branch, Educational Affairs Division, Mail Code FEE, NASA Headquarters, Washington, DC 20546; 202-358-1518.

Yodeling Cowboys

From Woody Guthrie to Woody Woodpecker, Indonesian temple gongs to roots gospel, the Folkway Records Archive is likely to have something to get you dancing. And if you ain't got rhythm, they also have plenty of spoken word recordings of historical figures and events. Even the soothing sounds of machines at work. There is a minimal cost for all recordings.

For a free catalogue contact: Folkways Records Archive, Center For Folklife Programs and Cultural Studies, 955 L'Enfant Plaza, SW, Suite 2600, Washington, DC 20560; 202-287-3262.

The Latest Technologies

The National Institute of Standards and Technology (NIST) is a major source of technical expertise for U.S. businesses seeking to use the latest technologies to improve their products and processes. A number of the NIST's programs are featured in videotapes and are available for interlibrary loan. Some of the titles include:

- "The Fun and Excitement of Invention"

- "Quest For Excellence V"

- "Mexico Earthquake"

For a free catalogue contact: Audiovisual Communications, Public Affairs Division, A903 Administration Building, National Institute of Standards and Technology, Gaithersburg, MD 20899; 301-975-2761.

Some Enchanted Evening

Enjoy a nice romantic afternoon or evening listening to the concert of your choice. This is not just a summer affair, but year round! Most performances are in the Washington area, however when on tour there are other performances along the East Coast. Don't miss out. Information is available through each of the Armed Forces Bands.

Air Force Band, 23 Mill St., Bolling Air Force Base, Washington, DC 20032; 202-767-4310

Navy Band, Washington Navy Yard, Building 105, Washington, DC 20032; 202-433-2394, 202-433-2525 recorded information line

Marine Band, 8th and I St., SW, Washington, DC 20390; 202-433-5809, 202-433-4011

Army Band, Building 400, Fort Myers, VA 22211; 703-696-3718, 703-696-3399 recorded information line

Silver and Gold

Minerals are important in our society and there is a need to conserve these finite resources. The Bureau of Mines has a series of films and videos available for free loan and cover a variety of minerals. The titles include:

- "Copper"

- "Silver"

- "Cast Iron: The Biography of a Metal"

- "Gold In Modern Technology"

- "Lead In Motion"

For a free descriptive catalog and ordering information contact: Audiovisual Library, Bureau of Mines, U.S. Department of the Interior, 2410 E St., NW, Washington, DC 20241; 202-501-9652.

Star Wars Speaker

The U.S. Department of Defense will send a speaker almost anywhere in the country to speak on Star Wars, MIAs/POWs, or many other current events. Your social group, school, or just a group of interested people can learn more about Defense Department topics simply by contacting the Speakers Bureau 6 to 8 weeks in advance. Some travel expenses may be required.

For a list of topics, contact: OASD Speakers Bureau, Public Affairs, Directorate for Community Relations, Pentagon, Room 1E776, Washington, DC 20301; 703-695-6108.

Foreign Affairs Films

The U.S. Department of State is in charge of advising the President in the formulation and execution of foreign policy. The Department has produced several films for free-loan on the topics of foreign policy and foreign relations including:

"The History of U.S. Foreign Relations" (a four-part series of 30 minute films) which recreate the history of U.S. foreign relations from the American Revolution to mid-1975. "From Where I Sit" explores how conflicting interests and opinions affect foreign policy issues and shape our objectives.

For information on these films and how to obtain them contact: Bureau of Public Affairs, U.S. Department of State, Washington, DC 20520; 202-647-6575.

Banking on Screen

The Federal Reserve Bank offers a variety of films, filmstrips, and videos available for free loan through your regional Federal Reserve Bank. The topics covered include the monetary system, electronic funds transfer, free enterprise, and the history of money. Some of the titles available include:

- "Both Borrower and Lender"

- "The Fed: Our Central Bank"

- "To Your Credit"

- "Money: Summing It Up"

- "Too Much, Too Little"

For a publications catalogue and lending information contact: Publications Services, Board of Governors of the Federal Reserve System, Washington, DC 20551; 202-452-3244.

For Your Retirement

Pension Central

The Pension Benefit Guaranty Corporation are the ones that monitor most private sector-defined benefit plans that provide a benefit based on factors such as age, years of service, and average or highest salary.

They have the following free publications:

- *Employer's Pension Guide* — provides a general overview of the responsibilities under federal law of employers who sponsor single-employer defined benefit pension plans.

- *Your Guaranteed Pension* — answers some of the most frequently asked questions about the Pension Benefit Guaranty Corporation and its termination insurance program for single-employer defined benefit pension plans.

- *Your Pension: Things You Should Know About Your Pension Plan* — serves as an explanation of pension plans; what they are, how they operate, and the rights and options of participants.

Contact: Public Affairs, Pension Benefit Guaranty Corporation, 2020 K St., NW, Room 7100, Washington, DC 20006; 202-778-8840.

Pensions –
An Investment for Your Future

Don't assume your pension is a sure thing. Make sure it is safe and secure.

The Pension and Welfare Benefits Administration helps to protect the retirement security of working Americans through the Employment Retirement Income Security Act.

They require administrators of private pension and welfare plans to provide plan participants with easily understandable summaries of plans, to file those summaries with the agency; and to report annually on the financial operation of the plans and bonding of persons charged with handling plan funds and assets.

They have many free publications dealing with pension plans including: *What You Should Know About The Pension Law* — which gives a summary of what is required of pension plans, and *How To File A Claim For Your Benefit* — which explains what you need to do to receive your benefit.

Contact: Division of Public Information, Pension and Welfare Benefits Administration, U.S. Department of Labor, 200 Constitution Ave., NW, Room N5666, Washington, DC 20210; 202-219-8921.

Social Insecurity

It's not enough you'll have to worry about your dentures slipping, but you might have to live on cat food, too.

The Social Security system will be in ruins and inflation will have rendered your pension laughable. What's a frightened taxpayer to do?

Request a free *Personal Earnings and Benefit Statement*. It includes a complete work history statement, outlining how much you will receive at age 62, as well as how much you would receive on disability or for your survivors.

You can request a form from Social Security by calling 800-772-1213.

Don't Let Yourself Become a Victim

Retirement is supposed to be a time of relaxation and enjoyment. But you must take some measures to protect yourself from unscrupulous thugs. *Elderly Victims* is a free report which outlines some problem areas, and steps you can take to avoid becoming another victim.

Contact: National Institute of Justice, NCJRS, Box 6000, Department AID, Rockville, MD 20850; 800-851-3420, 301-251-5500.

Social Security Speakers

Would your organization or group like to know more about possible benefits under Social Security?

The Social Security Administration will send speakers who can explain benefits, programs, and more. The service varies from region to region, so contact your local Social Security office.

For more detailed information or for help in locating your local office, contact: Public Affairs, Social Security Administration, U.S. Department of Health and Human Services, 6401 Security Boulevard, Baltimore, MD 21235; 410-965-1720.

For Your Soul

For that Special Day

The President doesn't want to miss a good party. He can only be so many places at once, but he will at least remember those special occasions such as graduations, weddings, and retirement with a special note. It is important to give enough notice in order to make sure cards arrive on time.

Contact: White House, Greetings Office, 1600 Pennsylvania Ave., NW, Washington, DC 20500; 202-456-2724.

Against Your Conscience

Once you hit 18, all males need to head to the post office to register for Selective Service. But what if you have some moral objection to the military or to war? The Selective Service System provides free fact sheets which contain information on certain aspects of the Selective Service System, including a publication *Alternative Service for Conscientious Objectors* which explains who can qualify and what type of service you need to complete.

For this publication or other on Selective Service contact: Public Affairs, Selective Service System, 1023 31st St., NW, Washington, DC 20435; 202-724-0790.

Need a Pick-Me-Up

How about a get well card from the President? All serious illnesses will be acknowledged after being notified by mail or through a fax. Remember, this is for serious illnesses, not the common cold. Also, a sympathy card can mean a lot to someone who has suffered a loss. Let the President send a note of condolence.

Contact: White House, Greetings Office, 1600 Pennsylvania Ave., NW, Washington, DC 20500; 202-456-2724; 202-456-2806 (fax).

Testimony to Service

The Presidential Memorial Certificate is available to the families of honorable discharge, deceased service members or veterans. This Certificate is an acknowledgment of a special contribution. To order your certificate a date of birth, death, and service number or social security number is needed.

Contact: Your regional Veterans Affairs office to order it, or U.S. Department of Veterans Affairs, 941 North Capitol St., NE, Washington, DC 20421; 800-827-1000.

Stars and Stripes

A flag is available to the families of deceased veterans who were honorably discharged and served during a war period. Requests should be made through the funeral home; however if this does not happen you can make a request within three years of the death.

Contact: U.S. Department of Veterans Affairs, 941 North Capitol St., NE, Washington, DC 20421; 800-827-1000.

Volunteer Service

Pictures and stories about disasters and trouble overseas at times rallies communities and individuals into service. Investigate the relief agencies a little before you sign on board.

Voluntary Foreign Aid Programs: Report of American Voluntary Agencies Engaged in Overseas Relief and Development Registered with the Agency for International Development (AID) describes the general nature of the work being carried out by Private and Voluntary Organizations (PVOs) which are registered with AID.

Included is such information as a PVO's geographic focus and sectorial concentration, as well as summaries of support, revenue, and expenditures. For your free copy contact: Bureau for Food and Humanitarian Assistance, Room 260, SA-8, U.S. Agency for International Development, Washington, DC 20523; 703-351-0201.

And They Said It Would Never Happen

It was a part of history that will never be forgotten. On September 13, 1993 the Peace Treaty between the Palestinian Liberation Organization (PLO) and Israel was signed. It was agreed to put an end to decades of confrontation and conflict.

A free copy of the treaty is available by contacting U.S. Department of State, NEA/P, Room 6243, Washington, DC 20520; 202-647-5150.

Don't Panic, Take Leave

The Family and Medical Leave Act of 1993 entitles an eligible employee to a total of 12 work weeks of leave during any 12 month period for any of the following reasons: 1) birth, 2) adoption, 3) serious health condition of family member, and 4) serious health condition of employee.

To find out additional information and to get a copy of the bill, write your Senator or Congressman or write directly to the Document Room. Contact: Document Room, Hart Building, Washington, DC 20510; or House of Representatives, Document Room, Washington, DC 20515; 202-224-3121.

Disabled Act On Your Rights!

Over 43 million Americans share one or more physical or mental disabilities. In order to provide a clear and comprehensive national mandate for the elimination of discrimination against individuals with disabilities, the American With Disabilities Act of 1990 was enacted. To get the specifics of this bill or any bill, write to your Senator or Congressman or directly to the Document Room.

Contact: Document Room, Hart Building, Washington, DC 20510; or House of Representatives, Document Room, Washington, DC 20515; 202-224-3121.

Are They Regular Voters?

Wonder if the Bill and Hillary Clinton voted in all the various elections? You can receive a copy of their voter registration ($0.50 each), which includes their date of birth, party affiliation, and their signature for each election. In many states voter registration cards are open records.

To find out about your state, contact your county clerk. To get a copy of Bill and Hillary's cards, contact: County Clerk, 201 S. Broadway, Room 101, Little Rock, AR 72201; 501-372-8330.

A New Set of Wheels

Is it time to retire your old car, and look into a replacement? The Federal Trade Commission (FTC) has a series of publications to help you learn your rights, and provide tips

and other information to help you with your search.

- *New Car Buying Guide* discusses questions you need to ask before you drive away.

- *Car Rental Guide* explains those confusing rental agreements and insurance deals.

- *Car Ads: Low Interest Loans and Other Offers* explains in easy to understand terms about car financing.

For your free copies contact: Federal Trade Commission, Public Reference Branch, Room 130, 6th and Pennsylvania Ave., NW, Washington, DC 20580; 202-326-2222.

Home Shopping

There are many reputable companies out there selling every type of merchandise imaginable over the phone or through the mail. But from time to time, problems do arise.

The Federal Trade Commission (FTC) receives complaints concerning problems with doing businesses by phone. The FTC also has several publications to help you resolve complaints, avoid scams, and more. Some of the titles include:

- *Buying By Phone*

- *Shopping By Mail*

- *Shopping By Phone and Mail*

- *Unordered Merchandise*

For your free copies contact: Federal Trade Commission, Public Reference Branch, Room 130, 6th and Pennsylvania Ave., NW, Washington, DC 20580; 202-326-2222.

Where Did You Begin

Where to Write for Vital Records: Births, Deaths, Marriages, and Divorces ($1.75) provides information about the availability of individual vital records maintained on file in State or local vital statistics offices. It includes a list of vital statistics offices for every State or locale, their addresses, estimated costs, and remarks for each type of record.

For your copy contact: Superintendent of Documents, U.S. Government Printing Office, Washington, DC 20402; 202-783-3238.

International Peace

The purpose of the United Nations (UN) is not just international peace and security but also to develop friendly relations among nations.

There are many publications available about the UN and its accomplishments, including *Charter of the United Nations and Statute of the International Court of Justice* which is free.

Additional information is available from the United Nations Information Centre and documents and films can be borrowed from the Centre's Library.

Contact: United Nations Information Centre, 1889 F St., NW, Ground Floor, Washington, DC 20006; 202-289-8670.

For Your Summer

Show Them the One that Got Away

Add some zip to your weekend get togethers with your fishing buddies or impress your teacher with a report on fish or fishing. The Audio Visual Department of the Fish and Wildlife Service has an extensive collection of both black and white pictures and color slides of fish and wildlife and there is no charge for their lending service.

Contact: Audio Visuals, Fish and Wildlife Service, 18th and C Sts., NW, Washington, DC 20240; 202-208-5611.

Secret Fishing Holes Revealed at Last

Some of the best kept secrets are kept by Uncle Sam. 491 National Wildlife Refuges on over 91 million acres of lands and waters enable you to catch a glimpse of a unique wildlife heritage. The publication *National Wildlife Refuges: A Visitor's Guide* lists refuges by state, as well as the facilities available such as foot trails, auto tour routes, bicycling, canoeing, hunting, fishing, bird watching, hiking, and more.

Contact: U.S. Fish and Wildlife Service, 4401 N. Fairfax Dr., Arlington, VA 22203; 703-358-1711.

Boating and You

Spending a lot of time on your boat this summer? Make sure you follow all the boating safety rules, so your fun-filled summer is accident free. For information on safety tips, the Coast Guard Hotline has a free "Boating Safety Information" packet, which includes fact sheets on safe boating, federal regulations, sources of boating education, and more. You can also request a free *Water 'N Kids* coloring book for 4-8 year olds, which explains basic concepts of water safety.

Contact: Boating Safety Hotline, Consumer and Regulatory Affairs Branch, (G-NAB-5), Auxiliary, Boating, and Consumer Affairs Division, Office of Navigation Safety and Waterways Services, U.S. Coast Guard, 2100 2nd St., SW, Room 1109, Washington, DC 20593; 800-368-5647.

Importing Pleasure Boats

Buying your speed boat or yacht somewhere other than in the U.S.? The free pamphlet, *Pleasure Boats*, explains the Customs formalities involving pleasure boats to help you plan your importation and reporting requirements, overtime charges, and provides other information relating strictly to pleasure boats.

Contact: Public Information Office, U.S. Customs Service, P.O. Box 7407, Washington, DC 20044.

Man Overboard

Actually, it is more common than you think. There were 458 vessels that capsized last year causing 248 deaths, and 433 vessels involved in people falling overboard with 212 deaths. Statistical information is available on a yearly basis in a free report titled *Boating Statistics*.

For your copy contact: U.S. Department of Transportation, U.S. Coast Guard, 2100 Second St., SW, Washington, DC 20593; 202-267-0955, 800-368-5647.

Go to the Source

Boater's Source Directory is a free booklet, produced under a Coast Guard grant, that describes boating services and publications (most of which are free) available from more than 100 resources. You can find information on marine radios, charts, boat registration, Coast Guard requirements, and more.

Contact: "The Source", BOAT/US Foundation, 880 S. Pickett St., Alexandria, VA 22304; 703-823-9550.

Stern and Bow

Before you solo, take a free lesson from the U.S. Coast Guard which offers beginner boating lessons free of charge.

To find the location nearest you contact: U.S. Department of Transportation, U.S. Coast Guard, 2100 Second St., SW, Washington, DC 20593; 202-267-0955, 800-368-5647.

Get Your Notice

Notice to Mariners is issued free each week by the U.S. Defense Mapping Agency, and is prepared jointly with the National Ocean Service and the Coast Guard. The Notice is intended primarily for deep-draft vessels. It details changes to channels and navigational aids and other information useful for updating the latest editions of nautical charts and publications.

Contact: Defense Mapping Agency, Office of Distribution Services Code DMO, 6001 MacArthur Blvd., Bethesda, MD 20816; 800-826-0342.

Updates for Mariners

The free *Local Notice to Mariners* is issued weekly by each of the 10 U.S. Coast Guard districts, for small craft owners using the intracoastal waterways, other waterways and small harbors. It includes items such as chart updates, information  on drawbridge operation, and warnings of a variety of events or activities.

For a subscription you should contact: Your local Coast Guard District Commander, or for referral to the correct address contact: Boating Safety Hotline, Commandant (G-NAB-5), U.S. Coast Guard Headquarters, Washington, DC 20593; 800-368-5647.

For Your Teacher

Save the Rainforests

We have all been told to save the rainforest, but do you want to learn more about its importance? A free teaching guide titled *Tropical Rainforests*, is available that highlights the workings of the rainforest, the adaptations of its animals and plants, their current status and future conservation. Teachers' and students' versions are available, and are designed for grades 5-12.

Contact: Smithsonian Tropical Research Institute, Office of Education, Unit 0948, APO AA 34002-0948.

Smokey the Bear and You

To make children aware of the campaign to fight forest fires, the Forest Service makes a variety of free materials available to children, including posters, signs, patches, bookmarks, bumper stickers, and comic books.

Call: This office to find the coordinator in your area who has a list of materials available. Smokey Bear Headquarters, U.S. Forest Service, 14th and Independence Aves., NW, Washington, DC 20250; 202-205-1510.

Your Guide to Outer Space

Want to know what is going on in outer space? You can get a direct line to the National Aeronautics and Space Administration (NASA) through their free quarterly report, *NASA Report to Educators*. This report contains educational information, including information on technology spinoffs, new publications and resource materials, conferences, and ongoing programs and competitions.

Contact: Distribution Officer, Mail Code XEP, NASA Headquarters, Washington, DC 20546; 202-453-1287.

Where the Heck Is Timbuktu?

Have students identify places with the funniest names, then find out more about the lay of the land. With a request on school letterhead, the Earth Science Center will put together special packages for teachers on mapping.

Contact: Earth Science Information Center, U.S. Geological Survey, National Center, US 507 Mail Stop, Reston, VA 22092, 703-648-5963.

Bring Your Paints to School

The Arts-In-Education Program is a partnership program through cooperative efforts of the Arts Endowment, state arts and education agencies, local communities, and others.

The Program's overall goal is to advance the arts as part of basic education. For free information on how you can help promote the arts from kindergarten through high school, request the following free publications:

- *Planning to Make the Arts Basic*

- *Special Projects Handbook Editions I and II*

- *State Arts Agency Arts in Education Profiles*

Contact: Arts-In-Education, National Endowment for the Arts, 1100 Pennsylvania Ave., NW, Room 602, Washington, DC 20506; 202-682-5426.

Armchair Archeologists

Participate in Archeology is a free brochure which provides some basic information on archeology, and lists magazines, books, videos, and agencies and organizations through which you can receive more information.

Contact: National Park Service, Office of Public Inquiries, U.S. Department of the Interior, P.O. Box 37127, Washington, DC 20013; 202-208-4747.

You and Your Wildlife

Many animals are more abundant in the U.S. now than in the past 100 years.

In Celebration of America's Wildlife: Teacher's Guide to Learning is a video and curriculum guide, which provides information about the Federal Aid in Wildlife Restoration Act, and lists activities and discussions related to the major concepts of the video.

For the curriculum guide, contact: U.S. Fish and Wildlife Service, 4401 N. Fairfax Dr., Arlington, VA 22203; 703-358-1711. For free loan of the video, contact U.S. Fish and Wildlife Service, 1849 C St., NW, Room 3444, Washington, DC 20240; 202-208-5611.

Free Flights of Fancy

Launch your own ground school for would-be pilots by contacting the Federal Aviation Administration's Office of Training and Higher Education. Curriculum guides, films, and other supplies dealing with aviation concepts and career opportunities are available free. Some of the publications include:

- *Aviation Science Activities for Elementary Grades* - pamphlet containing science demonstrations.

- *Curriculum Guide for Elementary Level* - deals with agricultural aviation as it helps meet basic needs of food.

- *Women In Aviation* - displays how women have changed in time.

- *Aviation Education Programs and Materials* - includes all FAA aviation education programs, as well as contacts.

- *A Model Curriculum* - hands-on activities and learning tasks demonstrating motivational aspects of aviation.

For a listing of materials contact: Office of Training and Higher Education, Federal Aviation Administration, U.S. Department of Transportation, 400 7th St., SW, Washington, DC 20590; 202-366-7500.

Send Your Students to the Moon

Rockets: A Teaching Guide for an Elementary Science Unit on Rocketry contains information on the history of rocketry, Newton's laws, and modern practical rocketry. Ten activities are included utilizing simple and inexpensive materials culminating in a model rocket launch.

For your free copy and other information available for teachers, contact: Publications, National Aeronautic and Space Administration, 300 E St., SW, Washington, DC 20546; 202-453-1287.

Them Bones, Them Bones

Anthropology is much more fun when you pass around real fossils instead of pictures. Bring history to life with artifacts from the Smithsonian archives.

Anthropological Materials Available From The Smithsonian Institution is a free list of educational materials, including resource packets, films, posters and more.

Anthropological Teaching Resources is a list of materials teachers can order, such as fossil reproductions, books, and artifact sets. Both are free and designed for grades K-12.

Contact: Anthropology Outreach and Public Information Office, National Museum of Natural History, MRC 112, Smithsonian Institution, Washington, DC 20560; 202-357-1592.

Environmental Hazards in Your School

New York City's public school asbestos problem in their schools is only the tip of the iceberg. Lead in drinking water, poor air quality, and more occur in schools across the country.

To find out about the dangers in a school and what you can do to protect your children, request a free copy of *Environmental Hazards In Your School: A Resource Handbook*, which outlines each problem and gives direction on who you need to contact to resolve the issue.

Contact: Indoor Air Quality Information Clearing-house, IAQ INFO, P.O. Box 37133, Washington, DC 20013-7133; 800-438-4318, 301-585-9020.

Connect the Dots to Pirate Booty and Ghost Mines

History isn't boring; history teachers are.

A free book called, *State Archaeological Education Programs*, shows how to educate the public about archeology by discovering ancient caves, abandoned gold mines, and frontier trails.

Write for your free copy to: National Park Service, Division of National Preservation Programs, Interagency Archeological Services, P.O. Box 25287, Denver, CO 80225.

Geology on Screen

Rather than just talk about it, show it! The U.S. Geological Survey has several films available on a free short-term loan to educational and scientific communities, professional and technical societies, civic and industrial groups, and other organizations. Some of the titles include:

- "1955 Eruption of Kilauea Volcano, Hawaiian Islands" - Elementary

- "Geology of the Berlize Barrier Reef" - High School, College

- "The 1923 Surveying Expedition of the Colorado River in Arizona" - Junior High

- "Flow in Alluvial Channels" - College

- "The Sea River" - High School

- "The Little Plover (River) Project, A Study in Sand Plains Hydrology" - High School

- "The Water Below" - Elementary

- "To Fill The Gap" - Elementary

- "National Petroleum Reserve in Alaska" - Junior High

- "Yakutat" - High School.

Contact: Visual Services, U.S. Geological Survey, 790 National Center, Reston, VA 22092; 703-648-4379.

Shaking in Their Seats

Earthquakes and volcanoes are like dinosaurs: time-less and totally awesome. Use this to your advantage when teaching geology.

The Geologic Inquiries Group has a free publication, *Educational Resources Available From The U.S. Geological Survey*, which describes teacher packets, booklets, and other resources available to teachers.

Please send your request on school letterhead to: Geologic Inquiries Group, U.S. Geological Survey, 907 National Center, Reston, VA 22092; 703-648-4383.

Cloudy With a Chance of Eagles

Want a tailor-made package of materials to hand out to teach students about the weather? The National Oceanic and Atmospheric Administration will pull one together - just specify grade and subject. Topics covered include the weather, oceans, whales, marine mammals, nautical charts, fisheries, and more.

Write: Education Affairs Division, National Oceanic and Atmospheric Administration, Room 317, 1825 Connecticut Ave., NW, Washington, DC 20235.

Art of the U.S.

All the great artists are not from Europe. The U.S. has their fair share. The National Museum of American Art focuses on these artists and their work and has assembled a collection of brochures, teaching guides, and exhibition catalogues.

- *American Landscape: 19th Century Selections* is a free brochure which highlights 12 landscape artists who depicted America's virgin forests, natural wonders, westward movement, and Native Americans.

- *Hispanic-American Art* is a free bilingual brochure of works of eight Hispanic American artists over the past 160 years.

- *The Art of the Nature Print* is an exhibition catalogue ($3) which traces the fascinating history of nature prints, from handprints by Stone Age cave dwellers to the works of Benjamin Franklin and late-20th century artists.

- *On Our Way* is a free booklet for kids in grades 1-4 which contains classroom exercises on looking at and discussing art. Topics explored include: What is a museum? What is the language of art? What are line, shape, color, texture?

Contact: National Museum of American Art, Office of Educational Programs, MRC 210, Smithsonian Institution, Washington, DC 20560; 202-357-3095.

Everything Old Is New Again

Have you ever wondered how the earliest inhabitants of North America lived? Interested in what goes on at an archeological dig? *Heritage Education* program is a very hands-on learning experience aimed at students K-12 with projects and traveling exhibitions.

For a free brochure and other information, contact: The Imagination Team, Bureau of Land Management, Anasazi Heritage Center, 27501 Hwy 184, P.O. Box 758, Dolores, CO 81323; 303-882-4811.

In the Footsteps of T-Rex... Utah Canyon Boasts Fossils Galore

Does the idea of a hike make your kids run the other way? What if the hike included a hunt for dinosaur bones? Mill Canyon Dinosaur Trail is a self guided walking tour on Bureau of Land Management Lands where you will see dinosaur bones and other wonderful fossils.

For a free map, write: Grand Resource Center, Bureau of Land Management, 885 South Sand Flats Rd., Moab, UT 84532.

Bring a Cast-Iron Umbrella

Acid Rain: A Student's First Sourcebook is a great way to teach kids about the environment and what needs to be done to protect it. Designed for grades 4-8 and their teachers, the sourcebook describes the effects of acid rain, solutions, experiments, and activities.

This office also has U.S. Environmental Protection Agency (EPA) Journal articles on acid rain, background information, and updates on EPA's activities.

Contact: Acid Rain Division (6204J), U.S. Environmental Protection Agency, 401 M St., SW, Washington, DC 20460; 202-233-9150.

English as a Second Language

Today's classroom doesn't look quite the same as it did twenty years ago. Teachers are finding more students are barely able to speak English.

The National Clearinghouse for Bilingual Education can help teachers and families by providing information, such as curriculum materials, models, and research findings on the education of limited English proficient students.

They have a free "Parent Involvement in Education" information packet, which contains information on how you can become involved and enhance your child's education, and an "Education for Teachers of Language Minorities" packet which provides resources and articles for teachers.

For a newsletter and publication catalog contact: National Clearinghouse for Bilingual Education, 1118 22nd St., NW, Washington, DC 20037; 800-321-6223

Speak Out

Teaching about the Civil Rights movement? *Protest and Patriotism: A History of Dissent and Reform* is a free teaching guide containing curriculum enrichment materials examining American protest movements.

It focuses on populism, civil rights, and environmentalism. The guide provides background essays, discussion questions, teaching suggestions, and a timeline. This is designed for grades 7-12.

For your copy contact: Office of Elementary and Secondary Education, Smithsonian Institution, Arts & Industries Building, Room 1163 MRC 402, Washington, DC 20560; 202-357-2425.

Make African Art Come Alive

Whether for art history or to study the various cultures in Africa, take advantage of your students' love of videos and use videos and slide kits available from the National Museum of African Art.

- "The Hands of the Potter" is a video demonstrating the magic of a Sundi potter as she forms moist clay to produce perfect pots.

- "Icons: Ideals and Power in the Art of Africa" is a slide survey of five themes in African art.

- "Masters of Brass: Lost-Wax Casting in Ghana" demonstrates the ancient technique among the Akan and Frafra peoples of Ghana in which a wax model is used to create a mold for casting a metal object.

For free loan information and to find out about the many other programs available contact: National Museum of African Art, U.S. Department of Education, MRC 708, 950 Independence Ave., SW, Smithsonian Institution, Washington, DC 20560; 202-357-4600.

Scientific Americans

Fire up the Bunsen burners and full speed ahead. Science teachers can send off for course materials, curriculum guides, and more on a wide range of science projects, courtesy of the National Science Resource Center (NSRC).

A free information packet is available by contacting the National Science Resource Center, Smithsonian Institution, Arts and Industries Building, Room 1201, Washington, DC 20560; 202-357-2555.

LEAP Back in Time

LEAP (Listing of Education on Archeological Programs) is an annotated listing of programs, special tours, and publications done by archeologists for the public and includes a contact person from whom additional and updated information can be obtained.

For your free copy write: LEAP Coordinator, DCA/ADD, National Park Service, P.O. Box 37127, Suite 210, Washington, DC 20013-7127.

Carbons to Computers

Carbons to Computers: The Changing American Office is a free teaching kit which includes curriculum enrichment materials exploring the relationship between technological change and cultural values as reflected in the American office, 1830 to the present. It contains background essays with illustrations, teaching guide with suggested activities, and photographs.

This kit is targeted for grades 7-12, and you can request your copy by contacting: Office of Elementary and Secondary Education, Smithsonian Institution, Arts and Industries Building, Room 1163, MRC 402, Washington, DC 20560; 202-357-2425.

Build a Better Light Bulb

Can creativity be taught?

Project XL is an outreach program designed to do just that by encouraging the inventive thinking process through the creation of unique inventions or innovations. They have developed an educator's resource guide, video, and a special curriculum.

Request your free copy of the *Inventive Thinking Project.* Contact: Office of Public Affairs, Patent and Trademark Office, U.S. Department of Commerce, 2011 Crystal Dr., Room 208B Washington DC 20231; 703-305-8341.

Take Your Class to the Park

Kids will learn more at the nearest national park than they will on any rainy day indoors. Most parks have education programs and will gladly share their wonderful resources with you.

A special 28 minute video, "Parks as Classrooms", is available at your nearest park and details the many ways teachers can work with the park service and incorporate the parks into their curriculum.

For information and location of parks near you contact: Office of Education and Interpretation, National Park Service Areas, U.S. Department of the Interior, P.O. Box 37127, Washington, DC 20013.

The Original Jurassic Playground

By now, most of America has seen the movie "Jurassic Park", but the real Jurassic story can be found on Bureau of Land Management lands in the West.

One of the largest areas is the Cleveland-Lloyd Dinosaur Quarry, which has yielded nearly 10,000 bones representing at least 14 species of animals from the Jurassic Period.

For a copy of a free brochure describing the quarry titled, *Al the Allosaurus*, write: Price River Resource Area Office, Bureau of Land Management, 900 North 700 East, Price, UT 84501.

Indian Ancestry

Make your American Indians section come alive in your classroom.

The Anthropology Outreach Office has a free teaching packet titled "North American Indians" for grades 1-12, which includes bibliographies, leaflets, lists of teaching materials available from the Smithsonian, photographs, suggestions for classroom activities, and even information on Native American pen-pals.

For your copy, contact: Anthropology Outreach and Public Information Office, National Museum of Natural History, Room 363, MRC 112, Smithsonian Institution, Washington, DC 20560; 202-357-1592.

Teaching Science Close to Home

Intrigued by the past? Teachers can show students the importance of past cultures and archaeology with *The Intriguing Past: Fundamentals of Archeology*. This teacher's guide is aimed at grades 4-7, and includes lesson plans and activity sheets.

Contact: The Imagination Team, Bureau of Land Management, Anasazi Heritage Center, 27501 Hwy 184, P.O. Box 758, Dolores, CO 81323; 303-882-4811.

Powwow with the Experts

Get a glimpse of the rich cultural heritage of our Native American history. Many tribes continue to celebrate customs that were old before Columbus reached shore.

The Bureau of Indian Affairs has a free publication, *American Indians Today*, which provides a brief overview, as well as providing a bibliography and other resources. This office can also provide you with other information on Indians including statistics, locations of reservations, and more.

Contact: Public Inquiries, Bureau of Indian Affairs, 1849 C St., NW, Washington, DC 20240; 202-208-3711.

Party Animals on Parade

"Let's Celebrate" is a slide set and teacher's handbook on celebrations around the world for grades 7-12. Not just religious festivals, but other world holidays and festivals, such as the Cow Festival in Nepal and the Child-Adult Initiation in Burma. This is available for free loan with the borrower paying return postage.

Contact: Department of Public Programs, Renwick Gallery, MRC 510, Smithsonian Institution, Washington, DC 20560; 202-357-2531.

Following in Godzilla's Footsteps

The Smithsonian is the granddaddy of museums, but like T-Rex, its size can be a bit of a problem. Fortunately there's a special booklet to help teachers get their bearings when navigating through the Smithsonian's musty closets. The free publication, *Smithsonian Resource Guide For Teachers*, lists workshops, courses, publications and newsletters for teachers across the country, most of which are free.

Contact: Office of Elementary and Secondary Education, Smithsonian Institution, Arts & Industries Building, Room 1163 MRC 402, Washington, DC 20560; 202-357-2425.

Free Land Films and Videos

The Bureau of Land Management has produced three films, three videos, and a slide show dealing with areas covered by BLM.

Titles include: "Promise of the Land" (film) - explains multiple use management on public lands. "Dapples, Bays, Pintos and Grays" (film) - presents wild horse and burro adopt a horse program. "Antiquities" (film) - details issue of looting and vandalism of our cultural resources. "Measuring America: The Cadastral Story" (slide show) - explains cadastral surveying. "BLM Backcountry Byways" (video) - looks at recreational opportunities provided by BLM's backcountry byways program. "Fish and Wildlife 2000" (video) - explains managing wildlife and fisheries habitat on public lands. "Automating the Past" (video) - details effort at automating old land records.

These films are often requested by educational institutions (elementary and junior high), as well as civic organizations interested in the outdoors or finding out how their tax dollars are being spent. Even the Boy Scouts have borrowed films for evening entertainment. Contact this office for more information on the films and videos available for free loan.

Contact: Division of Public Affairs, Bureau of Land Management, U.S. Department of the Interior, Washington, DC 20240; 202-208-6468.

Calling Mother India

Bring to life one of the oldest civilizations on the planet without leaving the classroom. "The Living Arts of India" is an instructional kit designed for elementary and secondary students, and contains books, pamphlets, catalogues, objects, videos, and more. Teach children's games, theater activities, and Indian fairs and festivals.

This kit is available for loan (shipping fee is charged) by contacting: Scheduler, Office of Education, Mail Stop 158, National Museum of Natural History, 10th St. and Constitution Ave., NW, Washington, DC 20560; 202-357-2747.

Wild and Woolly Neighborhoods

You don't have to hire a guide and rent tents to experience the wonders of a wildlife refuge. There's probably one tucked right around the corner from school. Snakes, turtles, even an injured owl will make your students sit up and take notice.

Many of the National Wildlife Refuges have established education programs where refuge managers may come to your class with animals in hand or your class may take a trip to the refuge. This varies from place to place, but give the wildlife refuge near you a call to see what services they offer.

For a publication titled *Refuge Managers List* contact: U.S. Fish and Wildlife Service, U.S. Department of the Interior, 4401 N. Fairfax Dr., Arlington, VA 22203; 703-358-1711.

Help Students Clean-Up

Kids intuitively grasp recycling and the need to keep the earth green and clean, so what's with their own rooms?

Let's Reduce and Recycle: Curriculum for Solid Waste Awareness provides lesson plans for grades

K-12, and includes activities, skits, bibliographies, and other resources.

School Recycling Programs: A Handbook for Educators describes a number of school recycling programs along with step-by-step instructions on how to start one in your school.

For these free publications contact: RCRA /Superfund Hotline, Office of Solid Waste, U.S. Environmental Protection Agency, 401 M St., SW, Washington, DC 20460; 800-424-9346, 703-412-9810.

Drug Abuse Teaching Aids

The Office of Educational Research and Improvement of the U.S. Department of Education has developed several publications dealing with substance abuse curriculum.

- *Learning to Live Drug Free: A Curriculum Model for Prevention* provides a framework for classroom-based prevention efforts in kindergarten through grade 12. The model includes lessons, activities, background for teachers and suggestions for involving parents and the community in drug prevention.

- *Prevention Resource Guide: Curriculum.*

- *Prevention Resource Guide: Elementary Youth.*

- *Prevention Resource Guide: Secondary School Students.*

Contact: National Clearinghouse for Alcohol and Drug Information, P.O. Box 2345, Rockville, MD 20847; 800-729-6686.

River and Water Films

The Bureau of Reclamation provides water for farms, towns, and industries, and is responsible for the generation of hydroelectric power, river regulation and flood control, outdoor recreation opportunities, and the enhancement and protection of fish and wildlife habitats.

There are films available for free loan on a variety of the Bureau's projects. Some of the titles include:

- "California Flooding"

- "How Water Won the West"

- "Rio Grande — Ribbon of Life"

- "To Build A Dream — The Story of Hoover Dam"

- "Take Pride in America"

- "Hydropower — A 20th Century Force"

- "Horizons"

- "For Want of Water"

- "Taming of Black Canyon".

These films are most often requested by elementary and junior high school teachers, or by people who have visited the dams while on vacation and would like to learn more about them. Contact the Bureau for more information regarding these videos.

Contact: Visual Communication Services, Bureau of Reclamation, P.O. Box 25007 D-1500, Denver, CO 80225; 303-236-6973.

The Mummy Walks at Midnight

Kids are fascinated by strange things. The Anthropology Outreach Office has two free leaflets available dealing with Egypt long ago.

Egyptian Mummies describes the art of mummification.

Egyptian Pyramids describes the various types of pyramids. Both leaflets include bibliographies and are applicable for grades K-12.

Contact: Anthropology Outreach and Public Information Office, National Museum of Natural History, Room 363, MRC 112, Smithsonian Institution, Washington, DC 20560; 202-357-1592.

The Idea Factory

Art to Zoo is a free quarterly publication of the Office of Elementary and Secondary Education and provides background information, lesson plans, classroom activities, and resource lists for teachers in science, social studies, and art.

Each issue focuses on a different topic, and is designed for grades 3-8.

For your free subscription contact: Office of Elementary and Secondary Education, Smithsonian Institution, Arts and Industries Building, Room 1163 MRC 402, Washington, DC 20560; 202-357-2425.

Your Travel Journal

Get your students to pretend to be reporters on the scene. *Collecting Their Thoughts: Using Museums as Sources for Student Writing* is a free teaching guide, containing curriculum enrichment materials suggesting ways for teachers to use museums and primary sources to teach writing.

The Guide provides background essays, lesson plans, activities, handouts, and samples of student writing.

Contact: Office of Elementary and Secondary Education, Smithsonian Institution, Arts and Industries Building, Room 1163 MRC 402, Washington, DC 20560; 202-357-2425.

Separation of Church and State?

To give equal time to all sides, many schools are teaching creationism. The Anthropology Outreach Office has put together a free teaching packet titled "Creationism" for grades K-12, which covers issues surrounding creationism and education for teachers and administrators from all disciplines. It includes reprints of articles on the subject by scientists, educators, and others.

For your copy, contact: Anthropology Outreach and Public Information Office, National Museum of Natural History, Room 363, MRC 112, Smithsonian Institution, Washington, DC 20560; 202-357-1592.

Science Horizons

Physics made easy? *Science Horizons* is a new publication (early 1994) disseminating information about education projects underway at the Science Education Department of the Harvard-Smithsonian Center for Astrophysics, including summer workshops for teachers, the development of software for the simulation of modern physics, and highly sensitive image-processing equipment for classroom use. It is free and designed for grades 1-12.

Contact: Harvard-Smithsonian Center for Astrophysics, Science Education Department, MS-71, 60 Garden St., Cambridge, MA 01238; 617-495-9798.

For those Budding Actors and Actresses

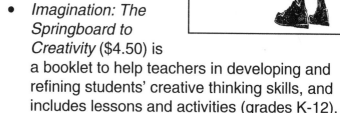

The Kennedy Center has an incredible array of information available about how you can introduce your students to the theater.

- *Imagination: The Springboard to Creativity* ($4.50) is a booklet to help teachers in developing and refining students' creative thinking skills, and includes lessons and activities (grades K-12).

- *Imagination at Work: Kids Invent Theater* ($4.50) introduces theater for elementary students. It outlines movement and story, and the activities introduce such aspects of theater as making sets and scenery, lighting, and costumes.

- *Performing Together: The Arts and Education* ($4.50) discusses why the arts are vital to every student's education, what characterizes outstanding school arts programs, and how parents and others can work with schools to provide a sound foundation in the arts. For these and other publications contact the Kennedy Center.

Contact: Education Department, John F. Kennedy Center for the Performing Arts, Washington, DC 20566; 202-416-8800.

Art Assistance

The National Gallery of Art has assembled teaching packets covering specific artists or time periods which are available for free loan. These packets usually contain a booklet, slides and study prints. A complete listing is included in the *Extension Programs* catalogue.

Some the packets available are:

- *Matisse in Morocco*

- *Art of the American Indian Frontier*

- *European Renaissance Art*

- *American Paintings*

- *French Impressionism and Post-Impressionism*

Contact: Department of Education Resources, Education Division, National Gallery of Art, 4th St. and Constitution Ave., NW, Washington, DC 20565; 202-842-6863.

The Noble Path

The Noble Path is a free booklet which provides an introduction to Buddhism and Buddhist art, with background information for teachers, activities for students, and a list of related videos and films.

Contact: Arthur M. Sackler Gallery, Education Department, MRC 707, Smithsonian Institution, Washington, DC 20560; 202-357-4880.

Celebrate the Asian Way

Southeast Asian New Year Celebrations is a free teaching guide which contains information, resources, and classroom activities about Vietnam, Cambodia, Laos, and Thailand. Activities are designed to stimulate hands-on memory experiences and to arouse awareness and recognition of the cultural heritage of Southeast Asians in the United States. This is designed for grades 4-6 and is available for 3-week loan only to teachers, with the borrower paying return shipping.

Contact: National Museum of Natural History, Office of Education, Room 212, MRC 158, Smithsonian Institution, Washington, DC 20560; 202-357-2066.

Draw Me a Map

The Power of Maps is a free teaching guide with suggestions on integrating the study of maps into school curricula based on the exhibition "The Power of Maps" at Cooper Hewitt. It includes suggestions for classroom activities, discussion questions, and a resource list.

Contact: Cooper-Hewitt National Museum of Design, Education Department, Smithsonian Institution, 2 East 91st St., New York, NY 10128; 212-860-6871.

Turn the Tide

Two-thirds of our planet is covered by oceans which are homes for thousands of species of plants and animals. Unfortunately ocean trash and other wastes are becoming a significant problem.

Turning the Tide on Trash: Learning Guide on Marine Debris is designed to increase students' awareness of the impacts of marine debris and to teach them about pollution prevention techniques. The activities also inspire an appreciation of the ocean and a commitment to the preservation of its water quality, and beauty.

For your free copy contact: U.S. Environmental Protection Agency, Information Access Branch, Public Information Center, 401 M St., SW, 3404, Washington, DC 20460; 202-260-7751.

One with Nature

Many Native American tribes believe we should live in harmony with nature. Here's a great coloring book to teach the concept to kids, courtesy of the Flathead Indian Reservation.

Living In Harmony coloring book ($1.35) is distributed by National Association of Conservation Districts, 408 East Main, P.O. Box 85, League City, TX 77574; 800-825-5547.

Social Studies Simplified

Elementary and secondary school teachers, policy-makers, even parents concerned about education in the social studies are likely to be interested in the activities and publications of the ERIC Clearinghouse on Social Studies, which monitors trends and issues about the teaching and learning of history, geography, civics, economics, and other subjects.

A free newsletter, *Keeping Up*, describes the latest information in the field. The Clearinghouse also produces several Digests, which are synopses of current literature on a topic of interest to social studies educators. The price of a Digest is $1, and some of the titles include:

- *Teaching About Japan*

- *Teaching The Bill Of Rights*

- *Teaching And Learning Economics*

- *Teaching Geography In The Elementary School*

- *Women In The Curriculum*

For a complete listing of publications contact: ERIC Clearinghouse For Social Studies, Indiana University, Social Studies Development Center, 2805 East 10th St., Suite 120, Bloomington, IN 47408; 812-855-3838.

Explore Mars

The Exploration of Mars: For Grades 8-12 gives a detailed overview of National Aeronautics and Space Administration (NASA) exploration from 1964 to 2003. It explains the major research capabilities of particular missions and expands on what further study is warranted on the red planet. Teachers are provided with four activities to further engage students and basic step-by-step directions on how to explore a planet are given.

Free from: National Aeronautics and Space Administration Educational Publications, Code FEP, Washington, DC 20546; 202-453-1287.

What's Happening in the World?

Geographic Notes, a free publication from the Office of the Geographer, contains brief analyses of current issues relevant to United States foreign policy. These analyses provide a geographical perspective on foreign policy-related topics such as boundary, sovereignty, and territorial disputes.

For your copy contact: Office of the Geographer, Bureau of Intelligence and Research, U.S. Department of State, 2201 C St., NW, Room 8742, Washington, DC 20520; 202-647-2022.

Every Day Should Be Earth Day

"Earth Day Every Day" is a free teacher's kit from the U.S. Environmental Protection Agency, and provides a wonderful overview of environmental science education for all grade levels. Each section lists activities, materials needed, discussion questions, vocabulary, and more. You can learn how to make a cloud, how substances are measured in water, and how rivers are formed.

For your free copy contact: U.S. Environmental Protection Agency, Information Access Branch, Public Information Center, 401 M St., SW, 3404, Washington, DC 20460; 202-260-7751.

Free Science Lab Equipment

Is the equipment in your college's laboratories broken, out-dated, or just worn out? The U.S. Department of Energy (DOE) will send your school energy-related lab equipment that they no longer need for free with you paying shipping and handling. The following free publications cover the program and the equipment available: *Energy-Related Laboratory Equipment Catalog*, and *Instruction and Information On Used Energy-Related Equipment Grants for Educational Institutions of Higher Learning*.

Contact: Postsecondary Programs Division, Office of University and Science Education, Office of Energy Research, DOE, ET-31, Washington, DC 20585; 202-586-8947.

For Your Travels

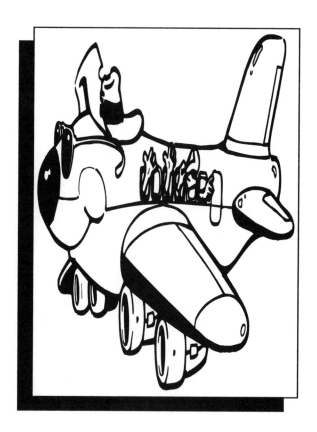

Know Before You Go

Can you bring back a kangaroo coat you purchased in Australia? What do have to declare? Can you mail packages home from abroad and not declare the items? All these are important questions to ask before you let your charge cards loose in a foreign country. The Customs Service has several interesting free pamphlets to get you headed in the right direction. *Know Before You Go* explains what you can and cannot bring into the country and explains what you must declare. *International Mail Imports* explains the rules regarding mailing packages from abroad.

For either of these publications write: U.S. Customs Service, P.O. Box 7407, Washington, DC 20044; 202-927-6724.

Right-On Write-Offs

There's still time to take advantage of leftover tax laws that favor the well-heeled. The Internal Revenue Service (IRS) has changed some of the rules regarding business deductions, but there are still ways you can write off parts of your summer vacation as a business expense. Anyone can do it even if you're just an employee. Find out how by calling the IRS at 800-829-3676 and asking for a free copy of Publications 463, *Travel, Entertainment, and Gift Expenses.*

far Shores, far Out

Want to study art in Italy? How about orangutans in Sumatra? The Youth Programs Division of the U.S. Information Agency sponsors a bunch of exchange programs for daring young rebels. Awards aren't made to individuals, but to the International Education Travel and Exchange Programs which in turn sponsor youth between the ages of 15 and 30.

A free listing of these programs titled *Advisory List of International Educational Travel and Exchange Programs* can be obtained from: Youth Programs Division, United States Information Agency, 301 4th St., SW, Room 357, Washington, DC 20547; 202-619-6299.

Where to Go

Deciding your vacation itinerary? The *Recreation Guide to BLM Public Lands* features a map outlining all of the public lands used as recreational areas. Designations on the map include campgrounds, visitors centers, national wild and scenic rivers, national wilderness areas, and national historic and scenic trails. Also included are the states that contain public lands, and state and district offices to contact for additional information.

Contact: Office of Public Affairs, Bureau of Land Management, U.S. Department of the Interior, 18th and C Sts., NW, Washington, DC 20240; 202-208-5717.

Fly Right

Which airline has the best ontime rate? Who loses the least amount of luggage? Which airport keeps on schedule the best? On which airline are you least likely to get bumped?

All of the answers to these questions and more are available from *The Air Travel Consumer Report*, a monthly report issued by the Office of Consumer Affairs at the U.S. Department of Transportation.

For your free copy contact: Office of Consumer Affairs, U.S. Department of Transportation, 400 7th St., SW, Room 10405, Washington, DC 20590; 202-366-2220.

Call Mother Nature

Tired of the rat race and need some time to contemplate the meaning of life? Head to the woods for some relaxation. To find out more about the National Parks, such as facilities, activities, and accommodations, request a free "National Parks Information" packet. This includes a listing of the most frequently visited parks, regional park service offices, reservation information, and more.

Contact: Office of Public Inquiries, National Park Service, U.S. Department of the Interior, P.O. Box 37127, Washington, DC 20013-7127; 202-208-4747.

Why Are You Taking My...?

Avoid the embarrassment in Customs when your suitcase is emptied and confiscated. Know what you can and cannot bring back to the U.S. before you go. *Travelers Alert!* alerts travelers to the requirement to declare all fruits, vegetables, meat, plants, and more. *Travelers' Tips* lists what food, plant, and animal products can an cannot be brought in the U.S. from foreign countries. *Why Are You Taking My...?* is for inspectors to give to travelers explaining why items were confiscated.

Contact: Animal and Plant Health Inspection Service, U.S. Department of Agriculture, Room G-195, Federal Building, 6505 Belcrest Rd., Hyattsville, MD 20782; 301-436-4478.

Travel Scams

Have you ever been tempted to buy one of those bargain-priced travel packages sold over the telephone? Be careful. Your dream vacation may turn into a misadventure if you fall victim to one of the many travel scams being sold over the phone which are defrauding consumers out of millions of dollars each month. If you feel you are a victim of just such a scam, or you want information on how to avoid them, request the free pamphlet, *Telemarketing Travel Fraud.*

Contact: Federal Trade Commission, Marketing Practices, 6th and Pennsylvania Ave., NW, Washington, DC 20580; 202-326-3128.

Camp USA

The National Forests are truly America's great outdoors. 155 National Forests stretch from Alaska to Puerto Rico and offer outstanding opportunities for outdoor recreation.

Wherever you are, you're probably no more than a day's drive from a National Forest, where you can hike, fish, camp, ski, or just sit back and enjoy the forest surroundings.

A Guide To Your National Forests is a free publication which lists regional Forest Service offices, as well as addresses and phone numbers for each National Forest. Request your free guide today.

Contact: Forest Service, U.S. Department of Agriculture, 12th and Independence, SW, P.O. Box 96090, Washington, DC 20090; 202-205-0957.

Take the Train

Fascinated by train travel? AMTRAK has a deal for you. They publish a travel planner which provides travel tips and services, as well as a listing of AMTRAK's vacation packages. For your free copy contact: AMTRAK, 60 Massachusetts Ave., NE, Washington, DC 20002; 800-USA-RAIL.

Travel on Uncle Sam's Expense Account

Are you an expert on a particular topic? Are you an artist? The U.S. Speakers Program will pay experts to travel abroad and participate in seminars, colloquia or symposia.

Subjects treated by the program include economics, international political relations, U.S. social and political processes, arts and humanities, and science and technology.

To see if you qualify, contact: U.S. Speakers, Office of Program Coordination and Development, U.S. Information Agency, 301 4th St., SW, Room 550, Washington, DC 20547; 202-619-4764.

Not Just a Trip, but an Adventure

Planning a trip to Florida and want to know about the tourist attractions? You can call or write the Senator of the state you plan to visit to get information on tourist attractions. There is also information available from the Department of Tourism located in each State Capitol.

Contact: Senator of your choice, The Capitol, Washington, DC 20510; 202-224-3121

George Washington Never Slept Here

The Advisory Council on Historic Places reviews Federal policies and procedures regarding preservation and enhancement of historic properties. They also maintain a free list of State Historic Preservation Officers, who can tell you about historic and archeological sites in their states, as well as direct you to the appropriate information sources.

Contact: Advisory Council on Historic Preservation, 1100 Pennsylvania Ave., NW, Suite 809, Washington, DC 20004; 202-606-8503.

Do Some Research

Going to a country where you've never been before? *Background Notes on the Countries of the World* is a series of short, factual pamphlets with information on the country's land, people, history, government, political conditions, economy, foreign relations, and U.S. foreign policy. Each pamphlet also includes a factual profile, brief travel notes, a country map, and a reading list.

Contact: Public Affairs Bureau, U.S. Department of State, Room 4827A, 2201 C St., NW, Washington, DC 20520; 202-647-2518.

You Can Only Bring So Many

Think there is no limit to the amount of something you can bring? You are wrong. *Trademark Information for Travelers* is a free publication which describes 800 articles popular with tourists and which are registered with U.S. Customs. You can generally only bring in limited numbers of these articles. So before you spend your money, check it out.

Contact: Information Services Division, Office of Logistics Management, U.S. Customs Service, U.S. Department of Treasury, 1301 Constitution Ave., NW. Washington, DC 20229; 202-927-2095.

3-2-1-Lift Off!

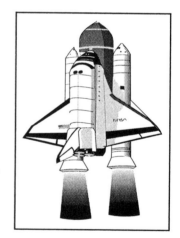

Want to see a shuttle lift off from the Kennedy Space Center, or just learn more about the Center? The John F. Kennedy Space Center will provide an information packet for those that what to learn more about the Space Center's accomplishments and function. Great for those wanting to learn more about space!

Contact: John F. Kennedy Space Center, NASA BOC-155, Kennedy Space Center, FL 32899; 407-867-4444.

The White House

No trip to Washington is complete without a stop at the White House. But know before you go. *White House Stone Carving: Builders and Restorers* ($3.25) describes planning and construction of the White House as a large stone building.

It shows the detailed carvings and mason markings in the stone exterior of the White House and illustrates the methods used to restore the stonework to its original condition.

For your copy contact: Superintendent of Documents, U.S. Government Printing Office, Washington, DC 20402; 202-783-3238.

Row, Row, Row Your Boat

Don't get lost up-creek without a paddle. The Army Corps of Engineers can teach you the proper way to handle a canoe or tie a line. They have a series of ten free brochures describing what recreation areas and services are available all over the country.

Contact: ACE Publications Depot, 2803 52nd Ave., Hyattsville, MD 20781; 301-436-2064.

Be Your Own Tour Guide

Stopping at all the historic places on your summer road trip?

The Office of Public Affairs can provide you with a list of publications available from the National Park Service.

They publish the *National Park Handbooks*, which are compact introductions to the great natural and historic places administered by the Park Service. Each is intended to be informative reading and a useful guide before, during, and after a park visit. Some of the titles include:

- *Antietam National Battlefield* ($2.50)

- *Craters of the Moon National Monument* ($2.25)

- *Gettysburg National Military Park* ($2.25)

- *John Brown's Raid* ($3.75)

- *Wright Brothers National Memorial* ($2.75)

To get a free catalogue contact: The Harpers Ferry Historical Association, P.O. Box 197, Harpers Ferry, WV 25425; 304-535-6881.

For Your Worries

The Bomb's in the Mail

The likelihood of you ever receiving a bomb in the mail is extremely remote, but in fact within the past five years, over 70 such incidents have occurred.

For help in recognizing such threats request a free publication titled *Bombs By Mail* (Notice 71) from: Congressional And Public Affairs Branch, U.S. Postal Service, 475 L'Enfant Plaza, SW, Washington, DC 20260-2175.

Before Your Boss Sends You on a Foreign Affair

The Overseas Security Advisory Council promotes security for businesses abroad. They have a data base and liaison staff which provides current unclassified threat information and directs you to local help in most areas of the world.

They have publications including *Security Guidelines for American Families Living Abroad* which outlines safety measures you can take and includes a videotape for kids.

Contact: Overseas Security Advisory Council, Bureau of Diplomatic Security, U.S. Department of State, 2216 Gallows, Dunn Loring, VA 22027; 703-204-6185.

Security Tips
for the Briefcase Bunch

Countering Terrorism: Security Suggestions for U.S. Business Representatives Abroad recommends some precautionary measures for employees to take at the office and at home and suggests rules of behavior in a hostage situation.

Contact: Office of Security Awareness, Bureau of Diplomatic Security, U.S. Department of State, Distribution Center, DS/SA 3rd Floor SA-10, Washington, DC 20522.

Experts TRAC Terrorists Here

Think terrorist activities only happen in the Middle East? Think again. *Terrorism In The United States* is a free publication that lists the number of incidents that have occurred in the U.S. and analyzes current threats that exist.

Contact: TRAC Unit, Federal Bureau of Investigation, J. Edgar Hoover Bldg., Ninth St. and Pennsylvania Ave., NW, Room 5431, Washington, DC 20535; 202-324-2064.

Bombs and Guns

Feel like you are living in the middle of a war zone? Find out what you are up against by requesting the following free publications. *Explosives Incidents Report* is an annual report, highlighting statistics of explosive incidents and stolen explosives and recoveries.

Identification of Firearms helps you in the identification of weapons, such as machine guns, rifles, and silencers. Just what you wanted to know!

Contact: Distribution Center, Bureau of Alcohol, Tobacco, and Firearms, U.S. Department of the Treasury, 7943 Angus Ct., Springfield, VA 22153; 703-455-7801.

Global Terrorism Tallied, Get the Free Report

Every day we hear about a bombing or suspicious fire overseas. *Patterns of Global Terrorism*, published by the Office of Counter Terrorism, is a free annual report which provides statistical information, as well as analyses and chronology of significant terrorist events.

Contact: Office of Public Information, 2201 C St., NW, Room 5831, U.S. Department of State, Washington, DC 20520; 202-647-6575.

Water Questions

Is your cup half empty or half full? How much water is in that flood? How little water is there in the drought?

The Hydrologic Information Unit answers questions like these and more. They have a free monthly publication, *National Water Conditions*, which is a summary of water-resource conditions across the U.S.

Contact: Hydrologic Information Unit, U.S. Geological Survey, 419 National Center, Reston, VA 22092; 703-648-6817.

It's Your Fault

If you really want to scare yourself silly, read *Preliminary Determination of Epicenters* before going to bed. This monthly publication is the bible of professional quake watchers, tracking seismic activity and predicting the next "Big One".

To get a copy of this publication or answers to your earthquake questions contact: National Earthquake Information Center, U.S. Geological Survey, Mail Stop 967, Box 25046, Federal Center, Denver, CO 80225; 303-273-8500.

The Worst Winter in a Hundred Years

The weather has gotten very strange lately, and people are always predicting the worst. But is better to be safe than sorry. The Federal Emergency Management Agency has produced several free publications on winter safety.

Safety Tips for Winter Storms (196) provides helpful hints if you are caught in a snow storm. *Winter Survival Coloring Book* (FEMA-26) includes safety precautions to be taken around the home before winter storms strike, and includes heating systems, room heaters and fireplaces, kitchen pipes, and emergency supplies.

Contact: Federal Emergency Management Agency, P.O. Box 70274, Washington, DC 20024; 202-646-3484.

The Check's in the Mail...or Is It?

Worried about sending a birthday check to Junior? A free booklet, *A Consumer's Guide to Postal Crime Prevention*, is full of helpful hints to discourage mail thieves. There is also information on how to deal with the problem of mail fraud.

Contact: Public Affairs Branch, The Postal Inspection Service, U.S. Postal Service, 475 L'Enfant Plaza, SW, Washington, DC 20260; 202-268-4293.

When a Disaster Strikes

We all think we'd know what to do in an emergency, but in reality, planning is the key.

- *Family Earthquake Safety Home Hazard Hunt and Drill* (FEMA-113) discusses how to identify and correct hazards in the home and practice what to do if an earthquake occurs.

- *Hurricane Safety: Tips for Hurricanes* (L-105) provides helpful suggestions on what should be done in the event of a hurricane.

- *Tornado Safety Tips* (L-148) outlines safe behavior when a tornado strikes.

Contact: Federal Emergency Management Agency, P.O. Box 70274, Washington, DC 20024; 202-646-3484.

Insured, I'm Sure

Some victims of the recent flood were covered under the government's National Flood Insurance Program (NFIP), many were not. To find out if you qualify, get the free brochure, *Answers to Questions About The National Flood Insurance Program* which explains NFIP, and the type of assistance it provides.

For information on rules, regulations, claims, and publications, contact: National Flood Insurance Program, 10101 Senate Dr., Lanham, MD 20706; 800-638-6620.

First Aid

Uncle Sam has a *First Aid Book* ($6.50) which recommends procedures for dealing with emergencies which require first aid. It includes

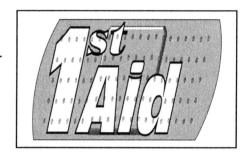

sections on CPR, shock, wounds, burns, and more.

It also contains numerous illustrations, a bibliography, and an index, so be prepared!

For your copy contact: Superintendent of Documents, U.S. Government Printing Office, Washington, DC 20402: 202-783-3238.

Panic City

Can't leave home? Do spiders send you fleeing? A free 40 page pamphlet, *Phobias and Panic* provides you with information on panic disorders, types of phobias, and various kind of treatments available. Don't let these fears run your life for you, learn to overcome them.

Contact: National Institute of Mental Health, 5600 Fishers Ln., Room 7C-02, Rockville, MD 20857; 301-443-4515.

Safe at Any Speed

Experiencing some car safety problems you feel are the manufacturer's fault? The toll-free Auto Safety Hotline is your chance to help identify safety problems in motor vehicles, tires, and automotive equipment and also get safety information.  Your complaint is logged and the manufacturer is notified.

If you are car or tire shopping, this hotline has a wealth of free information to help you with your decisions. The *Vehicle Crash Test Information* shows the relative crash protection provided front seat occupants in accidents at 35 mph. It also lists types of protection available and if anti-lock brakes are standard, optional, or available.

Regarding tires, the *Tire Quality Grading Report* provides information on the quality, mileage, and durability of various tires. Other information available includes *Anti-Lock Brake System* which explains this type of brake.

Contact: National Highway Traffic Safety Administration, Auto Safety Hotline NEF-11.2 HL, 400 Seventh St., SW, Washington, DC 20590; 800-424-9393.

Call in the National Guard

Curious about exactly who is the National Guard and what they do? The Guard publishes a brochure entitled *National Guard Update* which discusses the federal and state mission, force structure, overseas deployments, and personnel statistics, and an *Annual Review* of its work and accomplishments.

They also have a free "Heritage Series" of lithographs of historical events involving the Guard. For more information contact: National Guard Bureau, Public Affairs Office, Washington, DC 20317; 703-756-1923.

Army Downsizing

Find out if the Army is downsizing, what the Defense Department budget is for this year as compared to previous years, and more through two free publications.

The Army Posture Statement contains information on the Army's restructuring. *The Department of Defense Fiscal 1993 Budget* shows Defense allocations and where the money is being directed.

For your copies contact: U.S. Army Public Affairs, U.S. Department of Defense, The Pentagon, Washington, DC 20310; 703-697-7550.

A Boss with Itchy Fingers

Are you having some trouble at work with your boss sexually harassing you? To learn more about sexual harassment, you can contact the U.S. Equal Employment Opportunity Commission which has a series of publications on this topic, including:

- *Facts About Sexual Harassment*

- *Guidelines On Discrimination Because of Sex*

- *Laws Enforced by the U.S. Equal Employment Opportunity Commission*

- *Policy Guidance on Current Issues Of Sexual Harassment*

- *Questions and Answers About Sexual Harassment*

- *Sexual Harassment Resources*

For this and other information contact: Equal Employment Opportunity Commission, 1801 L St., NW, Washington, DC 20507; 202-663-4900; 800-669-3362.

This is Not a Drill

No one thinks that a fire can happen to them, but it can. You need to know how to protect yourself and your family. The U.S. Fire Administration has produced an array of free materials on such subjects as smoke detectors, alternate heater safety, characteristics of fire, and more.

"Curious Kids Set Fires" is a program curricula for ages 3-10 designed to raise awareness about the problem of curiosity fire setting. "Let's Retire Fire" is a multi-dimensional program targeting senior Americans with vital safety messages. *An Ounce of Prevention* is a booklet providing information on automatic sprinklers and early warning systems. *After the Fire: Returning to Normal* is a booklet providing helpful tips on what needs to be done after a fire for people who have experienced fire loss.

Contact: Office of Fire Prevention and Arson Control, U.S. Fire Administration, 16825 South Seton Ave., Emmitsburg, MD 21727; 301-447-1122.

Good News:
Aviation Accidents Are Down!
Bad News: Fatalities Are Up!

Last year the number of aviation accidents dropped; however more people were killed than in the previous year. The National Transportation Safety Board (NTSB) reports a total of 1,013 people died in 2,229 aviation accidents either in the U.S. or involving U.S. registered civil aircraft last year. These are just a few of the facts available in a free annual *End Report to Congress* from NTSB. Statistical information for the past ten years is also available.

Contact: National Transportation Safety Board, 490 L'Enfant Plaza, SW, Washington, DC 20594; 202-382-0660.

You've Survived the Flood,
Now What?

Your home and its contents may look beyond hope, but many of your belongings can probably be restored. *Repairing Your Flooded Home* is a free book published by the Federal Emergency Management Agency to help people who have been flooded and gives step-by-step advice you can use to clean-up, rebuild, and get help after a flood.

For your copy contact: FEMA Publications, P.O. Box 70274, Washington, DC 20024; 202-646-3484.

Who's Got the Energy?

The Energy Information Administration is responsible for the collection, processing, and publication of data in the areas of energy resource reserves, technology, and much more. A free *Directory of Energy Information* is available which lists the amount of energy used, trends for future, and the outlook in the energy field.

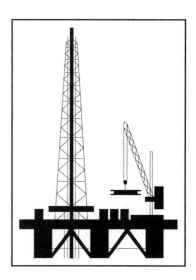

Contact: U.S. Department of Energy, National Energy Information Center, 1000 Independence Ave., SW, Washington, DC 20585; 202-586-5000.

Pipeline Safety

One of the U.S. Department of Transportation's missions is in the area of pipeline safety. To see if and how this is being accomplished, you can get a free copy of the *Annual Report on Pipeline Safety*.

Contact: U.S. Department of Transportation, Research and Special Programs Administration, Washington, DC 20590; 202-366-4595.

Did I Remember to Turn Off the ...

Whenever you go on a trip you always wonder if you turned off the coffee pot, iron, or stove. Electrical safety is not to be taken lightly. The U.S. Consumer Product Safety Commission (CPSC) has put together a series of free publications dealing with electrical safety. Some of the titles include:

- *Ranges and Ovens Fact Sheet*

- *Extension Cords Fact Sheet*

- *Portable Hair Dryers Fact Sheet*

- *Electrical Safety Room by Room Audit Checklist*

- *CPSC Guide to Home Wiring Hazards*

For your free copies or a complete publications list write: Publication Request, Office of Information and Public Affairs, U.S. Consumer Product Safety Commission, Washington, DC 20207.

On the Wrong Track

Information about railroad safety is available in a report known as the *Accident/Incident Bulletin*, which comes out annually.

There are three categories of reportable events; highway-rail accidents, train accidents, and any other event that results in a casualty. The report contains graphs and statistics.

For your free copy contact: U.S. Department of Transportation, Federal Railroad Administration, Office of Safety, 400 Seventh St., SW, Washington, DC 20591; 202-366-6299.

Your Guide to More Freebies

We just couldn't stop at 1,001. If you want more than what's in the book, here's your guide for getting your own freebies and cheapies. Listed below is a state-by-state directory of government offices that will help you find the freebies you're looking for at the federal, state, regional, and local levels. For each state, you will find the following sources:

- The Federal Information Center can connect you with the appropriate government agency which handles your topic of interest.

- The State Information Number can provide the same service on the state level.

- The Forest Service Regional number can answer all your Park Service questions and direct you to state resources.

- The Environmental Protection Agency Regional Office handles all environmental issues, and can also give you appropriate state information.

- The Cooperative Extension Service has offices located in almost every county across america and has a wealth of information regarding finances, child care, home economics, gardening, and more.

We wish you luck in your search for fabulous freebies and cheapies.

Directory of State Information

Alabama

Federal Information Center
Birmingham, Mobile; 800-366-2998
All Other Locations; 301-722-9098

State Information Office
205-242-8000

Forest Service
1720 Peachtree Rd., NW
Atlanta, GA 30367
404-347-4191

Environmental Protection Agency
345 Courtland St. NE
Atlanta, GA 30365
404-347-4727

Cooperative Extension Offices
Dr. Ann Thompson, Director
Alabama Cooperative Extension Service
109 A Duncan Hall
Auburn University
Auburn, AL 36849-5612
205-844-4444

Chinelle Henderson, Administrator
Alabama A&M University
Cooperative Extension Service
P.O. Box 967
Normal, AL 35762
205-851-5710

Dr. Moore, Director
Cooperative Extension Program
U.S. Department of Agriculture
Tuskegee University
207 N. Main Street, Suite 400
Tuskegee, AL 36083-1731
205-727-8806

Alaska

Federal Information Center
Anchorage; 800-729-8003
All Other Locations; 301-722-9098

State Information Office
907-465-2111

Forest Service
Federal Office Building
709 West Ninth St.
P.O. Box 21628
Juneau, AK 99802
907-586-8863

Environmental Protection Agency
1200 Sixth Ave.
Seattle, WA 98101
206-553-0479

Cooperative Extension Office
Hollis D. Hall, Director
Alaska Cooperative Extension
University of Alaska Fairbanks
P.O. Box 756180
Fairbanks, AK 99775-6180
907-474-7246

Arizona

Federal Information Center
Phoenix; 800-359-3997
All Other Locations; 301-722-9098

State Information Office
602-542-4900

Forest Service
Federal Building
517 Gold Ave., SW
Albuquerque, NM 87102
505-842-3292

Environmental Protection Agency
75 Hawthorne St.
San Francisco, CA 94105
415-744-1702

Cooperative Extension Office
Jim Christenson, Director
Cooperative Extension Office
University of Arizona
Forbes 301
Tucson, AZ 85721
602-621-7205

Arkansas

Federal Information Center
Little Rock; 800-366-2998
All Other Locations; 301-722-9098

State Information Office
501-682-3000

Forest Service
1720 Peachtree Rd., NW
Atlanta, GA 30367
404-347-4191

Environmental Protection Agency
1445 Ross Ave.
Dallas, TX 75202
214-655-6444

Cooperative Extension Offices
David Foster, Director
Cooperative Extension Service
P.O. Box 391
Little Rock, AR 72203
501-671-2000

Dr. Mazo Price, Director
Cooperative Extension Service
1200 N. University
Box 4005
University of Arkansas at Pine Bluff
Pine Bluff, AR 71601
501-543-8131

California

Federal Information Center
Los Angeles, San Diego, San Francisco, Santa
Ana; 800-726-4995
Sacramento; 916-973-1695
All Other Locations; 301-722-9098

State Information Office
916-322-9900

Forest Service
630 Sansome St.
San Francisco, CA 94111
415-705-2874

Environmental Protection Agency
75 Hawthorne St.
San Francisco, CA 94105
415-744-1702

Cooperative Extension Office
Kenneth Farrell, Vice President
University of California
Division of Agriculture and Natural Resources
300 Lakeside Drive, 6th Floor
Oakland, CA 94612-3560
510-987-0060

Colorado

Federal Information Center
Colorado Springs, Denver, Pueblo; 800-359-3997
All Other Locations; 301-722-9098

State Information Office
303-866-5000

Forest Service
740 Sims
Golden, CO 80401
303-275-5350

Environmental Protection Agency
999 18th St., Suite 500
Denver, CO 80202
303-293-1603

Cooperative Extension Office
Milan Rewets, Director
Colorado State University
Cooperative Extension
1 Administrative Building
Fort Collins, CO 80523
303-491-6281

Connecticut

Federal Information Center
Hartford, New Haven; 800-347-1997
All Other Locations; 301-722-9098

State Information Office
203-240-0222

Forest Service
310 W. Wisconsin Ave., Room 500
Milwaukee, WI 53203
414-297-3963

Environmental Protection Agency
JFK Federal Building
Boston, MA 02203
617-565-3420

Cooperative Extension Office
Associate Director
Cooperative Extension System
University of Connecticut
1376 Storrs Road
Storrs, CT 06269-4036
203-486-4125

Delaware

Federal Information Center
All Locations; 301-722-9098

State Information Office
302-739-4000

Forest Service
310 W. Wisconsin Ave., Room 500
Milwaukee, WI 53203
414-297-3963

Environmental Protection Agency
26 Federal Plaza
New York, NY 10278
212-264-2657

Cooperative Extension Offices
Dr. Richard E. Fowler, Director
Cooperative Extension
131 Townsend Hall
University of Delaware
Newark, DE 19717-1303
302-831-2504

Dr. Starlene Taylor
Assistant Administrator
Delaware State College
Cooperative Extension Service
1200 N. DuPont Highway
Dover, DE 19901
302-739-5157

District of Columbia

Cooperative Extension Office
Reginald Taylor, Acting Director
Cooperative Extension Service
University of the District of Columbia
901 Newton Street, NE
Washington, DC 20017
202-576-6993

Florida

Federal Information Center
Ft. Lauderdale, Jacksonville, Miami, Orlando, St.
Petersburg, Tampa, West Palm Beach;
800-347-1997
All Other Locations; 301-722-9098

State Information Office
904-488-1234

Forest Service
1720 Peachtree Rd., NW
Atlanta, GA 30367
404-347-4191

Environmental Protection Agency
345 Courtland St. NE
Atlanta, GA 30365
404-347-4727

Cooperative Extension Offices
John T. Woeste, Director
Florida Cooperative Extension Service
P.O. Box 110210
University of Florida
Gainesville, FL 32611-0210

Lawrence Carter, Director
Cooperative Extension Service
215 Perry Paige Building
Florida A&M University
Tallahassee, FL 32307
904-599-3546

Georgia

Federal Information Center
Atlanta; 800-347-1997
All Other Locations; 301-722-9098

State Information Office
404-656-2000

Forest Service
1720 Peachtree Rd., NW
Atlanta, GA 30367
404-347-4191

Environmental Protection Agency
345 Courtland St. NE
Atlanta, GA 30365
404-347-4727

Cooperative Extension Offices
Wayne Jordon, Director
Cooperative Extension Service
University of Georgia
1111 Conner Hall
Athens, GA 30602
706-542-3824

Dr. Fred Harrison, Jr., Director
Cooperative Extension Service
P.O. Box 4061
Fort Valley State College
Fort Valley, GA 31030
912-825-6269

Hawaii

Federal Information Center
Honolulu; 800-733-5996
All Other Locations; 301-722-9098

State Information Office
808-548-6222

Forest Service
630 Sansome St.
San Francisco, CA 94111
415-705-2874

Environmental Protection Agency
75 Hawthorne St.
San Francisco, CA 94105
415-744-1702

Cooperative Extension Office
Dr. Po'Yung Lai, Assistant Director
Cooperative Extension Service
3050 Maile Way
Honolulu, HI 96822
808-956-8397

Idaho

Federal Information Center
All Locations; 301-722-9098

State Information Office
208-334-2411

Forest Service
Federal Building
200 East Broadway St.
P.O. Box 7669
Missoula, MT 59807
406-329-3511

Environmental Protection Agency
1200 Sixth Ave.
Seattle, WA 98101
206-553-0479

Cooperative Extension Office
Dr. LeRoy D. Luft, Director
Cooperative Extension System
College of Agriculture
University of Idaho
Moscow, ID 83844-2338
208-885-6639

Illinois

Federal Information Center
Chicago; 800-366-2998
All Other Locations; 301-722-9098

State Information Office
217-782-2000

Forest Service
310 W. Wisconsin Ave., Room 500
Milwaukee, WI 53203
414-297-3963

Environmental Protection Agency
77 W. Jackson Blvd.
Chicago, IL 60604
312-353-2000

Cooperative Extension Office
Donald Uchtmann, Director
University of Illinois
Cooperative Extension Service
122 Mumford Hall
1301 W. Gregory Drive
Urbana, IL 61801
217-333-2660

Indiana

Federal Information Center
Gary; 800-366-2998
Indianapolis; 800-347-1997
All Other Locations; 301-722-9098

State Information Office
317-232-1000

Forest Service
310 W. Wisconsin Ave., Room 500
Milwaukee, WI 53203
414-297-3963

Environmental Protection Agency
77 W Jackson Blvd.
Chicago, IL 60604
312-353-2000

Cooperative Extension Office
Dr. Wadsworth, Director
1140 AGAD
CES Administration
Purdue University
West Lafayette, IN 47907-1140
317-494-8489

Iowa

Federal Information Center
All Locations; 800-735-8004

State Information Office
515-281-5011

Forest Service
310 W. Wisconsin Ave., Room 500
Milwaukee, WI 53203
414-297-3963

Environmental Protection Agency
726 Minnesota Ave.
Kansas City, KS 66101
913-551-7000

Cooperative Extension Office
Dr. Robert Anderson, Director
Cooperative Extension Service
315 Boardshear
Iowa State University
Ames, IA 50011
515-294-9434

Kansas

Federal Information Center
All Locations; 800-735-8004

State Information Office
913-296-0111

Forest Service
740 Sims
Golden, CO 80401
303-275-5350

Environmental Protection Agency
726 Minnesota Ave.
Kansas City, KS 66101
913-551-7000

Cooperative Extension Office
Mark Johnson, Interim Director
Cooperative Extension Service
Kansas State University
123 Umberger Hall
Manhattan, KS 66506
913-532-5820

Kentucky

Federal Information Center
Louisville; 800-347-1997
All Other Locations; 301-722-9098

State Information Office
502-564-3130

Forest Service
1720 Peachtree Rd., NW
Atlanta, GA 30367
404-347-4191

Environmental Protection Agency
345 Courtland St. NE
Atlanta, GA 30365
404-347-4727

Cooperative Extension Offices
Dr. Absher, Director
Cooperative Extension Service
310 W.P. Garrigus Building
University of Kentucky
Lexington, KY 40546
606-257-1846

Dr. Harold Benson, Director
Kentucky State University
Cooperative Extension Program
Frankfort, KY 40601
502-227-5905

Louisiana

Federal Information Center
New Orleans; 800-366-2998
All Other Locations; 301-722-9098

State Information Office
504-342-6600

Forest Service
1720 Peachtree Rd., NW
Atlanta, GA 30367
404-347-4191

Environmental Protection Agency
1445 Ross Ave.
Dallas, TX 75202
214-655-6444

Cooperative Extension Offices
Bruce Flint, Director
Cooperative Extension Service
Louisiana State University
P.O. Box 25100
Baton Rouge, LA 70894-5100
504-388-4141

Dr. Adell Brown, Assistant Administrator
Cooperative Extension Program
Southern University and A&M College
P.O. Box 10010
Baton Rouge, LA 70813
504-771-2242

Maine

Federal Information Center
All Locations; 301-722-9098

State Information Office
207-582-9500

Forest Service
310 W. Wisconsin Ave., Room 500
Milwaukee, WI 53203
414-297-3963

Environmental Protection Agency
JFK Federal Building
Boston, MA 02203
617-565-3420

Cooperative Extension Office
Vaughn Holyoke, Director
Cooperative Extension Service
University of Maine
5741 Libby Hall, Room 102
Orono, ME 04469-5741
207-581-3188

Maryland

Federal Information Center
Baltimore; 800-347-1997
All Other Locations; 301-722-9098

State Information Office
410-974-2000

Forest Service
310 W. Wisconsin Ave., Room 500
Milwaukee, WI 53203
414-297-3963

Environmental Protection Agency
26 Federal Plaza
New York, NY 10278
212-264-2657

Cooperative Extension Offices
Dr. Nan Booth
Regional Directors Office
Cooperative Extension Service
Room 2120, Simons Hall
University of Maryland
College Park, MD 20742
301-405-2907

Dr. Henry Brookes, Administrator
Cooperative Extension Service
UMES
Princess Anne, MD 21853
410-651-6206

Massachusetts

Federal Information Center
Boston; 800-347-1997
All Other Locations; 301-722-9098

State Information Office
617-722-2000

Forest Service
310 W. Wisconsin Ave., Room 500
Milwaukee, WI 53203
414-297-3963

Environmental Protection Agency
JFK Federal Building
Boston, MA 02203
617-565-3420

Cooperative Extension Office
Dr. John Gerber, Associate Director
210C Stockbridge Hall
University of Massachusetts
Amherst, MA 01003
413-545-4800

Michigan

Federal Information Center
Detroit, Grand Rapids; 800-347-1997
All Other Locations; 301-722-9098

State Information Office
517-373-1837

Forest Service
310 W. Wisconsin Ave., Room 500
Milwaukee, WI 53203
414-297-3963

Environmental Protection Agency
77 W. Jackson Blvd.
Chicago, IL 60604
312-353-2000

Cooperative Extension Office
Gail Emig, Director
Michigan State University Extension
Room 108, Agriculture Hall
Michigan State University
East Lansing, MI 48824
517-355-2308

Minnesota

Federal Information Center
Minneapolis; 800-366-2998
All Other Locations; 301-722-9098

State Information Office
612-296-6013

Forest Service
310 W. Wisconsin Ave., Room 500
Milwaukee, WI 53203
414-297-3963

Environmental Protection Agency
77 W. Jackson Blvd.
Chicago, IL 60604
312-353-2000

Cooperative Extension Office
Patrick Borich
Minnesota Extension Service
University of Minnesota
240 Coffey Hall
1420 Eckles Avenue
St. Paul, MN 55108
612-625-3797

Mississippi

Federal Information Center
All Locations; 301-722-9098

State Information Office
601-359-1000

Forest Service
1720 Peachtree Rd., NW
Atlanta, GA 30367
404-347-4191

Environmental Protection Agency
345 Courtland St. NE
Atlanta, GA 30365
404-347-4727

Cooperative Extension Offices
Danny Cheatham, Director
Cooperative Extension Service
Mississippi State University
P.O. Box 9601
Mississippi State, MS 39762
601-325-3034

LeRoy Davis, Dean
P.O. Box 479
Alcorn Cooperative Extension Program
Lorman, MS 39096
601-877-6128

Missouri

Federal Information Center
St. Louis; 800-366-2998
All Other Locations; 800-735-8004

State Information Office
314-751-2000

Forest Service
310 W. Wisconsin Ave., Room 500
Milwaukee, WI 53203
414-297-3963

Environmental Protection Agency
726 Minnesota Ave.
Kansas City, KS 66101
913-551-7000

Cooperative Extension Offices
Ronald J. Turner, Interim Director
Cooperative Extension Service
University of Missouri
309 University Hall
Columbia, MO 65211
314-882-7754

George Enlaw, Director
Cooperative Extension Service
Lincoln University
110A Allen Hall
P.O. Box 29
Jefferson City, MO 65102-0029
314-681-5550

Montana

Federal Information Center
All Locations; 301-722-9098

State Information Office
406-444-2511

Forest Service
Federal Building
200 East Broadway St.
P.O. Box 7669
Missoula, MT 59807
406-329-3511

Environmental Protection Agency
999 18th St., Suite 500
Denver, CO 80202
303-293-1603

Cooperative Extension Office
Andrea Pagenkopf
Vice Probost for Outreach and Director of Extension
212 Montana Hall
Montana State University
Bozeman, MT 59717
406-994-4371

Nebraska

Federal Information Center
Omaha; 800-366-2998
All Other Locations; 800-735-8004

State Information Office
402-471-2311

Forest Service
740 Sims
Golden, CO 80401
303-275-5350

Environmental Protection Agency
726 Minnesota Ave.
Kansas City, KS 66101
913-551-7000

Cooperative Extension Office
Lloyd Young, Director
University of Nebraska
S.E. Research and Extension Center
211 Mussehl Hall, East Campus
Lincoln, NE 68583
402-472-3674

Nevada

Federal Information Center
All Locations; 301-722-9098

State Information Office
702-687-5000

Forest Service
Federal Building
324 25th St.
Ogden, UT 84401
801-625-5354

Environmental Protection Agency
75 Hawthorne St.
San Francisco, CA 94105
415-744-1702

Cooperative Extension Office
Bernard M. Jones, Director
Nevada Cooperative Extension
University of Nevada, Reno
Mail Stop 189
Reno, NV 89557-0106
702-784-1614

New Hampshire

Federal Information Center
All Locations; 301-722-9098

State Information Office
603-271-1110

Forest Service
310 W. Wisconsin Ave., Room 500
Milwaukee, WI 53203
414-297-3963

Environmental Protection Agency
JFK Federal Building
Boston, MA 02203
617-565-3420

Cooperative Extension Office
Peter J. Horne
Dean and Director
UNH Cooperative Extension
59 College Road
Taylor Hall
Durham, NH 03824
603-862-1520

New Jersey

Federal Information Center
Newark, Trenton; 800-347-1997
All Other Locations; 301-722-9098

State Information Office
609-292-2121

Forest Service
310 W. Wisconsin Ave., Room 500
Milwaukee, WI 53203
414-297-3963

Environmental Protection Agency
26 Federal Plaza
New York, NY 10278
212-264-2657

Cooperative Extension Office
Mr. Helsel, Director
Rutgers Cooperative Extension
P.O. Box 231
New Brunswick, NJ 08903
908-932-9306

New Mexico

Federal Information Center
Albuquerque; 800-359-3997
All Other Locations; 301-722-9098

State Information Office
505-827-4011

Forest Service
Federal Building
517 Gold Ave., SW
Albuquerque, NM 87102
505-842-3292

Environmental Protection Agency
1445 Ross Ave.
Dallas, TX 75202
214-655-6444

New York

Federal Information Center
Albany, Buffalo, New York, Rochester, Syracuse;
800-347-1997
All Other Locations; 301-722-9098

State Information Office
518-474-2121

Forest Service
310 W. Wisconsin Ave., Room 500
Milwaukee, WI 53203
414-297-3963

Environmental Protection Agency
26 Federal Plaza
New York, NY 10278
212-264-2657

Cooperative Extension Office
Lucinda Noble, Director
Cornell Cooperative Extension
276 Roberts Hall
Ithaca, NY 14853
607-255-2237

North Carolina

Federal Information Center
Charlotte; 800-347-1997
All Other Locations; 301-722-9098

State Information Office
919-733-1110

Forest Service
1720 Peachtree Rd., NW
Atlanta, GA 30367
404-347-4191

Environmental Protection Agency
345 Courtland St. NE
Atlanta, GA 30365
404-347-4727

Cooperative Extension Offices
Dr. Robert C. Wells, Director
Cooperative Extension Service
North Carolina State University
Box 7602
Raleigh, NC 27695
919-515-2811

Dr. Daniel Godfrey, Director
Cooperative Extension Program
North Carolina A&T State University
P.O. Box 21928
Greensboro, NC 27420-1928
919-334-7956

North Dakota

Federal Information Center
All Locations; 301-722-9098

State Information Office
701-224-2000

Forest Service
Federal Building
200 East Broadway St.
P.O. Box 7669
Missoula, MT 59807
406-329-3511

Environmental Protection Agency
999 18th St., Suite 500
Denver, CO 80202
303-293-1603

Cooperative Extension Office
Bob Cristman, Director
Cooperative Extension Service
North Dakota State University
Morrill Hall, Room 311
Box 5437
Fargo, ND 58105
701-237-8944

Ohio

Federal Information Center
Akron, Cincinnati, Cleveland, Columbus, Dayton,
Toledo; 800-347-1997
All Other Locations; 301-722-9098

State Information Office
614-466-2000

Forest Service
310 W. Wisconsin Ave., Room 500
Milwaukee, WI 53203
414-297-3963

Environmental Protection Agency
77 W. Jackson Blvd.
Chicago, IL 60604
312-353-2000

Cooperative Extension Office
Keith Smith, Director
OSU Extension
2120 Fiffe Road
Agriculture Administration Building
Columbus, OH 43210
614-292-6181

Oklahoma

Federal Information Center
Oklahoma City, Tulsa; 800-366-2998
All Other Locations; 301-722-9098

State Information Office
405-521-1601

Forest Service
1720 Peachtree Rd., NW
Atlanta, GA 30367
404-347-4191

Environmental Protection Agency
1445 Ross Ave.
Dallas, TX 75202
214-655-6444

Cooperative Extension Offices
Dr. Ray Campbell
Interim Associate Director
Oklahoma Cooperative Extension Service
Oklahoma State University
139 Agriculture Hall
Stillwater, OK 74078
405-744-5398

Dr. Ocleris Simpston, Director
Cooperative Research and Extension
P.O. Box 730
Langston University
Langston, OK 73050
405-466-3836

Oregon

Federal Information Center
Portland; 800-726-4995
All Other Locations; 301-722-9098

State Information Office
503-378-3131

Forest Service
333 SW 1st Ave.
P.O. Box 3623
Portland, OR 97208
503-326-4154

Environmental Protection Agency
1200 Sixth Ave.
Seattle, WA 98101
206-553-0479

Cooperative Extension Office
O.E. Smith, Director
Oregon State Extension Service Administration
Oregon State University
Ballard Extension Hall #101
Corvallis, OR 97331-3606
503-737-2711

Pennsylvania

Federal Information Center
Philadelphia, Pittsburgh; 800-347-1997
All Other Locations; 301-722-9098

State Information Office
717-787-2121

Forest Service
310 W. Wisconsin Ave., Room 500
Milwaukee, WI 53203
414-297-3963

Environmental Protection Agency
26 Federal Plaza
New York, NY 10278
212-264-2657

Cooperative Extension Office
Dean Hood, Director
Pennsylvania State University
Room 217, A.G. Administration
University Park, PA 16802
814-863-0331

Rhode Island

Federal Information Center
Providence; 800-347-1997
All Other Locations; 301-722-9098

State Information Office
401-277-2000

Forest Service
310 W. Wisconsin Ave., Room 500
Milwaukee, WI 53203
414-297-3963

Environmental Protection Agency
JFK Federal Building
Boston, MA 02203
617-565-3420

Cooperative Extension Office
Kathleen Mallon, Director
Cooperative Extension Education Center
University of Rhode Island
East Alumni Avenue
Kingston, RI 02881-0804
401-792-2900

South Carolina

Federal Information Center
All Locations; 301-722-9098

State Information Office
803-734-1000

Forest Service
1720 Peachtree Rd., NW
Atlanta, GA 30367
404-347-4191

Environmental Protection Agency
345 Courtland St. NE
Atlanta, GA 30365
404-347-4727

Cooperative Extension Offices
E.V. Jones, Director
Clemson University
Cooperative Extension Service
P.O. Box 995
Pickens, SC 29671
803-868-2810

Director
Cooperative Extension Service
P.O. Box 7265
South Carolina State University
Orangeburg, SC 29117
803-536-8928

South Dakota

Federal Information Center
All Locations; 301-722-9098

State Information Office
605-773-3011

Forest Service
740 Sims
Golden, CO 80401
303-275-5350

Environmental Protection Agency
999 18th St., Suite 500
Denver, CO 80202
303-293-1603

Cooperative Extension Office
Mylo Hellickson, Director
SDSU
Box 2270D
AG Hall 154
Brookings, SD 57007
605-688-4792

Tennessee

Federal Information Center
Chattanooga; 800-347-1997
Memphis, Nashville; 800-366-2998

State Information Office
615-741-3011

Forest Service
1720 Peachtree Rd., NW
Atlanta, GA 30367
404-347-4191

Environmental Protection Agency
345 Courtland St. NE
Atlanta, GA 30365
404-347-4727

Cooperative Extension Offices
Billy G. Hicks, Dean
Agricultural Extension Service
University of Tennessee
P.O. Box 1071
Knoxville, TN 37901-1071
615-974-7114

Cherry Lane Zon Schmittou, Extension Leader
Davidson County Agricultural Service
Tennessee State University
800 Second Avenue N., Suite 3
Nashville, TN 37201-1084
615-254-8734

Texas

Federal Information Center
Austin, Dallas, Fort Worth, Houston, San Antonio;
800-366-2998
All Other Locations; 301-722-9098

State Information Office
512-463-4630

Forest Service
1720 Peachtree Rd., NW
Atlanta, GA 30367
404-347-4191

Environmental Protection Agency
1445 Ross Ave.
Dallas, TX 75202
214-655-6444

Cooperative Extension Offices
Dr. Zerle Carpenter, Director
Texas Agricultural Extension Service
Texas A&M University
College Station, TX 77843-7101
409-845-7967

Hoover Carden, Director
Cooperative Extension Program
P.O. Box Drawer-B
Prairie View, TX 77446-2867
409-857-2023

Utah

Federal Information Center
Salt Lake City; 800-359-3997
All Other Locations; 301-722-9098

State Information Office
801-538-3000

Forest Service
Federal Building
324 25th St.
Ogden, UT 84401
801-625-5354

Environmental Protection Agency
999 18th St., Suite 500
Denver, CO 80202
303-293-1603

Cooperative Extension Office
Dr. Robert Gilliland
Vice President for Extension
and Continuing Education
Utah State University
Logan, UT 84322-4900
801-750-2200

Vermont

Federal Information Center
All Locations; 301-722-9098

State Information Office
802-828-1110

Forest Service
310 W. Wisconsin Ave., Room 500
Milwaukee, WI 53203
414-297-3963

Environmental Protection Agency
JFK Federal Building
Boston, MA 02203
617-565-3420

Cooperative Extension Office
Larry Forchier, Dean
Division of Agriculture, Natural Resources,
and Extension
University of Vermont
601 Main
Burlington, VT 05401-3439
802-656-2990

Virginia

Federal Information Center
Norfolk, Richmond, Roanoke; 800-347-1997
All Other Locations; 301-722-9098

State Information Office
804-786-0000

Forest Service
1720 Peachtree Rd., NW
Atlanta, GA 30367
404-347-4191

Environmental Protection Agency
26 Federal Plaza
New York, NY 10278
212-264-2657

Cooperative Extension Offices
Dr. William Allen, Interim Director
Virginia Cooperative Extension
Virginia Tech
Blacksburg, VA 24061-0402
703-231-5299

Lorenza Lyons, Director
Cooperative Extension
Virginia State University
Petersburg, VA 23806
804-524-5961

Washington

Federal Information Center
Seattle, Tacoma; 800-726-4995
All Other Locations; 301-722-9098

State Information Office
206-753-5000

Forest Service
333 SW 1st. Ave.
P.O. Box 3623
Portland, OR 97208
503-326-4154

Environmental Protection Agency
1200 Sixth Ave.
Seattle, WA 98101
206-553-0479

Cooperative Extension Office
Harry Burcalow, Interim Director
Cooperative Extension
411 Hulbert
Washington State University
Pullman, WA 99164-6230
509-335-2811

West Virginia

Federal Information Center
All Locations; 301-722-9098

State Information Office
304-558-3456

Forest Service
310 W. Wisconsin Ave., Room 500
Milwaukee, WI 53203
414-297-3963

Environmental Protection Agency
26 Federal Plaza
New York, NY 10278
212-264-2657

Cooperative Extension Office
Rachael Tompkins, Director
Cooperative Extension
305 Stewart Hall
P.O. Box 6201
West Virginia University
Morgantown, WV 26506-6201
304-293-3408

Wisconsin

Federal Information Center
Milwaukee; 800-366-2998
All Other Locations; 301-722-9098

State Information Office
608-266-2211

Forest Service
310 W. Wisconsin Ave., Room 500
Milwaukee, WI 53203
414-297-3963

Environmental Protection Agency
77 W. Jackson Blvd.
Chicago, IL 60604
312-353-2000

Cooperative Extension Office
Aeyse Somersan, Director
432 North Lake Street, Room 601
Madison, WI 53706
608-262-7966

Wyoming

Federal Information Center
All Locations; 301-722-9098

State Information Office
307-777-7011

Forest Service
Federal Building
324 25th St.
Ogden, UT 84401
801-625-5354

Environmental Protection Agency
999 18th St., Suite 500
Denver, CO 80202
303-293-1603

Cooperative Extension Office
Jim Debree, Director
CES
University of Wyoming
Box 3354
Laramie, WY 82071
307-766-3567

Index

A

Abandoned gold mines 335
Accidents
    fatal highway 97
Accounting services 43
Acid rain 340
Acne 115
ACTION ....86 - 87
Adjustable rate mortgages 252
Administration on Aging 144
Adobe architecture 216
Adolescence 157
Adopt a horse 348
Adoption 113, 258
Advertising, outdoor 86
Aerial flyover, Blue Angels 275
Aeronautics 61, 217, 297
Aerospace careers 61
Aerospace Internship Competition 242
African art 342
African violets 125
AgExport information 20
Agriculture
    exports 20, 48
    imports 20
    internships 68
    news 253
    products 368
Agriculture, Department of 68, 128
AIDS 147, 228
    children 154
    hotline 266

Air pollution 33, 94, 208
Air quality, indoor 27
Airlines 367
Airports 297
Alcohol 154
Alcohol use
    adolescent 162
    hotline 269
    pregnancy 10
    women 10
Alcoholics, children of 154
Allergies, food 102
Alluvial channels 336
Alzheimer's disease 136
American art 84, 338
American Disabilities Act 165
AMTRAK 369
Animal and Plant Health Inspection Service 126, 368
Animal welfare 283
Animals 214, 290, 332
Anniversary greetings 140
Anorexia nervosa 101
Anthropology 54, 334
Anti-drug programs 86
Anti-lock brakes 384
Antietam National Battlefield 374
Apollo 17 217
Appliance labeling 184
Archeology.. 331
    summer fieldwork... 54
    education programs.................................... 335, 343
    map of dinosaur trail.. 339
    teacher's guide 346
Archives 142
Armed Forces Bands 299
Armed Services 237
Army 385

Army Corps of Engineers 373
Art 84, 171, 331
    African 342
    American 338
    Asian 172
    Buddhist 357
    Chinese 172
    community programs 89
    education 338
    fraud 196
    French impressionism 357
    Hispanic-American 338
    history 357
    Indonesia 85
    Renaissance 357
    state agencies 331
Arthritis 141
Arthur M. Sackler Gallery 172, 357
Artists
    postage stamp designs 69
Arts-In-Education 331
Asbestos in schools 334
Asia 358
Asian art 172
Assault 181
Asthma 159
Astronauts 69, 222
    training 67
Astrophysics 355
Athletic scholars 244
Atomic Clock 253
Audubon, John James 85
Auto mechanics 74
Auto Safety Hotline 266, 287, 384
Auto theft 181
Aviation 204, 208, 296, 332
    accidents 388

Aviation (continued)

    careers 61

    flying lessons 119, 122

    science activities 332

Awards

    Blue Ribbon School Award 239

    Congressional Medal of Honor 237

    E Award 237

    E Star Award 237

    Lowry Award 241

    Malcolm Baldrige National Quality Award 244

    National Distinguished Principals 243

    National Medal of Technology 239

    Presidential Awards For Excellence

        in Science and Mathematics Teaching 238

    Presidential Scholars 244

    Presidential Sports Award 243

    Quigg Excellence in Education Award 241

    Small Business Person of the Year 238

B

Background Notes on the Countries of the World 371

Bald eagles 90

Band, Armed Forces 275, 299

Banking 302

Base closures 89

Battlefields 374

    photographs 170

Beagles 281

Bed and breakfasts 30

Behavior problems 157

Berlize Barrier Reef 336

Bicycle safety 221

Biking 169

Bill of Rights 360

Bilingual education 340
Billboards 86
Birdfeeders 174
Birds 85, 174
Birth announcements 9
Birth control 113, 226, 230
Birth records 317
Birthday greetings 135
Black Canyon 352
Black holes 217
Blue Angels 275
Blue Ribbon School Award 239
Boater's Source Directory 323
Boating
    hotline 268
    lessons 324
    safety 322, 325
    services 323
    statistics 323
Bombs 377, 379
Bond market 251
Books, free for nonprofit organizations 273
Botanic Garden, U.S. 254
Boy Scouts 214
Breast implants 228
Breastfeeding 7, 12
Breath alcohol testing 115
Brokerage firms 197
Buddhism 357
Bulimia 101
Bureau of Alcohol, Tobacco, and Firearms 379
Bureau of Engraving and Printing 256
Bureau of Indian Affairs 118, 347
Bureau of Labor Statistics 55, 59, 74
Bureau of Land Management 172
Bureau of Mines 195
Bureau of the Census 63

Burglary 181
Bus safety 215
Business 238, 244
    credit 29
    deductions 365
    home-based 41
    hotline 266
    loans 30, 35
    management .... 43 - 44
    minorities in 24
    opportunities 49
    overseas 19
    planning 44
    relocation 44
    security .... 377 - 378
    women-owned 22
    working women 24

C

C-Sections 7
Cable television 95, 257
Cadastral surveys 348
Calcium 103
California condors 90
Cambodia 358
Cancer
    diet 102
    hotline 267
Cancer Information Service 267
Canning 107
Canoeing 321, 373
Capital, raising 35
Capitol, U.S. 207, 253
Car 81
    Auto Safety Hotline 287, 384

buying guide 316

electric 96

loans 316

rental guide 316

Careers

aerospace 61

astronauts 67

aviation 61, 332

biology 55

business 58

computers 59

conservation 55

decision making 64

disc jockeys 58

engineering 59, 121

Fish and Wildlife Service 60

future trends 58

graphic design 62

health technology 59

hotline 256

oceanography 55

pilots 122

renewable energy 57

sales 59

weather reporter 56

Carpal tunnel syndrome 31, 46

Carpenters 74

Cartography 63

Cast iron 300

Cataracts 137

Cats 283

CD-ROM 120

Celebrations 347, 358

Cellulite 103

Cement careers 59

Center for Veterinary Medicine 283

Centers for Disease Control 152, 266

Central Intelligence Agency 62
Cerebral Palsy 164
Cervical cap 226
Cesarean childbirth 7
Charitable contributions 278
Chemicals 80
Chesapeake Bay 219
Childbirth, Cesarean 7
Children
       AIDS 154
       disabled 158
       drug abuse 160
       educational development 220
       gifted 151
       handicapped 151
       health 105
       mental disorders 157
Chinese art 172
Cholesterol 104, 110
Chronic pain 164
Cigarettes 136
Citizenship 258
Civics 360
Civil Rights movement 341
Civil War 170
Cleveland-Lloyd Dinosaur Quarry 345
Clinton, Bill 315
Clinton, Hillary 315
Coal 241
       training 59
Coast Guard, U.S. 203, 289, 322
Colds 148
College
       community 119
       preparation 113
Colorado River 336

Coloring books
    air pollution 208
    boating safety 322
    Coast Guard 203
    endangered species 222
    Environment 219
    nature 359
    toy safety 218
    wetlands 222
    winter safety 381
Commemorative coins 195
Commerce Department News 247
Commerce, U.S. Department of 247
Commodity Futures Trading Commission 194
Community arts 89
Community college 119
Complaint handling 18
Complaints, consumer 79
Complex carbohydrates 108
Computers 63, 120, 344
    careers 59
    CD-ROM 120
    floppy disks 120
    internships 68
Concerts, free 299
Condoms 227, 230
Confusion 134
Congressional Budget Office 265
Congressional internships 122
Congressional Medal of Honor 237
Congressional votes 262
Conscientious objectors 311
Conservation 96
Conservation and Renewable Energy Inquiry
    and Referral Service 190
Constipation 138

Consumer
    assistance 79
    complaints 18, 179, 268, 317
    fraud 252, 291
    hotline 255
    mail order 24
Consumer Price Index 248
Consumer Product Safety Commission 218, 255
Consumer's Resource Handbook 79
Contraception ....113, 225 - 226
    condoms...230
    Norplant 230
    oral contraceptives.................................231
    vasectomies 161, 231
Contractors
    fraud...289
    government 30
Contributions, charitable 278
Cooking times 109
Cooper-Hewitt National Museum of Design 358
Cooperative Education Program ....63 - 64
    Energy, U.S. Department of 73
    National Security Agency 68
    Peace Corps..60
    Treasury, U.S. Department of..........................70
Cooperative Extension Service 92
Copper 300
Copyrights 45
Cordless phones 263
Counterfeit merchandise 291
Countries of the world 371
Cowpokes, photographs 172
Crash test results 384
Craters 374
Creationism 355
Creative writing 354
Creativity 344, 356

Credit

    business 29

    counseling 188

    protection 193

    rights 20

Credit history 20

Crime 79

    confessions under hypnosis 270

    control 91

    drug related 86, 262, 290

    mail 381

    statistics 181

    stolen art 196

    victims 292

Crime Stoppers 91

Crime Victims Fund 292

Current affairs 361

Customs Service, U.S. 291, 322, 365, 368, 372

D

DaVinci, Leonardo 85

Day care 17

Death records 317

Defense Department bands and color guards 275

Defense Mapping Agency 324

Defense, Department of 66, 89

    budget 385

Depression 133

Desktop publishing 27

Detector dogs 281

Diabetes and nutrition 138

Dial-a-porn 36

Diet and cancer 102

Diet books 103

Dietary guidelines 108

Digestive problems 138
Dinosaurs 339, 345
Disabilities 158, 165, 315
Disability insurance 47
Disasters
     food distribution 277
     overseas 313
Disc jockeys 58
Divorce records 317
Do-it-yourself 188
Dogs .... 282 - 283
Down Syndrome 150
Drug abuse 86, 154, 351
     community programs 86
     high school 163
     hotline 269
     juvenile 160, 162
     pregnancy 10
     workplace 34, 38
Drug Enforcement Administration 290
Drug testing 35
Drug trafficking 262
Dumps 269
Dyslexia 150

E

E Awards 237
Earnings 75
     women 23
Earth Day 362
Earth Science Information Center 330
Earth sheltered homes 187
Earthquakes 202, 337, 380, 382
Eating disorders 101
Economic development 30

Economic indicators 250
Economic outlook 265
Economics 250, 360
Education 210
    adult 39
    anthropology 334
    art 338
    awards 241
    bilingual 340
    civil rights 341
    community college 119
    development 220
    engineering 121
    exchange programs 366
    financial aid 265
    mapping 330
    NASA 330
    Native Americans 118
    nutrition 106
    public school budgets 263
    science 355
    U.S. Department of Energy 71
    veterans benefits 114
    vocational/technical 64
Egypt 353
Eldercare 17, 144
Elderly
    exercise 133
    nutrition 138
    service hotline 144
    victims 307
Electric vehicles 96
Electrical safety 390
Electricians 74
Electronic funds transfer 302
Ellis Island 134
Emergencies 382

Emergency Planning and Community
   Right-To-Know Act 80
Employees 46
   benefits 46
   federal 37
   federal retirement 255
   health programs 32
   rights 22
   training 46
Employment 249
   assistance programs for women 23
   government jobs 256
   trends 248
Employment Cost Index 248
Employment Retirement Income Security Act 306
Endangered species 90, 214, 222
Endometriosis 148
Energy
   conservation 96
   efficiency 184, 190
   information sources 44, 389
   internships 73
   job opportunities 57
   solar 96, 190, 204
   wind 92
Energy conservation careers 57
Energy Information Administration 44
Energy metabolism 101
Energy, U.S. Department of 71, 73
Engineering careers 59, 121
English as a second language 340
Environment 219
   awareness 96
   glossary 91
   hazards 334
   issues 295
   science education 362

volunteer jobs 66
Environmental Protection Agency, U.S. 42, 288
Epicenters, earthquake 380
Equal Employment Opportunity Commission 386
ERIC Clearinghouses
    Adult, Career, and Vocational Education 64
    Community Colleges 119
    Elementary and Early Childhood Education 220
    handicapped and gifted children 151
    Information Resources 120
    Reading and Communication Skills 218
    Social Studies 360
Exchange programs 120, 366
Exercise 101, 133
Explosives 379
Export Import Bank 65
Export Information System 19
Exporting 237
    agricultural 20, 48
    trends 19
Extension cords 390
Extraterrestrial life 261

F

Fad diets 103, 114
False Claims Act 289, 291
Family and Medical Leave Act of 1993 .... 22, 314
Family folklore 211
Family leave 47, 314
Family Life Information Exchange 113, 160
Family planning 113, 160, 230
Fast foods 103
Fat intake 108
Fatal accidents, highway 97
Federal Aviation Administration 61, 296

Federal Bureau of Investigation 287, 378
Federal Communications Commission 36, 58, 95, 257
Federal Emergency Management Agency 381
Federal employees
    retirement benefits 255
Federal Highway Administration 80, 97
Federal Procurement Data Center 30
Federal Reserve Bank 302
Federal Student Aid Information Center 265
Federal Trade Commission 24, 182, 252
Fiber 108
Films
    foreign policy 301
Financial aid 265
Financial management 43
Financial Management Service 70
Fire Administration, U.S. 387
Fire safety 205, 387
Firearms 379
Fires 387
First aid 383
First Cat 169
Fish hotline 176
Fish and Wildlife Service, U.S. 60, 64
Fisheries 295, 337
Fishing 321
    activities 169
Flags 207
    free 313
Flash floods 56
Flight schools 119
Flood insurance 382
Floods 56, 388
Floppy disks 120
Flu 148
Flu shots 148
Flying lessons 122

Folk music 298
Folklore, family 211
Folkway Records Archives 298
Food
    allergies 102
    canning 107
    consumption survey 233
    distribution program 277
    handling 109
    labeling 108
    News for Consumers 110
    organic 103
    preparation 103
    safety .... 103, 109 - 110
Food and Drug Administration 103, 108
Food and Nutrition Information Center 106, 110
Food Labeling Education Information Center 108
Foodborne illness 109
Foreign Aid Programs 313
Foreign countries 371
Foreign labor trends 19
Foreign policy 301, 361
Foreign trade 19
Forest fires 329
Forest Service 140, 169, 175, 329
Forestry, photographs 175
Forests, national 369
Fossils 339
Foster grandparents 87
Franchise seminars 36
Franchises 26
French Impressionism 357
Fruit 108
Fuel economy 81
Fulbright grants 120
Future Aircraft/Spacecraft Design 240
Futures market 194

G

Gardening 129, 254
Gas 241
General Services Administration 30
Geographic Names database 261
Geographic Notes 361
Geography 63, 261, 360
    learning 210
    Southwest 216
Geological Survey, U.S. 258
Geology .... 336 - 337
Gestational diabetes 13
Get rich quick 196
Get well card from the President 312
GI Bill 114
Gifted children 151
Girl Scouts 214
Glass Ceiling Commission 24
Gold 173, 300
Gold mines, abandoned 335
Gold prospecting 170
Golden Age Passport 135
Golden Knights 275
Government jobs .... 256 - 257
Graduation 117
Grants 275
Graphic design 62
Green cards 258
Greeting from the President 9, 140
    birthday card 135
    Greetings Office 311
    scouting 214
Gross National Product 250
Guthrie, Woody 298
Gypsy moths 126

H

Hair dryers 390
Handicapped children 151, 158
Harvard-Smithsonian Center for Astrophysics 355
Hazardous substances 80, 288
Hazardous waste disposal 269, 288
Head hunter services 53
Health and the workplace 32
Health care
    children 9
    infants 7, 14
    low-income mot 155
    special needs 161
Health Care Financing Administration 142
Health insurance 147
Health spas 166
Hearing
    aids 137
    loss 137
Heart disease 104
Heat pumps 184
Heating 186
Herb gardening 129
High blood pressure 32, 104
Highway beautification 80, 86, 97
Highway safety 97
Hiking tours 339
Historic preservation 183, 371
History 335, 360
Home shopping 316
Home-based business 41
Homeless 276
Homeowner counseling 188
Homes
    building 188

Homes (continued)
 buying 185, 189
 earth sheltered 187
 preservation 183
 veterans 179
 water treatment 82
Hoover Dam 352
Horse adoption 348
Horticulture 125, 128
Hotlines
 AIDS 266
 alcohol 154
 alcohol abuse 269
 asbestos 93
 auto safety 266, 384
 boating 268
 boating safety 322, 325
 breast implants 228
 cancer 267
 child learning 210
 Department of Housing
  and Urban Development 188
 disabled children 158
 drinking water 82
 drug abuse 154, 160, 269
 drug-related crime 262
 eldercare 144
 energy conservation 190
 financial aid 265
 flood insurance 382
 government jobs 256
 hearing loss 137
 meat and poultry 109, 268
 Medicare 267
 museums 259
 neurological disorders 164
 product safety 255

    1001 Government Freebies and Cheapies

RCRA/Superfund 269
resource conservation 83
road safety 215
seafood 176
sexual harassment 386
sexually transmitted diseases 232
small business 266
smoking 156, 162
Social Security 264
solar energy 204
stroke 164
Sudden Infant Death Syndrome 153
Superfund 351
T-bills 251
tax 264
tax fraud 288
veterans 179
wetlands protection 88
wind energy 93
House of Representatives, U.S. 262
Human Nutrition Information Service 233
Hunting 321
Hurricanes 56, 382
Hydroelectric power 352
Hyperactivity 150
Hypnosis 270

I

Illegal dumping 288
Immigration and Naturalization Service 258
Immunizations 14, 152
Importing boats 322
Imports, agricultural 20
Impotence 226
Impressionism 84

Income 251
India 349
Indonesian art 85
Indoor air quality 27, 93
Infertility services 230
Information Agency, U.S. 120
Injury compensation 37
Insects 129
Insulation 184
Insurance
    disability 47
    flood 382
    health 147
Interior landscaping 33
Internal Revenue Service 21, 181, 274, 288
International exchange programs 366
International peace 318
Internships 63
    agriculture 68
    banking 65
    cartography 63
    Central Intelligence Agency 62
    computers 63, 68
    congressional 122
    Department of Defense 66
    energy 71, 73
    finance 70
    Fish and Wildlife Service 64
    geography 63
    photography 62
    Presidential Management Program 72
    Smithsonian 54
    Washington, DC 122
Interplanetary Art Competition 240
Interstate Commerce Commission 179
Interstate highways 80
Inventions 25, 45, 344

Inventive thinking 344
Investment companies 25
Investment fraud 196
Investment income 249
Iron 300
Israel Peace Treaty 314

J

Japan 360
Jefferson, Thomas 85
Job Corps 75
Jobs
    government 74, 256
    hunting 53
    information 257
    interviews 53
    market ....58, 65, 74 - 75
    search methods 65
    summer 54, 70
    training ....57, 74 - 75, 119
    trends 58
    women 74
John F. Kennedy Center for the Performing Arts 89, 356
Junkyards 80
Jurassic Park 345
Juvenile delinquency 160

K

Kennedy Space Center 372
Kilauea volcano 336
Kindergarten 220
King, Martin Luther, Jr. 117

L

Lab equipment 362
Labeling
    food 108
    wine 171
Labor Market activity 249
Labor statistics 58, 248
Lactation 13
Land disposal 269
Land fills 82
Land management 172, 348
Land sale scam 182
Landscaping 129
Laos 358
Lasers 116
Lawn care 126
Lead 300
    drinking water 82
Lead poisoning 149
Leading economic indicators 247
Learning strategies 210
Leaves 201
Legislation 262
Library of Congress 273
Literacy education 39
Little Plover Project 336
Loans, business 30, 35
Loch Ness Monster 214
Lowry Award 241
Lungs 32

M

Machine guns 379
Mail bombs 377

Mail fraud 40
Mail order 24, 41
Malcolm Baldrige National Quality Award 244
Maps 330, 358
Marine animal protection 290
Marine debris 359
Marine mammals 337
Mark Trail 201
Marriage 225
Marriage records 317
Mars 361
Mars Science Experiment Project 242
Martin, August 208
Masons 74
Maternity leave 47
Mathematics 210, 238
Matisse 85
Meat and Poultry Hotline 109
Meat preparation 109, 268
Medicare 143
    fraud 291
    hotline 267
Medicines 139
Medigap 143
Memory loss 134
Menopause 229
Mental health 157, 163
    depression 133
    phobias..383
    stress 116
Mental retardation 150
Merchandise transactions 249
Merchant Marine Academy 121
Mexico 299
Mileage guides 81
Military base closings 89
Mine Safety and Health Administration 59

Minerals 195, 300
Mining 59, 170, 195
Minorities in business 24
Mint, U.S. 195
Mission To Planet Earth 242
Money 205, 256
    history of 302
    small business 35
    veterans education 114
Money management 189
Monuments, photographs 170
Moon craters 374
Mortgages 182, 185
    adjustable rate 252
    Veterans Administration 179
Mothers, working 22
Motor oil 83
Mount Shasta 202
Moving
    companies 179
    expenses 181
Mugging victims 292
Mummies, Egyptian 353
Murder 181
Museums 259, 354
Music .... 298 - 299

N

National Aeronautics and
    Space Administration (NASA) 61, 330
    educational programs 361
    posters... 217
    puzzle kit 221
    science competitions.. 240, 242
    speakers.. 297

National AIDS Information Clearinghouse 147
National Archives and Records Administration 142, 254
National Clearinghouse for Alcohol
        and Drug Information 11, 269
National Clearinghouse
        for Primary Care Information 106, 155
National Displaced Homemakers Network 147
National Distinguished Principals 243
National Energy Information Center 44
National Forests 369
National Gallery of Art 84, 171
National Guard 385
National Heart, Lung, and Blood Institute 105
National Highway Traffic Safety Administration 215
National Information Center for Children
        and Youth with Disabilities 159, 165
National Institute for Occupational Safety
        and Health 31
National Institute of Justice 79, 307
National Institute of Mental Health 116, 157
National Institute of Standards and Technology 115, 298
National Institute on Aging 133
National Institute on Deafness
        and Other Communication Disorders 137
National Marine Fisheries Service 290
National Maternal and Child Health
        Clearinghouse 7, 105
National Medal of Technology 239
National Museum of African Art 342
National Museum of American Art 338
National Museum of Natural History 54
National Oceanic and Atmospheric Administration 206
National Park Service 135, 331
National parks 135, 345, 367, 374
        photographs 170
National Science Foundation 296
National Science Resource Center 343

National Security Agency 68
National Victims Resource Center 270
National Weather Service 56
National Wildlife Refuges 321
Native Americans 346, 359
    education programs 118
    history 347
    pottery.. 216
Natural history 54
Nature 359
Nautical charts 337
Naval Observatory 253
Navigational aids .... 324 - 325
Navy ships 141
Neighborhood watch 79
New Mexico 216
Non-profits
    food programs 277
    grants 275
    tax exempt status 274
Norplant 230
Nursing homes 142
Nutrition 103, 108, 110, 138
    childhood 105
    education 106
    labeling 103
    pregnancy 105
    research 110
    seafood 176
    services 106

O

Obesity 101
Occupational diseases 37
Occupational Outlook Handbook 58

Occupational Outlook Quarterly 57
Occupational Safety and Health Administration 28
Occupational trends 58
Occupations 57
Ocean dumping 289
Oceanography careers 55
Oceans 206, 359
Odometer tampering 287
Office of Educational Research Improvement 263
Office of Personnel Management 66, 72
Office of Seafood, FDA 176
Office of Technology Assessment 49
Office of Thrift Supervision 252
Office plants 33
Office technology 344
Oil 241
        automobile 83
Organic foods 103
Osteoporosis 133, 141
Outdoor activities 169
Outdoor advertizing 86
Ovens 390
Overseas Security Advisory Council 377

P

Pain, chronic 164
Palestinian Liberation Organization 314
Pandas 214
Panic disorders 383
Parachute show, Golden Knights 275
Parks, National 135, 345, 367
Parrots 295
Parvo 283
Passports 258
Patent and Trademark Office 40

Patents 25, 40, 45, 344
Peace Corps 60, 256
Peace Treaty, PLO/Israel 314
Pennsylvania Avenue Development Corporation 253
Pension Benefit Guaranty Corporation 250
Pension plans .... 250, 305 - 306
Performing arts 356
Personal income 251
Pesticides 127, 180, 187, 189
Pets
    care 282
    food 283
Petroleum reserves 336
Phobias 383
Photographs 172
    art 171
    fish and wildlife 175
    Fish and Wildlife Service 321
    forestry 175
    National Parks 170
    nature 173
    President Clinton 169
Photography 62
Physical fitness 213, 243
Physics 355
Pictorial survey of the U.S. 173
Pilots 122, 208
Pimples 115
Pipeline 389
Planets 260
Plant closings 37
Plants 33, 125, 128
Playground safety 212
Pleasure boats 322
Plumbers 74
Poinsettias 125
Police radar 115

Pollution 94, 201, 209, 219
   air 208
   indoor air 33, 93
   water 359
Ponzi schemes 196
Portraits 84
Postage stamp designs 69
Postal crime 40
Postal Service, U.S. 40, 69, 175, 209
   bombs 377
   crime 381
Posters
   AIDS 229
   anthropology 334
   drug abuse 10, 163
   fire safety 329
   Forest Service 140
   good health and the workplace 32
   National Aeronautics
      and Space Administration 217
   outdoor activities 169
   outdoors 215
   smoking 12, 156
   trees 203
Pottery 216
Poultry preparation 109, 268
Pregnancy 7, 11, 160
   alcohol use 10
   diabetes 13
   endometriosis 148
   nutrition 105
   prenatal care 8
   smoking 12
   tests 230
Prenatal care ....7 - 8
Prescription drugs 139
Preservation of homes 183

President Clinton 169, 214
President's Challenge 243
President's Council on Physical Fitness and Sports 243
Presidential Awards for Excellence
    in Science and Mathematics Teaching 238
Presidential Management Internship Program 72
Presidential Memorial Certificate 312
Presidential Scholars 244
Presidential Sports Award 243
Pricing guides 43
Primary care 106
Principals 243
Procurement, federal 30
Producer price index 255
Project Blue Book 254
Project XL 344
Prospectors, photographs 172
Protest movements 341
Public companies 42
Public debt 259
Public school budgets 263
Public service careers 72
Public speaking 117
Publishing 27
Puzzle
    solar system 221
Pyramid schemes 196
Pyramids 353

Q

Quality control 244
Quigg Excellence in Education Award 241

1001 Government Freebies and Cheapies

R

Radar 115
Radio interference 263
Radon 184
Railroad safety 391
Rainforests 329
Rangeland, photographs 172
Reading 213, 218
Reading is Fundamental 213
Real estate brokers 183
Records of vital statistics 317
Recreational areas 366, 373
Recycling 96, 350
    programs 82
    used oil 83
Relocation, business 44
Renwick Gallery 347
Representatives, U.S. House of 262
Resource Conservation and Recovery Act Hotline 83
Retail sales 247
Retired Senior Volunteers 87
Retirement 250
    federal employees 255
    Social Security 264
Rewards
    Auto Safety Hotline 287
    Coast Guard 289
    contractor fraud 289
    Customs Service 291
    Drug Enforcement Administration 290
    Environmental Protection Agency 288
    Federal Bureau of Investigation 287
    Internal Revenue Service 288
    Medicare fraud 291
    National Marine Fisheries Service 290

Rifles 379
Rio Grande 352
Rivers 352
Roadside improvements 97
Robbery 181
Rock collecting 176
Rockets 216, 333
Roses 129
Rural economic development 30

S

Saccharin 103
Safe Drinking Water Hotline 82
Safety
     auto 266, 384
     bicycle 221
     boating 268, 322
     bus 215
     electrical 390
     fire 387
     food 109
     mining 59
     occupational 28
     pesticide 187, 189
     playground 212
     railroad 391
     toy 218
     winter 381
Salary statistics 55
Salt 103
Savings bonds 194, 251, 258
Scholarships 122
Scholastic Aptitude Tests (SATs) 121
School bus safety 215
Schools, hazards in 334

Science 296, 343, 355

    awards...238

    competitions..240, 242

    films and videos 296

    lab equipment 362

    projects 116, 343

    Space Camp...216

Seafood hotline 176

Securities 193

Securities and Exchange Commission 42, 193

Security 378

Security abroad 377

Selective Service 311

Senate, U.S. 260

Senior Companions 87

Sesame Street 205

Sexual harassment 386

Sexually transmitted diseases 161, 232

Sharks 212

Ship passenger lists 142

Ships 247

    historical data 141

Shopping

    abroad 365

    by mail 316

    by telephone 316

Sick building 27

Silencers 379

Silicone implants 228

Silver 300

Single people 225

Skiing 169

Skywatchers Report 260

Small business

    complaint handling 18

    money 35

    tax guide 21

Small Business Investment Companies 25
Small Business Person of the Year Award 238
Smithsonian Institute 259
    internships 54
    Resource Guide 348
Smokey Bear 329
Smoking 156
    cessation 162
    elderly 136
    pregnancy 12
Social Security Administration 264, 307
    speakers 308
Social studies 360
Socks,first feline 169
Sodium intake 108
Soil
    conservation 130
    erosion 130
    surveys 130
Soil Conservation Service 130
Solar energy 190, 204
Solar system 221
Solid waste reduction 94
Soup kitchens 277
Southeast Asia 358
Space 222, 372
    educational resources 330, 361
    posters 217
Space Camp 216
Space flight program 69
Space Science Student Involvement Program 242
Space Shuttle 217
Space Shuttle rides 69
Speakers
    Department of Defense 300
    National Aeronautics
        and Space Administration 297

Social Security Administration 308
travel 370
Speech writing 117
Speeding tickets 115
Sports 243
Sports nutrition 102
St. Lawrence Seaway 247
Stamp collecting 175
Stamp designs 69
Star Wars 300
Stars 260
Statue of Freedom 207
Statue of Liberty 134
Sterilization operations 161
Steroids 163
Stock brokers 197
Stolen art 196
Stress 116
Striped bass 295
Student jobs
    Bureau of the Census 63
    Fish and Wildlife Service 64
    National Security Agency 68
    U.S. Department of Energy 73
    U.S. Department of the Treasury 70
Student programs 62, 72
    volunteer 66
Study abroad 120
Sudden Infant Death Syndrome 153
Summer Aid Program 71
Summer jobs ....68, 70 - 71
    Central Intelligence Agency 62
Sun lamps 118
Superfund hotline 269, 351
Surplus
    books 273
    food 277

Surplus (continued)
    property 274
    real property 276
Survey of the U.S., pictorial 173

T

T-bills 251
Tanning safety 118
Tax Guide for Small Business 21
Taxes
    hotline 264
    moving expenses 181
    non-profits 274
    public education spending 263
    small business 21
    travel expenses 365
Teachers 241
Technical Assistance Directory 42
Technology 239, 298, 344
    wheelchairs 49
Teens
    job training 75
    summer jobs 73
Tele-Tax 264
Telemarketing fraud 368
Telephone services 36
Television interference 263
Terrorism .... 378 - 379
Thailand 358
Theater 356
Thermostats 184
Thunderbirds 275
Tides 359
Timber industry 175
Time 253

Tinworking 216
Tires 384
Tobacco 156
Tornadoes 56, 382
Tourism 85, 370
Toy safety 218
Trade practices 252
Trademarks 40, 45
Training
    mining 59
    teens 75
Training employees 46
Trains 369
    accidents 391
    travel 369
Travel 85
    airlines 367
    business deductions 365
    deductions 365
    expenses 365
    fraud 368
    market research 85
    speakers 370
    train 369
Travel and Tourism Administration, U.S. 85
Treasury bills 251
Treasury, U.S. Department of 70
Trees 203, 211
Tropical plants 125
Tropical rainforests 329
Turkey 109, 268

U

Unidentified Flying Objects (UFOs) 254, 261
Unemployment rate 249

Unions and plant closings 37
United Nations 318
United States Mint 195

V

Vacation 366
Vaccinations 14
Vasectomy 161, 231
Ventilation 184
Vertebrate zoology 214
Veterans
    education money 114
    free flags 313
    home buying 179
    Presidential certificates 312
Veterans Benefits Administration 114
Veterinary medicine 283
Veterinary terminology..283
Victims of Crime Act of 1984 292
Video display terminals 31
Videos
    African art 342
    airplanes 296
    alcohol abuse and the workplace 38
    animals 283
    archeology 331
    art 84
    aviation 61, 296
    banking 302
    Buddhism 357
    drug abuse and the workplace 34, 38
    Fish and Wildlife Service 60
    fishing 295
    immunizations 14
    India 349

inventions 299, 344
minerals 300
National Parks 345
nutrition 102, 106, 110
pollution 201
Postal Service 209
public lands 348
science 296
security abroad 377
sharks 212
technology 298
United Nations 318
water 353
weight control 110
wetlands 295
wildlife 295, 332
Vietnam 358
Violent crime victims 292
Vital statistics 317
Vitamins 103
Vocational education 119
Volcanoes 173, 202, 337
Volunteer Service Program 66
Volunteers 66, 87
Peace Corps 256
United States Geological Survey 258
Voter registration cards 315

W

Wages 251
Walking tour 339
Washington, DC 253
Waste recycling 96
Water 206, 352, 380
pollution 289, 359

Water (continued)
    testing 82
Weapons 379
Weather 206, 337
    forecasting 56
    safety 381
Weight control 101, 110, 114
Welders 74
Wetlands 222, 295
    protection hotline 88
Whales 337
Wheelchairs 49
White House 9, 135, 140
    awards 244
    construction 373
    first cat 169
    get well card 312
    Greetings Office 311
    scouting 214
Wholesale sales 247
Wildlife 332
    endangered species 90
    pets 281
    photographs 175
    refuges 135, 321, 350
Windmills 92
Wine 171
Winter safety 381
Wiring hazards 390
Women
    alcohol use 10
    business credit 29
    business owners 22
    calcium 103
    credit history 20
    disabled workers 23
    earnings 23

health insurance 147
job discrimination 24
labor trends 23
low-income 155
non-traditional jobs 74
sterilization 161
training programs 74
working 23, 24
Women's Bureau 23
Women-owned businesses 22
Wood preservation 93
Wood siding 188
Woodstoves 186
Woodsy Owl 209
Woody Woodpecker 298
Work and Family Clearinghouse 17
Work visas 258
Worker adjustment programs 37
Workers' Compensation 37
Working mothers 22
Workplace
and the family 17
drug abuse 34
hazards 28
literacy 39
World trade markets 19
Wright brothers 204, 374
Writing, creative 354

Y

Yakutat 336
Yani, Wang 172

Z

Zoning 87
Zoology 214
Zoos 354

1001 Government Freebies and Cheapies